CRISIS
of character

CRISIS
of character

Building Corporate Reputation
in the Age of Skepticism

PETER FIRESTEIN

UNION SQUARE PRESS
An imprint of Sterling Publishing Co., Inc.

New York / London
www.sterlingpublishing.com

STERLING and the distinctive Sterling logo are registered trademarks of
Sterling Publishing Co., Inc.

Library of Congress Cataloging-in-Publication Data

Firestein, Peter.
Crisis of character: building corporate reputation
in the age of skepticism / Peter Firestein.
    p. cm.
  Includes bibliographical references and index.
  ISBN 978-1-4027-6246-8
  1. Business ethics. 2. Industrial management. I. Title.
  HF5387.F564 2009
  658.4'08--dc22
                                                    2009013960

10 9 8 7 6 5 4 3 2 1

Published by Sterling Publishing Co., Inc.
387 Park Avenue South, New York, NY 10016
© 2009 by Peter Firestein
Distributed in Canada by Sterling Publishing
c/o Canadian Manda Group, 165 Dufferin Street
Toronto, Ontario, Canada M6K 3H6
Distributed in the United Kingdom by GMC Distribution Services
Castle Place, 166 High Street, Lewes, East Sussex, England BN7 1XU
Distributed in Australia by Capricorn Link (Australia) Pty. Ltd.
P.O. Box 704, Windsor, NSW 2756, Australia

Design and layout by Adam Bohannon

Sterling ISBN 978-1-4027-6246-8

For information about custom editions, special sales, premium and
corporate purchases, please contact Sterling Special Sales
Department at 800-805-5489 or specialsales@sterlingpublishing.com.

for
Sheree

AND IN MEMORY OF
Eleanor Firestein

Inclusion is Everything

✳ JOSCHKA FISCHER

CONTENTS

Introduction

The conduct of corporate life provides one of the defining characteristics for any age. In post–World War II America, business virtually carried the country on its back as corporations translated the organizing principles they had developed in the war effort to create one of the greatest bursts of growth and productivity ever. As shareholders became well-to-do, unions also flourished. The opportunity to create healed many of the wounds of the generation that had endured the depression of the 1930s and the war.

That was then.

The publication of this book comes amid one of the greatest financial—and therefore human—crises in the history of the modern world. What began as a normalization of inflated home prices in the U.S. exposed unimaginable abuse of the financial system by some of its managers. The creation of mortgage-based derivative securities—most with no underlying collateral except their reference to each other—had reached staggering proportions. While no one knew the exact figure, the total face value of these and other derivative products far exceeded the world's annual economic output—perhaps by a factor of ten.

Remarkably few saw the disaster coming. Many people were making a great deal of money, and examining the source of these riches was not only inconvenient, but clearly a waste of time. Emblematic of the spirit of the age were a number of the investors in funds offered by Bernard Madoff, who allegedly bilked clients out of approximately $50 billion. Some of those investors had long thought Madoff was engaged in illegal activities. They believed he was abusing his role as a broker dealer, misappropriating privileged information to trade ahead of his customers in that business. They saw themselves as beneficiaries of such misdeeds. None considered that they might be victims of a Ponzi scheme.

Madoff's investors who suspected him, but remained invested, offer insight into the psychology of the age. Financial markets had become a secular religion, centered on the belief that government regulation limited progress and that markets and their participants were best qualified to regulate themselves. The tragic result of this absence of accountability was a financial system gone haywire.

When markets for many derivative securities dried up in mid-2008, there was no way to tell what they were worth. So it became impossible to know what the banks who held those securities were worth. Unable to determine their own solvency, these banks became incapable of lending. Businesses of all kinds withered for lack of credit, forcing millions out of work. Rises in unemployment tracked credit card defaults almost exactly. To make up for those losses, many banks raised interest rates on cardholders who were still paying their bills, forcing them into more dire straits. Rates of home foreclosures multiplied. People cut back on spending and purchased only the things they needed, imposing further stress on consumer goods companies already starved for credit.

The U.S. financial crisis spread across the globe like an epidemic. European institutions began to suffer the same solvency problems as their U.S. counterparts. U.S. and European demand for manufactured goods plummeted, forcing thousands of Asian exporters out of business with near-catastrophic effects on employment there. President Obama's new CIA director testified within weeks of taking office that global unrest due to unemployment had surpassed terrorism as the primary threat to the U.S. In countries that had moved toward free-market economic models—as in Eastern Europe after the fall of the Soviet Union and Latin America in the wake the "Washington Consensus," which promoted democratic reforms and open markets—pressures toward protectionism gained ascendancy. Globalization, which had created enormous economic power and wealth over the prior two decades, seemed in danger of shifting into reverse.

Public bitterness raged against both the bankers whose smoke-and-mirrors path to personal wealth had caused this crisis, and against the outgoing administration of George W. Bush that had let them do it. As President Obama began to implement plans to save what was salvageable of the banking system, reduce the rate of home foreclosures, and stimulate economic activity, Americans glanced back at the Great Depression and wondered whether they were doomed to live it again. We had considered the 1930s an experience far in the past, from which our modernity had made us immune. Yet—few dared say it—if those times weren't repeating themselves now, what we were experiencing veered uncomfortably close to them. Could it possibly be as bad this time?

The writer Stetson Kennedy, who lived through the depression

of the 1930s, pointed out that we may have been more poorly prepared to survive a depression in the early 21st century than we'd
been in the 1930s. Contemporary life had moved us light years
from the skills that would enable us to survive in tough circumstances. Steinbeck's Okies loaded everything they had on a truck
and went to California. We couldn't fit more than a fraction of
what we'd come to rely on in even the largest SUV. And besides,
there were no more promised lands to go to.

Had we progressed at all over the last seven or eight decades?
Or was our experience telling us that real progress is a nonsensical
idea? Were we, instead, trapped in a long-wave cycle that contained
the best and worst of times, but always returned us to places we'd
been before? Was the economic cycle written in our DNA?

One of our more impressive combinations of ideas and technology may reside in the software we've designed to analyze and
manage financial risk. It has become complex almost beyond belief.
But its sophistication has not enabled us to identify real risk, and
so we have to ask ourselves whether our ability to create such complexity has actually taken us anywhere at all. It seems that the
technology we design contains our faults. Commentary after the
meltdown by those who understood risk programs told us that they
were limited by the array of possible results with which they'd been
programmed. If a program designer wanted to include every outcome that had occurred since 1960—and four decades or so might
have seemed a long time—lessons learned from the collapse of the
banking system in the early 1930s would have been excluded. That
programmer may have seen such data as so far from his or her
experience as to be irrelevant. The problem, of course, was that the
possibility of such a collapse had remained with us.

*   *   *   *

As individual experiences shape perceptions of risk, so they influence the writing of books such as this. Presuming to write a book

is to animate the supposition that one's own views have some kind of universality. That, of course, is for the reader to decide. Because one of the primary ideas of this book is the necessity for candor in corporate life, I offer a bit of candor regarding the far-off origins of the book itself.

I grew up in South Bend, Indiana, which, during my youth in the 1950s and '60s, was a classic mid-American industrial town populated by immigrants from Poland and Hungary who had been living there in neat, narrow-yarded houses for half a century. They had come to work for Studebaker, Bendix, Oliver, and other large manufacturing concerns of the kind that created American power as we knew it, but today are remembered mostly in sepia-tinted murals that decorate restaurant walls in a town that feels better dwelling on its history than its present.

The downtown of my youth was dense with department stores, jewelry stores, banks, hotels, and theaters. The Palace Theater was an ornate classic of the vaudeville age. Not only the town's citizens, but farmers and small-business owners from a 50-mile radius in northern Indiana and southern Michigan crowded the sidewalks as they bought diamonds and refrigerators on credit.

By far the most prominent of the companies at which the town's residents worked—and from which the town itself drew its security—was Studebaker, the last major American auto company outside Detroit. Studebakers were well-engineered, stylish cars whose models ranged from the useful to the luxurious. Today, movie companies wanting to represent an American street between 1945 and 1960 often rent one of the last remaining Studebakers. During World War II, Franklin D. Roosevelt sent 10,000 Studebaker trucks to the Soviet Union for defense on the German front. On a visit to Moscow in the mid-1980s, I needed only mention that I came from the place where they made Studebakers to receive an unmistakably Russian embrace from people of a certain age who claimed they'd driven those dependable vehicles through the frozen wartime winters.

When I was away at college, Studebaker closed down forever. The company's management had not performed up to the level of its engineers and designers. Adequate cost controls had been absent for a long time. I knew employees of my parents' generation who punched the time clock in the morning, disappeared for the day, and returned to punch out at four in the afternoon without repercussion. The result was that the enormous plant on South Main Street, with its dedicated railroad sidings, went dark and silent.

Within two years, the vibrant downtown looked as though it had been bombed. At least half the stores had closed. And within five years, their structures had been removed. Over the next couple of decades, a number of banks and vertical parking lots went up. They looked like concrete shoe boxes on a hard-baked plain. I never saw them without thinking of the vibrant town, now lost, that had formed me. And, as I got older, I became conscious of the fragility of the thread from which it all had hung. The world that had seemed the only world to me as a child had turned out to depend on a few men in management jobs who—I'm guessing here—may have spent too much time on the golf course.

The experience of witnessing the decline of my hometown has influenced business decisions I've taken much later in life. Approximately a quarter century after the disappearance of Studebaker, a job offer came my way from the financial products marketing group at the investment bank Drexel Burnham Lambert. I was to serve as senior writer of the media presentations used to market high-yield debt offerings—also known as junk bonds—that originated with the group headed by Michael Milken. I had been impressed with the way Milken had convinced capital markets that portfolio diversification made low-rated debt, which had been around for a century or more, less risky and worth more than the market had ever thought. This seemed a remarkable accomplishment.

What was more important to me, however, was the piece of the junk bond rationale that said refinancing American companies, and installing fresh management who could run them at sufficient profit to service the new debt, would save both the aging companies and the communities that depended on them. Because of my experience in my hometown, this theme resonated with me, and it was part of the reason I took the job.

Three years into my time at Drexel the U.S. Attorney for the Southern District of New York, Rudolph Giuliani—later two-term mayor of the city—indicted Milken on a series of financial improprieties. Drexel soon went the way of Studebaker. A brilliant, enormously productive boss had been caught engaging in illegal acts that were utterly unnecessary to his wealth and legendary success. All of us who worked in the company lost our jobs as the organization dissolved around us.

For me, these experiences distill into a single insight, which is that the individuals who run significant companies hold much more than the companies themselves in their hands. Their influence extends to where the children of their employees can go to college, and whether the communities that surround them survive. It is from this point that the rest of this book ensues.

It is no longer reasonable to argue that corporations exist in a social vacuum where their sole obligation is to provide economic choices. The Nobel Prize–winning economist Milton Friedman spent his life making this argument. But, as the boundaries between corporations and the life that exists around them continue to blur, the ability to force such old delineations fades.

People look to corporations as they look to their politicians. They want corporations to reflect their own values. As a consequence, the question arises: Why should the conduct expected of corporations and individuals differ from each other? Why should we not hold both to the same standards? A corporation's strong social identity can cast its light across products and services, and onto the attitudes of investors, legislators, regulators, and prospective business partners. The only requirement is that this stature be earned. And, in earning it, the last thing the company needs is a sense that it is excepted from the norms of human affairs.

* * * *

In 1976, the biologist Richard Dawkins introduced the concept of the meme—an idea that takes hold in many different minds, and in many different places, at roughly the same time. The delusional brand of risk analysis that seized some of the world's best financial minds and led to the subprime crisis was a meme. People were invaded by these ideas, and, in various stages of accepting them, gave each other license to continue along the same path.

This book is dedicated to breaking the meme of the corporation as a fortress divorced from its social context. Today, and in the future, the viability of corporations and other large groups requires a break from traditional norms in the relationships between organizations and society's interests—including those associated with the environment. Doing what has been done in the past will not yield the same results as the past. The results will be worse because society, itself, has moved far from where it was.

This is new territory in the practice of corporate management, and its contours are unlikely to have been learned at a parent's knee. The way forward for any individual—and for the ultimate reputation of the group in which he or she participates—lies in personal experience and judgment. Which brings us to the title of chapter 1...

PART ONE

The New Corporate Landscape

CHAPTER 1

It's Always Personal

The film *Citizen Kane*, which many consider the greatest movie ever made in America, opens with the death of a newspaper tycoon who, with his last breath, utters the word "Rosebud." Cadres of reporters then deploy across the land to seek out the significance of that mysterious word. We, the audience, learn at the end that it's the name of a sled the great man owned as a child.

The stature of the film lies partly in the ability of its creator, Orson Welles, to link the inner and the outer man. *Citizen Kane* makes the point that, no matter how great we may become, we remain the same person we've always been. No matter where you go, so to speak, there you are.

The story riveted Welles' audiences when he released the film in 1941. Its notion of the unity of the inner and outer person is a principle that modern corporate leaders should burnish and hold in a prominent place among the things they know. Understanding how the inner man, or woman, plays out across the great external stage is more important today than ever because the concerns of the individual have taken on an unprecedented role in the life of the corporation.

End of the Corporate Exception

The freedom of companies to adhere to codes of conduct that are distinct from those of society is disappearing. The "corporate exception," in other words, is an endangered species and unlikely to be saved. Corporate oversight has been democratized, and companies today face an unprecedented level of scrutiny. The Internet has created a public super-consciousness, delivering extraordinary access to information, accompanied by a sense of entitlement on the part of virtually any group or member of society to hold an opinion and have it heard. Non-governmental organizations (NGOs), the press, and shareholder activists of all stripes stand ready to expose corporate misbehavior. It seldom matters whether misdeeds are real or imagined. Groups in opposition to corporations can now organize both message and massive action with the click of a computer mouse or the transmission of a text message.

Because a company can no longer hide its actions from investors and the public, the question of its reputation has moved to the forefront as a determining factor in its ability to grow and sustain itself. Its reputation derives directly from its actions. All of its constituencies—customers, shareholders, employees, the media, communities, and activist groups—form their opinions out of what the company has done, or not done. A company's reputation is the sum total of these opinions. Reputation determines the value of a company's shares, the cost of its capital, its ability to attract talent, its treatment in the press, and its relationships with interest groups who influence the attitudes of legislators and the decisions of customers. If you're a CEO, therefore, developing a solid corporate reputation—and repairing it when necessary—is Job One. Your company and your career depend on it.

I began with the Rosebud story because the role of a corporate leader's personal history in his or her professional actions receives only occasional attention in the general conversation about leadership. This book maintains that the whole individual is required to lead.

The company lives in a social environment. Even institutional investors—to say nothing of social activists, consumers, and legislators—base their decisions in part on subjective impressions of company managements. They watch how CEOs communicate, and they analyze the process by which company leadership makes decisions. Managers can't respond adequately to the complexities of the real world armed only with lessons learned in business school and on-the-job experience. That's not where conviction and authenticity come from. They come, instead, from the qualities in the individual that have placed him or her in a position to lead.

The rules of the game have changed because the fundamental nature of the corporation has changed. Companies today have subcontracted much of their manufacturing and many of their services overseas, freeing them to become idea factories that concentrate on analyzing markets and building strategies. They are marketers, creators of ideas, and manipulators of public emotion. The battlefield on which they compete has therefore moved from the factory floor to the marketing, information technology, PR, and investor relations departments. Their competitiveness (and reputation) hinges on the stories their actions enable them to tell.

What Is a Stakeholder?

We talk a great deal today about a company's stakeholders, and it's probably worthwhile to describe them. Stakeholders are those individuals, organizations, and communities who are affected by a company's activities. The nature of being stakeholders defines their relationships to the company, particularly with regard to expectations for the company's behavior.

Employees—as stakeholders—expect the company to stand by its word with reference to working conditions, compensation, benefits, fair treatment, and opportunities for advancement.

Investors—as stakeholders—expect management to be honest in reporting its financial condition and outlook on its business.

Communities—as stakeholders—expect the company to act as though its interests for the community are similar to those the community has for itself. The term "community" can refer not only to the locality around a facility, but to nations and even groups of nations.

Interest groups, such as environmental- or human rights–oriented NGOs, expect the company to comply with specific standards. Such NGOs are stand-ins for broader social interests. No company can respond to all social interests, but every company is responsible for identifying those that represent norms to which it should adhere.

A company's relationship with its stakeholders always comprises a mixture of explicit and implicit obligations. The importance of implicit obligations makes corporate behavior a much bigger subject than legal compliance. The term "stakeholder" implies a compact of good faith. And it's that good faith for which markets and society most frequently reward companies.

Reputation and Survival

Reputation is the strongest determinant of any corporation's sustainability. Stock price can always come back. Business strategies can always be changed. But when your reputation is gone, its retrieval is difficult, long-term, and uncertain.

The world has witnessed spectacular reputational collapses over recent years. The big names of the scandal era, Enron and WorldCom, represented simple cases of thievery and fraud. An admonition not to steal hardly requires a book, however. Of far greater interest, and more instructive of the dangers that can lurk in any corporation's DNA, is the kind of decline of reputation that occurred at Merck from its marketing of the painkiller Vioxx. Over its long history Merck had established a reputation for unsurpassed excellence in technology and business practices. But the selective disclosure of scientific research aimed at inflating the perceived effectiveness of Vioxx constituted a significant departure from its traditional ethical rigor. It is doubtful that management ever decided to become a different kind of company. Merck's decline derived instead from an incremental erosion of corporate culture driven by demands for ever-improving financial performance. The results have included loss of careers, a fall in shareholder value, and long-term weakness in business.

Well-intentioned managers and students of business everywhere who have observed Merck's embarrassment, as well as similar reputation declines at other companies, may ask themselves how they can avoid such a fate. This book is for them. They must come to understand, first of all, that vulnerabilities of reputation cannot be addressed through classical business solutions. Neither PR, advertising, branding, name changes, nor sleek logos can disguise underlying weaknesses. Instead, developing and maintaining a strong reputation requires engagement with a company's constituencies across the entire range of its activities.

This book presents a series of stories that show how some companies have prevailed in the face of immense challenges to their reputations, and why others have not. Investors are increasingly aware of the reputational vulnerabilities companies face. And if outside perceptions of their companies don't grab managers' attention, the impact that those perceptions exert on share price certainly will.

The dynamics of corporate engagement and its major component, a gift for listening to constituencies, make up the greater part of this book's content. Listening is a prerequisite for any company's understanding of its stakeholders. It provides the only basis on which the company can legitimately respond to them.

The book plots a path that any manager or company can follow for making allies of potential enemies, thereby removing an enormous component of risk. It provides a foundation for the external relations a company needs in order to grow securely into its future.

What Does a Strong Reputation Look Like?

A company with a strong reputation is one for whom investors and the public have high expectations. If it produces superior products, as Apple and GE have done, the public sees those products as arising from a bedrock of excellence. Over the long run, the company's shares trade at a premium compared to its peer group, based on expectations of higher future value. When things go wrong, it receives the benefit of the doubt. Its version of events is heard with a normal degree of skepticism, of course, but also with interest. The best available employees seek to work there. Its current employees show pride in belonging and take the company's fortunes personally. Its thinking is solicited by others; its processes become case studies.

The fundamental insight that drives such a company is that

its engagement with constituencies in capital markets and society will determine its fate. Management understands that the process begins with its attitude toward the entire financial and social environment. A company with a strong reputation is one that knows it must, first of all, make itself subject to an open dialogue. Its leader also understands that it cannot productively manipulate that dialogue through strategies and tactics.

Only by engaging can you influence. But engaging also means you will *be* influenced. In a world where information on companies is more accessible than ever, and powerful currents of opposing opinion live side by side, this exchange of influence provides the only route to long-term stability. Later in this book, in the chapter on telling your corporate story (Strategy 5 in chapter 12), I'll discuss the communications of convergence and how becoming part of the greater dialogue helps a company influence the terms the world uses to discuss its affairs.

There is, of course, a flip side to the reputation dynamic. A second, more problematic kind of approach causes management to think and act like a victim. Such a management considers journalists who write unfavorable stories to be ill-informed and pernicious; investors who question the company's credibility are viewed as "dense"; and NGOs that criticize the company are incapable of understanding the pragmatic demands of business. Companies who see their experiences in such terms generally view the world with mistrust, and the resulting lack of transparency prevents investors and others from developing the kinds of clear definitions of the company that engender confidence.

Traditional wisdom says that a reputation can take a century to build and a minute to lose. And when things go bad, it doesn't matter who's at fault or whether critics are being fair—management is responsible. Crises are failures of performance. Most corporate crises are years in the making, arising not from the tanker hitting underwater rocks, but from the absence of procedures to prevent such an accident. The cancer of incrementalism, marked by standards eroding slowly over years, may be the most detrimental way a company can abdicate its standing in the world. The CEO's job is to instill principles every day that will make accidents and rogue practices virtually impossible.

The good news is that a strong reputation is something a committed leader can decide to have, and he or she can set out to achieve it through specific actions. Market bias and public opinion aren't like the weather—any CEO can elevate the company's reputation, and therefore his or her own. And, while these two reputations are not the same, the CEO can't build his own without first taking care of the corporation's. Companies, after all, generally survive crises of reputation; the careers of the managers involved in them usually do not.

So, whether strong or weak, reputation becomes a self-fulfilling prophecy and tends to perpetuate the current experience. A strong reputation not only propels a company's positive momentum, it enhances the CEO's power to bring needed change.

The seven strategies on which this book is based (see box, page 19), and which I will explore in depth in part two, offer a comprehensive approach to building a positive, protective corporate reputation. These strategies will transform the position a company and its leadership hold in the minds of its constituents. The investors in such a company, and the public, will seek out management's view of its markets, and they will look to the company as a standard setter for the best practices in its industry. They will come to judge the company's competitors on how well those competitors measure up to the standards the company has set. Both the company and its leadership will attain a level of influence they may not even have sought in earlier times.

Even though these strategies address the management of a company's relationships with everyone it affects, they bear no relationship to altruism. Instead, they reflect a new realism. They describe the terms of predictable survival for a company and its leaders in this new "age of consensus."

THE SEVEN STRATEGIES
OF REPUTATION LEADERSHIP

STRATEGY 1 Establish Core Values and Reputation Will Follow: Core Values and the Authentic Leader

STRATEGY 2 See Yourself through Stakeholders' Eyes: Market Intelligence and the Art of the Perception Study

STRATEGY 3 Define Your Company's Landscape: The Power of Stakeholder Mapping

STRATEGY 4 Build Your Reputation from the Inside Out: Become the Company You Want the World to See

STRATEGY 5 Tell Your Corporate Story: Engagement and the Communications of Convergence

STRATEGY 6 Prepare for Crisis: How the CEO Saves the Company Every Day

STRATEGY 7 The Governance Imperative: Oversight, Informing the Board, Compliance

---

These strategies work only when they've become everyday operating procedure. In accommodating the strategies, the corporate structure must allow management to develop and implement a set of core values agreed upon by all. It must also offer a process for gathering constituents' views so that business practices and communications address their concerns. It must provide a means of analyzing and mapping the stakeholder universe so the necessary parties contribute to the conversation. The structure must also encompass a communications discipline that ensures transparency and prepares for times of crisis. And it must deliver the means of assessing all the company's efforts in the reputation domain. These attributes of structure closely match the seven strategies. The correlation between structure and strategy is essential because no management can simply bolt the strategies onto a company that doesn't otherwise support them. The need to build reputation and accommodate the necessary actions must saturate the entire organization.

These strategies should appeal far beyond the leader by reaching those whose partnership he or she requires. They're intended to help orient the board as it identifies decisions that affect reputation and attempts to make those decisions with the broadest view of their potential impact. They will also provide the board with the tools it needs to assess results.

The strategies will also help individuals and teams supporting the chief executive, including those who communicate with investors and manage the company's public relations. They will help the heads of businesses understand how their strategies play out in the minds of investors. They will, in fact, address all those who think they may be headed for corporate leadership.

In focusing on the link between corporate leadership and reputation, the strategies show how to lead reputation change. Authority, of course, always comes from the top. Actions and tactics can be delegated, but the rationale behind them, and therefore the accountability for them, originates with the boss. The job is never finished, but a real, lasting, and valid reputation follows naturally after the process is well underway—when the company's various constituencies understand that their concerns have been considered and they recognize management behavior that will sustain the organization's new direction. This comprehensive program will not only show the leader how he or she can restructure corporate processes to build reputation, but how to demonstrate its efficacy. Although reputation is notoriously difficult to measure, this book will set forth the means to conduct reputation audits and develop specific points of confirmation that track the progress of a reputation development program. And it will show how such tracking plays a critical role in the CEO's relationship with the group that pays his salary—the board of directors.

Changes in the corporate atmosphere since the spectacular scandals that marked the early 2000s and the credit crisis that began in 2007 have been dramatic. Early in the decade the public watched handcuffed executives paraded across their TV screens and heard the sad stories of betrayed employees who lost livelihoods and sometimes their homes and families. No one escaped the effects of the financial crisis that began to emerge in 2007, and the world looked on in disbelief as corporate executives, many sitting before Congressional committees, pointed fingers in an attempt to assign responsibility to others. Directors whose job it is to look after the interests of investors now endure an unprecedented level of scrutiny for the actions of management. As a result, they are judging their managements—and hiring and firing them—with a view toward how well management protects the company.

Accentuating this new atmosphere is the need for board members not only to fulfill their responsibilities to shareholders, but to protect themselves from legal liabilities if they fail to do so. Their management of the company's reputation through the CEO has therefore become critical, and no leader of a corporation or any other kind of organization is going to last long without an agreement with the board about matters of reputation. The strategies set forth here provide both the board and the chief executive with an objective basis on which to approach their mutual responsibilities to the company and to all those whose lives it affects.

CHAPTER 2

The Great Stealth Factor in Business

Reputation is the great stealth factor in business. Executives and analysts customarily attribute business failures to familiar causes. They see the roots of product failures in market competition, pricing pressures, or other market factors. But too often they fail to consider the effect of consumers' opinions of the company as a source of business weakness and of specific failures.

Today, consumers make billions of dollars' worth of purchasing decisions on the basis of concerns for the environment, human rights, child labor practices, ethics, and the use of animal testing. In fact, consumers select the companies from which they buy much as they choose their politicians: on the examples they set and the values they portray. The relationship between consumer and corporation has become an emotional one.

These new kinds of customers are aware of the resources used to make goods, the environmental costs of the manufacturing process, and the effects on the environment of their own use of various products. Such scrutiny applies to most things people buy and use, from laundry detergent to clothes to automobiles. The great resource of the Internet and other media enables consumers to inform themselves about ways they and the businesses they support can become preservers rather than destroyers of the environment.

People with an awareness of the social and environmental implications of spending choices are sometimes referred to as conscience consumers. And not only are they everywhere, but they predominate among some of the most important shoppers—those under thirty. These are the most vibrant consumers and will be doing their shopping for the longest time.

There's a great temptation to resort to spin in order to manipulate attitudes toward a company. This is understandable, as we live in an age of unprecedented sophistication in perception management. Modern polling techniques allow us to determine what everybody thinks about everything. The use of focus groups has become a refined art. Technicians can assess minute emotional changes by electronic means. In this environment, many corporate leaders make the mistake of thinking they can extricate themselves from troubled circumstances through artful communication alone, without making fundamental changes.

The lure of perception engineering can be irresistible for

executives facing public pressure to reveal failings whose disclosure would prove damaging or embarrassing. They are prone to try one story and then another. But, like those financial derivatives with no underlying collateral that contributed to the financial crisis, narratives cannot work unless they reflect some fundamental reality. If they don't, the truth will emerge over time anyway, and then the damage may be virtually limitless.

Perrier of France found this out in the early 1990s when the public learned that some of its bottled water contained benzene, a carcinogen. Perrier management, unsure what to do, gave out a series of conflicting statements about the source of the benzene, all of which turned out to be guesses. Sales dropped dramatically, and, because the firm's credibility failed to recover, so did its revenues. The ultimate cost to management was the company itself when Nestlé bought it two years later.

The story didn't end there, however. While management was ousted in the sale of the company, the area of Les Bouillens, where the Perrier spring is located, still maintained the status and financial benefits it had enjoyed since 1898 as source of the world-famous water. Then, in 2004, Nestlé began acting like the multinational it was. Having bought the company and name, Nestlé said it had the right to move production anywhere it wanted—perhaps to the Czech Republic—and still call the water Perrier. It also explored the possibility of labeling water from Les Bouillens something other than Perrier.

The local mayor approached the French courts to change the name of the spring to one that reflected the Perrier name (Source Perrier—Les Bouillens), thereby preventing Nestlé from slapping the name Perrier on any other water. No resolution has arrived as of this writing, but the distinct possibility exists that a place in France will lose a substantial part of its heritage. Perrier management lost control of its story, and the cascade of events that loss triggered continues more than a decade later—all because of one company's disingenuous communications strategy.

Communication Starts with Listening

Throughout this book we will revisit the importance of authenticity in communication. Part of that discussion will involve communication within the company directed toward building an internal culture that supports a strong reputation. Another part will address the need to develop the company story, tell it to the world, and apply it to events as they occur. Yet no effective communication can take place without an understanding of the audience.

Companies make huge investments in creating impressions. They spend millions on advertising, public relations, investor relations, lobbying, and public affairs. But, except for consumer research on products, it is generally a one-way conversation from the company outward. Management is therefore denied the information and influence needed to win true allies. Uninformed communication is comparable to shooting an arrow while wearing a blindfold. On the other hand, becoming a participant in a dialogue enables the company to exert an influence that it could never achieve as a mere transmitter of spin.

Few companies have ever confronted a more promising business opportunity than Monsanto did in the mid-1990s when its scientists assumed the lead in developing genetically modified organisms (GMOs) that could help the world's farmers feed a global population that had grown to six billion. Today, however, GMOs have a dubious reputation—due, in large part, to Monsanto's failure a decade ago to participate in a dialogue with the public rather than attempt to dictate to it.

Monsanto's advances had created the prospect of a real reduction in world hunger. Scientists had learned to adapt the genetic makeup of crop seed in ways that would enable farmers in the poorest countries to grow food in places that had previously been too dry or too wet, too cold or too hot. Rice, the world's most prevalent food, could be engineered to carry enough vitamin A to reduce disease and malnutrition for millions. Tomatoes could be planted with slow-ripening characteristics that would allow them to travel on some of the world's poorest transportation systems and reach market while still fresh. It was now possible to grow bananas containing hepatitis B vaccine, and enough of them could be cultivated on a relatively small amount of land to immunize a medium-sized country.

Using GMO technology, Monsanto modified seeds for various food crops to make them resistant to its Roundup weed killer. Called "Roundup Ready," these seeds enabled farmers to spray Monsanto's Roundup herbicide directly on the fields during growing season. Roundup Ready seeds saved farmers money by freeing them from more specialized herbicides. It also reduced their overall need for chemicals. Three years after the introduction of Roundup Ready seeds, 40 million hectares of them had been planted worldwide. They dominated every market in which they were sold. Monsanto CEO Robert Shapiro's strategy of focusing the company on biotechnology made believers of Wall Street, and the stock price more than quadrupled between 1994 and 1998.

To maximize its advantage, Monsanto came up with a unique plan to market its seeds. In fact, it no longer wanted to sell them at all, but would deliver them under licenses that pertained to the genetic technology the company had placed inside them. In other words, Monsanto had decided to distribute the seeds not as physical products but as intellectual property that assumed the commercial characteristics of proprietary software.

Monsanto's licensing contracts required farmers to use only Monsanto seed and only Roundup herbicide. The company sent out detectives to check up on compliance, and their findings resulted in approximately 500 lawsuits against farmers who it claimed had failed to comply with its licensing agreements.

The company had now embarked on a path that began to arouse opposition from anti–genetic modification activists. Still, Shapiro pursued his strategy, which began to take on other unpopular features. Since ancient times, farmers have harvested seed from crops for planting the following season. In the case of Roundup Ready seeds, Monsanto claimed seed-saving was tantamount to illegal duplication of its intellectual property, and the company identified a potential means of stopping it that seemed preferable to suing farmers in court. Shapiro acquired a company that had developed a seed that produced crops whose own seeds were sterile. Quickly dubbed the "Terminator Gene" by opponents, this technology would prevent farmers from using seeds from prior crops in future plantings, forcing them to buy all fresh seed for each new growing season only from Monsanto.

What angered farmers and Terminator Gene opponents most was the spectacle, as they saw it, of Monsanto creating a highly beneficial technology, then withholding it in monopolistic fashion. It seemed to many that Big Brother had arrived on the north forty. And Monsanto had painted a large target on its back.

The environmental activist group Greenpeace charged the company with attempting to use the Terminator Gene to control world food supplies. The press picked up the scent, and skepticism about GMOs suddenly aroused many fears related to the sensitive politics of food. GMOs posed unknown health risks, it was said. Cross-pollination of GMO food crops with wild plants would give rise to unkillable superweeds. The arguments were highly emotional, none of them proven.

Opposition was particularly vehement in Europe. Monsanto's response was to spend approximately $1.6 million on advertising in the British media. The purpose of the advertising was to insist to the public it was wrong. "Worrying about starving future generations won't feed them," the ads said. "Food technology will."

It didn't work. Monsanto's stock price lost half its value during one of the strongest stock market booms in history. The European Union declared what became, in effect, a five-year moratorium on all genetically modified foods—shutting Monsanto and all of its peers out of the European market.

In a weakened state, Monsanto agreed to a merger with Pharmacia-Upjohn, which was shortly thereafter absorbed into Pfizer. In October 1999, after the EU's declaration of its moratorium on genetically modified foods, a dispirited Robert Shapiro addressed a London Greenpeace conference: "Because we thought it was our job to persuade," he said, "too often we forgot to listen."

Pfizer spun off Monsanto in 2002, making it an independent company again. The Monsanto of today has entirely different leadership from the company that submitted to a takeover in 1999.

Throughout the Monsanto story Shapiro remained a likeable figure, despite the company's arrogance and profound errors in judgment. One can think of him as a hero with a tragic flaw—which he himself named in admitting his failure to listen. The study of corporate experience over the last several decades tells us that Shapiro's story is not unusual. The age is studded with similar failures by truly intelligent and often well-meaning, but misguided, corporate leaders who thought they could create the appearance of accommodating public interests without really doing so.

The Decline of Royalty: A Prince and a Lord

Two corporate leaders in particular showed the ability to hold inspired visions of how to run large companies in a world that demands socially responsive behavior. But both of these leaders failed—or refused—to allow what they knew to penetrate their company cultures beyond a superficial level. One of these was Charles O. Prince III of Citigroup. The other was Lord John Browne of BP. Both knew how to lead companies and shape a corporation's culture. But both did it only halfway. And both ended up as ex-CEOs, looking incompetent and cynical.

Citigroup CEO Chuck Prince must have felt snakebit as he stepped aboard a Tokyo-bound plane one October day in 2004. In the year since he'd succeeded the legendary Sanford Weill, the news about what was then the largest of all financial institutions had turned negative in sudden, startling bursts.

From the moment Prince assumed his position, investors and analysts had wondered how strong a successor he would make. Weill had built the bank by acquiring and then cobbling together such legendary names as Travelers Insurance, Smith Barney, Salomon Brothers, and, finally, Citibank itself. For 20 years, Prince had worked as corporate counsel to Weill. If he'd been known at all, it had been as a behind-the-scenes negotiator, the guy who stayed up all night to pound out difficult agreements. But now, as CEO, he sat in full view. And though little of the new adversity could be attributed to his management, it did nothing to increase the market's confidence in him or the bank.

During the long hours of the Tokyo flight, it may have seemed to Prince that there would be no end to the bad news. In May, the bank had paid $2.6 billion to settle a lawsuit filed by investors affected by the bankruptcy of WorldCom, whose CEO, Bernard Ebbers, would soon begin a 25-year prison term for fraud and conspiracy. WorldCom was the largest accounting scandal ever recorded, and Citigroup stood accused of underwriting new loans shortly before the implosion. Then Citi had to set aside another $5.2 billion to cover possible claims related to additional corporate collapses, including Enron.

Then on a quiet August morning, with many European traders on holiday, the bank's European bond desk sold €11 billion worth of bonds in a two-minute period, depressing the market, and bought back €4 billion half an hour later, making a profit of about €17 million. This bold manipulation was so abusive of the trading system that it forced regulators to reexamine the fundamental rules of the market. Called "Dr. Evil" by the traders who executed it, Citi's strategy outraged precisely the people that the bank, as an underwriter and dealer, needed as friends—European government banking officials, who now foresaw that the regulations needed to stop such practices would reduce liquidity and limit access to capital.

The fallout from the bond trade could be damaging in crucial ways. If the measures needed to prevent such abuses constrained the market, capital could become more expensive. It could impact employment and social programs with distinctly negative political consequences for sitting governments. "This was a mixture of greed and arrogance," one official said of Citi's bond trade.

The SEC shared the view of many observers that Citigroup had lost control of its processes. The regulator imposed a moratorium on significant acquisitions until management could show that it had retaken control of the company. The share price was stuck in neutral. At the same time, Chuck Prince also confronted major business challenges in reviving Citi's consumer bank and building its presence in China. The market was rife with doubts about his ability to bring it all off, and he suffered particularly in the view of many when compared to Weill.

After his plane landed in Tokyo, Prince went to a press conference, and there, before cameras transmitting his image around the world, he bowed his head in the traditional Japanese gesture of remorse. He offered this bow to Japanese regulators who had just thrown Citigroup's private banking operation out of the country. The ejection followed years of complaints against Citi for deceiving customers, rejecting regulators' demands for stronger internal controls, "profiteering," conducting business relationships with organized crime figures and money launderers, and for falsely claiming to have cleaned up all these problems three years before. "I sincerely apologize to customers and the public for the company's failure to comply with legal and regulatory requirements in Japan," Prince said.

Citi's reputation lay in tatters, and Prince knew that his career and legacy depended on rebuilding it. To do this, he had to change the culture of a 300,000-person global organization. Through an exhaustive consultative process that included internal panels, surveys, and personal visits to other CEOs to ask advice, he established a clear and simple set of principles, which he called his "Five-Point

Plan." It focused on training, communications, staff development, pay-for-performance, and controls. He also championed a group of three principles he called "Shared Responsibilities"—responsibilities to clients, colleagues, and the bank's franchise. As part of his program to instill a sense tradition, he showed employees a carefully produced video portraying the bank's long and storied history.

Then for months he traveled the world to sell the plan to his employees. He spoke before 40,000 people at Citi locations virtually everywhere. And it worked. Virtually all of the misconduct stopped, and Prince began to look as though he had—against all odds—gotten the Citigroup empire under control. The kinds of events that had brought on the crisis simply stopped.

It turned out, unfortunately, that these efforts represented merely a good tactic instead of a fundamental change. Prince, the accomplished lawyer, clearly understood what he had to do to get the regulators off Citi's back. But, once that was done, he embarked on a series of actions that appeared to undermine the bank's ability to grow its businesses. Prince fired several senior executives who were key strategists and planners in some of Citi's most important business segments. Although it wasn't clear if their firings were the result of poor performance, among them were individuals who had received attention as his possible successor in the top spot.

The endgame arrived with the credit crisis that began in the summer of 2007. In July, a reporter asked Prince whether he was concerned about strains appearing in the credit markets that had been driving corporate buyouts, real estate speculation, and markets in opaque derivative securities. Prince conceded that liquidity would dry up at some point, but in a statement that soon became a signature of the wishful thinking of the age, he said, "As long as the music is playing, you've got to get up and dance. We're still dancing."

While it was dancing, Citi paid insufficient attention to risk. That November, Prince submitted his resignation at a special board meeting. The bank's loss for the fiscal quarter in which he left fell just short of $10 billion.

By the following spring, Citi had written approximately $35 billion off its balance sheet. It was forced to raise approximately $39 billion through new debt and stock sales. The stock price dropped more than 50 percent. Prince's first high-profile appearance on the public stage after resigning came when he sat before a Congressional committee answering questions about how he had earned his reported $68-million departure package.

Chuck Prince's story is more than a tale of corporate greed. It's even sadder than that. He had shown the capacity for true inspiration when he taught Citi's global workforce the proper conduct of a corporation. In the process, he gave us a textbook example of how to do it. But when he had put out the fire, he seemed to go on unaffected by the trial he'd endured.

Citigroup didn't suffer the subprime crisis because of an absence of values, and Prince wasn't the only Wall Street CEO to depart during that period. He was, however, alone among them in having brought a major institution back from the brink. Yet even with that experience behind him, he proceeded with business as usual once the regulatory cuffs were off. Prince lost, Citi lost, and so did the thousands of families who lost their livelihoods as the bank reduced its size to cut expenses and, ultimately, to comply with the terms of the government's bailout.

Which brings us to a theme that will recur throughout this book: Business reputation isn't just about business.

* * * *

If Chuck Prince wrote the book on changing corporate culture, John Browne of BP did the same for social responsibility in the kinds of immense infrastructure projects that often disrupt large swaths of landscape and the communities that lie within it. The story of BP under Browne offers us the spectacle of an elaborate, highly public program of reputation-building that, despite the investment of tens of millions of dollars, never penetrated to the core of the organization.

Achievement of a strong reputation requires the CEO to align every part of the company with its core values. Little is accomplished by taking innovative measures in protecting the environment and the rights of those whom a company affects if management doesn't conduct all of its day-to-day business according to the principles expressed by such actions. Browne's sad demise offers poignant evidence of this.

In the late 1990s and early 2000s, Browne made BP a leader in the enlightened rebranding of traditional industry. Having changed the company's name from British Petroleum, Browne initiated a campaign that claimed the letters "BP" now stood for "Beyond Petroleum." He intended to show that the company's new direction would focus on alternative energy sources, including solar, which would reduce greenhouse gas emissions. The company's logo became a sunburst against a green background.

But Browne did much more than rebrand his company. He used construction of its 1,000-mile pipeline from the Caspian to the Mediterranean to establish new standards in corporate social responsibility. During the early 2000s, it was the largest infrastructure project underway in the world. In a later chapter on the ways companies earn the "social license to operate," we'll describe how plotting the pipeline's route and BP's involvement with communities along the way brought the inclusion of an unprecedented array of interested parties.

Later the roof fell in on BP. Despite its unsurpassed record of demonstrating engagement with external stakeholders, a series of deeply embarrassing—and, in one case, tragic—setbacks revealed its failure to integrate the philosophy it expressed externally into the roots of its business. Senior management's deafness to its field teams' warnings on safety and basic infrastructure maintenance led to a series of operational and human disasters that severely compromised the company's credibility.

A preventable explosion at a Texas refinery killed 15 people and injured 180. Regulators later cited BP management for failing to respond to repeated warnings of substandard safety practices at the site. Then the failure of the company to follow fundamental pipeline monitoring procedures led to oil leaks in its pipelines across the Alaskan tundra. The result was a shutdown of many months, disrupting production equivalent to 8 percent of total U.S. crude output. Investigators found the company had inexplicably neglected to run standard corrosion tests. In light of the inspired measures the company had taken to assure that its Caspian pipeline not only met, but advanced, social and environmental standards, journalists, regulators, and other corporate observers struggled to reconcile the two BPs.

The company claimed it was just having a run of bad luck. But a BP-sponsored inquiry led by former U.S. Secretary of State James A. Baker concluded that senior management had ignored numerous warnings in both cases. The panel's report stated that such failures were not a coincidence of unrelated misfortunes, but instead were systemic to BP.

The failure to align the entire corporation with his best principles caused the early departure of CEO Browne, whom the BP board chairman a short time earlier had called the greatest British business leader of his generation. The disclosure that Browne had given inaccurate information to a court on a personal matter only hastened his exit. One of the early acts of his successor, Tony Hayward, was to restructure reporting and communications lines to reestablish management contact with its line operators on the ground.

In the end, BP had made great strides in engaging with influential constituencies, but these achievements came out of tactical thinking, not from core principles that should have permeated the entire business. The failure to make that simple distinction brought on the downfall of Lord Browne.

Sin and Redemption

The purpose of this book is to set forth the manner by which leaders can build strong organizational reputations and, by doing so, advance their own. Such a book, to be useful, must be explicit about ways a leader can fail to build the desired reputation, and so it must set forth a few cautionary tales. While it is customary to draw neat, uncomplicated conclusions in making a business case, the neatness is nearly always false. And that can be good news because, in failure, the possibility of redemption and rebirth remains.

In the years leading up to the subprime credit crisis corporate leaders dismissed by their boards often left with immense pay packages, and one might wonder what all that money meant to them. Stan O'Neal, ousted as CEO at Merrill Lynch for failing to manage risk, walked away with $161.5 million. Hank McKinnell resigned as CEO of Pfizer amid growing board and investor dissatisfaction, taking $213 million with him. Angelo Mozilo, CEO of Countrywide Financial, one of the companies most directly responsible for home mortgage excesses, pocketed $470 million over his last 5 years with the company.

The marriage of business failure and huge payouts provided an overarching theme in the wake of the subprime mortgage collapse. Yet one wonders where former executives go with all that money when they are shown the door. Is retirement with a boatload of gold the end of their stories? Henry Cisneros, the Democratic politician and former Countrywide board member, described Mozilo in late 2008 as "sick with stress—the final chapter of his life is the infamy that's been brought on him, or that he brought on himself." Stan O'Neal, on the other hand, reportedly played 20 rounds of golf during August and September 2007 as Merrill Lynch registered its largest quarterly loss ever. He left that October, and his performance before departing makes it easy to imagine his life afterward.

Depending on the nature of the individual, however, the story does not have to end in moneyed disgrace. John Profumo was not a businessman but a British politician who was born to wealth. In the early 1960s he served as Secretary of State for War in the Conservative government of Harold Macmillan. At a summer party in 1961 he met the 19-year-old Christine Keeler emerging from a swimming pool and began an affair with her. He was 46. Their relationship lasted but a few weeks before Profumo broke it off. And although rumors about it began to circulate, the British respect for privacy that still prevailed in those days kept the gossip relatively contained. When asked confidentially by colleagues, Profumo denied the affair.

Keeler's extreme allure, however, had a quality that induced dramatic events, and one of them caused the wheels to come off Profumo's denials. When one of her former lovers fired a pistol at Keeler as she looked out from the flat of another male acquaintance, a police inquiry began, and the press followed close behind. Another of Keeler's qualities was that she couldn't keep her mouth shut. Her statements to the police and friends that she hoped this episode would not damage Profumo were enough to open the floodgates.

The story splashed across front pages of virtually every newspaper in the world. And it quickly became a subject of debate in the House of Commons, primarily because Keeler also happened to be the mistress of a spy, Yevgeny Ivanov, Naval attaché to the Soviet embassy in London. The Cold War was at its height, and Profumo's sensitive position as Secretary of State for War suggested the possibility of a catastrophic security breach. (The vulnerability of secrets was overblown. For one thing, Ivanov said years later that Keeler could not have kept a story straight if her life, not to mention that of the free world, depended on it.)

Profumo repeated his denials openly to the House of Commons. And while the government heard what it wanted to—that no breach of morals or security had occurred—newspapers continued to pursue the rumor.

On a trip to Venice that spring, Profumo broke down and confessed the truth to his wife, the actress Valerie Hobson (star of movies that ranged from *Bride of Frankenstein* to *Great Expectations*). She urged him to return to London and tell all, which he did. It had been one thing to mislead his friends and fellow ministers. But lying to Commons was insurmountable, and he resigned immediately in disgrace. The scandal's stress on the government is widely held to have contributed to the resignation later that year of Prime Minister Macmillan and to Labor's ascendance to power in national elections a year later. It has been reasonably argued that Keeler, whom Profumo had met emerging from a swimming pool draped in nothing but a wet towel, contributed to the end of an extended period of Conservative rule in Britain.

Profumo, having been regarded as a possible future prime minister, now retreated to his 20-room Georgian mansion, scorned and ostracized by virtually all society. The first half of his story closes on him as a broken politician.

But not a broken man. The second half begins a few weeks later with his appearance at Toynbee Hall, a 19th-century settlement house and refuge dedicated to aiding the poor. Profumo turned up saying he would like to do anything to help out. Some reports say he started by cleaning toilets. His son wrote that he began by taking in the laundry of residents and working in the kitchen while maintaining the lowest profile he could.

Over time, the community at Toynbee Hall recognized that he was not using it as a vehicle to rehabilitate himself socially and politically. While not a broken man, he had become a different man, and he remained dedicated to the place for nearly 40 years until shortly before his death. Eventually, he brought his talents into play and raised funds that enabled Toynbee Hall to broaden its support for the poor with significant new programs. His wife, the former movie star, changed her life in parallel and became a leading advocate for those suffering from leprosy.

Thirty years after Profumo's political demise Margaret Thatcher invited him to her 70th birthday celebration and seated him next to the queen. "It's time to forget the Keeler business," Thatcher said. "His has been a very good life."

The Myth of Immunity

Business narratives are full of examples that support their author's themes, and the savvy reader will recognize that the world of business successes and failures is diverse enough to supply backup for virtually any idea. In this light, an executive might construe the stories of Perrier, Monsanto, Citigroup, BP, and the like as memorable headlines, but, by being headlines, as exceptions to the experience an individual may expect in his career and life. After all, we've read many tales of hurricanes, tsunamis, volcanoes, mad bombers, and earthquakes—and still we step out into the world each morning in the belief that such events are anomalies in the context of our lives.

Any executive, however, must reflect on the likelihood of a career-altering reputational crisis appearing in the course of his or her business life. There is, of course, the temptation to diminish the probability that lightning will strike the very spot where one is standing.

In his book *The Black Swan*, Nassim Nicholas Taleb maintains that we encounter, on a continuous basis, events that seemed remote in their likelihood until the point when they actually occurred. The terrorist attacks of September 11, 2001, come first to mind.

Financial markets, which absorb a great proportion of the world's intellectual capital and attention, have proved a rich source of the monumentally unexpected. In the last two decades or so we've seen the stock market crash of 1987, the Asian financial crisis of 1997, and the 1998 collapse of the hedge fund Long-Term Capital Management, which used trading strategies designed by two winners of the Nobel Prize in economics. Its rescue required quick action by the most powerful institutions on Wall Street to avert a systemic financial crash. More recently, the financial crisis that began in the U.S. home mortgage market took less than a year to engulf the world. All these events share a number of characteristics: They all seem unrelated to other occurrences. Not one was foreseen before it happened, but the logic of why it happened dawned on everyone immediately afterward. And, while they all seemed to represent exceptions, as a group they make the occurrence of unique, devastating events appear rather common. Though their particulars are always a surprise, as a type of experience, they're almost predictable.

If we allow it to, our simple observation of what happens can call into question our expectations of world and financial events, as well as those events that shape our working lives. Can a manager today expect that the odds are with him in his wish to escape scandals and corporate collapses in the course of a career? Those thousands of people who went to work at Enron every morning and did their jobs honestly know that the actions of those with whom you associate can dramatically affect your own life. At Enron, it was mostly top management who went off the rails. But this dynamic can work the other way, as well. A CEO who fails to establish a solid structure and culture in his organization significantly reduces the predictability of that organization and therefore makes his own destiny more uncertain.

Our strategic approach to the future depends on the interpretation of the world we choose for ourselves. George Soros traces the roots of the subprime crisis to the belief, which had prevailed for two decades, that markets are best left to self-regulation. This philosophy, which goes back to Adam Smith, received renewed sponsorship in the 1980s from Ronald Reagan and Margaret Thatcher.

Soros observes that the idea of market self-regulation plays well to the interests of those who wish to avoid oversight by the authorities. This freedom from scrutiny was undoubtedly popular among those in the finance world who designed and sold the shaky derivative securities that contributed to the subprime meltdown.

Soros points out that confidence in market self-regulation is closely tied to the idea of reversion to the mean, a statistical concept that says no matter how far certain values diverge from their historical relationships with each other—the ratio of stock price to corporate earnings, for example—traditional correlations will eventually reestablish themselves. This is an attractive proposition because it softens concerns around the riskiness of any strategy by implying that the market will always correct for mistakes. But Soros says experience teaches us that markets do not necessarily revert to a mean, and the belief that they inevitably will has contributed to governmental acceptance of light market regulation under which financial crises have continued to occur.

Whether markets revert to a mean or not, the idea is laughably irrelevant as a predictor of experience. In financial markets, a mean can represent data that varies 5 percent or 90 percent on either side of it. So the same mean can be derived from data that shows virtually no variation, or it can indicate a boom-and-bust cycle in which experience hardly ever comes close to the mean—though, over time, it lies equally on either side of it.

In much the same way, the career of any executive has little certainty of matching his or her idea of normal experience. Taleb makes the point that one of the most striking features of our inability to forecast events (though we explain them so easily in hindsight) is that we are blind to our inadequacies—despite the many recurring opportunities we have to observe them in action. Our mental hardwiring simply prevents us from seeing risks that lie outside our risk vocabulary—that is, outside the traditions of business thinking we've inherited.

The Risk Manager's Dilemma

For many CEOs, processes that support and enhance reputation don't come naturally. Their careers may have been free so far of adverse experiences associated with reputation. Or they may have adopted an "it can't happen here" outlook. This attitude is sometimes called "presumptive integrity," and those who hold it believe their fundamental honesty—and that of their staff—places them beyond the temptations of moral compromise.

A CEO's belief in his organization's presumptive integrity may also indicate other qualities. It may, for example, reveal a chief executive who is willing to allow a certain amount of reputation risk in order to maintain a freer hand at running the company. This CEO might view the committees and information-sharing structures necessary to manage reputation as a bureaucratic burden or a source of unwanted internal scrutiny. Such CEOs occasionally regard internal consultations as interference. At times, then, an attitude of presumptive integrity that seems on the surface to represent positive thinking and a charitable view of human nature may actually turn out to be a refusal to engage in the diverse conversations necessary to lead.

Risk management, often called "enterprise risk management," is one of the most strenuously examined topics among senior executives and boards of directors. Consultants, many associated with insurance companies, have applied massive resources to generating risk-management products and services. They tend to cover information systems, internal audit controls, physical assets, security (including protection against terrorism), regulatory compliance systems, product liabilities, environmental damage, and human rights and labor matters. But seldom is reputation included on a list of risk-management issues.

Nevertheless, a survey conducted among more than 100 companies by insurance broker AON a few years ago determined that, after business interruption, reputation loss was considered the greatest hazard these companies faced. At the same time, only 22 percent of those interviewed had implemented a formal strategy to manage reputation risk.

How could this be?

CEOs have trouble recognizing reputation development as a distinct business discipline partly because it was rarely taught in engineering or business schools until the last decade or so. Leading a corporation toward a strong reputation requires a fundamentally different kind of thinking than that which customarily drives executive decision-making. Business traditionally focuses on metrics, on the ability to measure margins and other ratios of performance known to determine success or failure. Stock price is connected in great part to current and expected income, as well as to balance-sheet and cash-flow factors. Executive compensation usually turns on the metrics of productivity. Capital investment decisions are determined by expected return. Measurement, therefore, is one of the pillars of business culture—and rightly so, because without measurement, accountability is impossible.

But there's no comparable way to measure return on investment in the building of structures, training, and communications aimed at developing a solid reputation. If you have implemented a program to teach your employees ethical behavior, for example, it's impossible to calculate how much the misconduct that *didn't* occur would have cost you. (In Strategy 7, I will describe ways to assess the results of a reputation-building program.) The CEO who restricts reputation strategy to that which is objectively measurable essentially abandons the field of play.

Why? Because reputation exists in the subjective beliefs of others, and so requires subjective talents on the part of those who wish to influence it. These talents involve an understanding of the dynamics of dialogue and perception, and they derive as much from the executive's life experience as his business training. The CEO must instill in his organization a conviction that the company acts across a broad moral canvas. To approach reputation strictly on the basis of normal business measurement criteria is to risk the corporation.

CHAPTER 3

Structural Corruption

The panorama of reputational failure over recent years teaches us that a hypercompetitive corporate environment can induce good people to do ill-advised things. Furthermore, there's a stealth quality to the process of reputation loss. The decline of corporate conduct seldom happens all at once, but, rather, in slow, barely noticeable increments—until one day the company finds itself staring over a precipice.

The nature of a business environment can, in some cases, make it difficult for even the best-intentioned executives to maintain acceptable standards of conduct. What do you do when norms of practice in your company or industry are illegal and any hesitation to compete on a level (though crooked) playing field can put you at a severe—and possibly lethal—disadvantage? There is no easy answer to this question. In fact, there may be no way at all for an executive intent on a viable long-term career to continue under such conditions. And getting out can mean a costly abandonment of investment in time and effort—and often equity. Though at first this scenario may seem extreme, no one should consider himself or herself immune from having to face such circumstances. One may have enough luck to avoid them, but anyone committed to a long career should also understand that there may come a time when he or she is denied the luxury of observing them from a distance. Sometimes they simply engulf a business and everyone in it.

In his book *The Tipping Point*, Malcolm Gladwell says that the way some ideas gain acceptance with ever-increasing momentum is similar to the manner in which epidemics begin and spread. The disease metaphor can also help describe the contagious nature of business and financial misconduct. I use the term structural corruption to refer to a specific kind of risk-taking in which an entire enterprise, industry, or market deviates from accepted norms of behavior in a dangerous way. Often the pressures of business performance override the kinds of good judgment that managers would otherwise apply.

Structural corruption doesn't materialize out of nothing. It begins with a private but clearly stated agreement within a small group to cut corners, to find ways of doing things that appear to be in its favor but fail to account for their broader implications. The behavior then spreads to the wider workforce that hasn't been party to the original consensus, but which now views the practices that have resulted as standard operating procedure. Often years pass before it becomes clear that the breadth of the original agreement to engage in questionable conduct exposes the entire organization to compromise and reputation loss.

During the subprime credit crisis, executives of collapsed banks and corporations spent a great deal of time pointing fingers at one another. Richard Fuld, who had presided over the implosion of Lehman Brothers, admitted to a Congressional committee that he'd made mistakes, but so had a great many other people, he said. He was right. In fact, a consensus had taken form on Wall Street to value derivative securities in ways that served bankers' short-term interests but did not account for the real risks these securities carried. To promote this very profitable fiction, everyone who needed to sign on to the illusion did so, including ratings agencies who were supposed to maintain an independent view. This was a case of structural corruption. The lie was in the system.

Regulation and Its Discontents

If the axiom that you can't legislate behavior is true, then you *really* can't legislate behavior in financial markets. Certain segments of a population of smart, motivated people who gravitate to large amounts of capital will, in the long run, find ways around the scope of existing legislation, which is often decades old and out of date. But, more immediately, they will easily rebuff the regulatory enforcement bureaucracy. Some will be found out and indicted, but by the time this occurs, the problem will generally have become so pervasive as to rock an entire industry.

If, during the market bubble of the mid- and late 1990s, you had listened to company conference calls in which management discussed quarterly financial results with equity analysts, you would have heard a curious camaraderie between the executives and the analysts on the other end of the line who were supposed to be assessing them. The job of an analyst was to scrutinize companies for the benefit of the analyst's clients—institutional money managers who were entrusted with the investments of mutual funds, pension assets, and other reservoirs of capital important to the retirement and well-being of millions. The ingratiating attitude these analysts typically adopted toward management was therefore curious in the extreme. "Nice quarter, guys," was often the phrase that introduced a supposedly neutral analyst's conversation with management.

The abdication by many analysts of their fiduciary responsibilities to clients became generally apparent. Jack Grubman, telecom analyst for Salomon Smith Barney, part of Citigroup, had been found to be consorting with WorldCom in ways that were hazardous to his objectivity. He had advised CEO Bernard Ebbers on such matters as WorldCom's takeover of MCI. Grubman made at least one presentation to the WorldCom board of directors on financial strategy while he was supposed to be judging the company's viability as an investment for his clients.

The Trouble with a Business Model Built on Illegal Practices

A reputation challenge facing a corporate leader can be complex and daunting. How, for example, do you preserve your reputation while competing in an industry whose very structure is corrupt? That was the case in much of the insurance industry in the late 1990s and early 2000s, as one of its most powerful brokers, or middlemen, pursued a business model based on deception. But what does it look like when a group of associated companies undertakes risky behavior across a host of industries? The experience of Marsh & McLennan offered just such an unhappy spectacle, as three of its affiliated companies fell into what one insurance commentator called "a perfect storm."

In October 2004, New York Attorney General Eliot Spitzer filed suit against Marsh—the world's largest insurance broker—and others for bid rigging and taking illegal kickbacks in the sale of large industrial insurance policies. There was no secret in the industry that brokers, in connecting large buyers of insurance with insurance underwriters, had been collecting commissions from both sides. They received customary commissions from their clients, the purchasers, but they also collected fees, called contingent commissions, from the underwriters who sold the product. Brokers naturally channeled business to those underwriters who paid the highest contingent commissions.

This lucrative arrangement had brought Marsh $800 million the year before. To create a stable flow of contingent commissions, the company asked some underwriters to bid high on certain contracts in a scheme that allowed those who had previously held the contracts to retain their business. Those who gave way by bidding high, and therefore losing, were favored under similar situations in the future. As a result, underwriters were able to offer insurance under noncompetitive bids, receive higher premiums, and hold onto their business at the same time. The contingent commissions compensated Marsh for making the underwriters' lives more predictable and profitable. The losers, of course, were the customers—large companies, their investors, and governments at all levels—whom Marsh steered to the higher-priced insurance products.

Not only was this practice prevalent in the industry, it was Marsh who had made it so. To create the appearance of a free market, it was necessary that other large brokers pursue the same ruse, and Marsh convinced them to do so. In his statement on filing the suit, Spitzer said, "These charges go to the heart of Marsh's and the industry's business model. There was craven disregard for ethics and the law at some of our nation's largest companies."

As the drama played out, it became clear that Marsh was not prepared to deal with the assault from Spitzer, who accused management—and particularly CEO Jeff Greenberg—of a lack of candor in early communications with the attorney general's office. Spitzer told Marsh's board to examine its management closely, claiming it had "corrupted the marketplace." He said, in fact, that he would not negotiate with current management, and CEO Greenberg suddenly resigned. (Mr. Greenberg's father, Hank Greenberg, left the chairmanship of AIG in an accounting fraud just two months later.)

Under an agreement with Spitzer, Marsh committed $850 million to a restitution fund for customers. This was roughly equal to revenues the company had received in contingent commissions the prior year and left it open to billions in claims from defrauded customers. Hoping to mitigate this exposure, Marsh issued a public apology for its "unlawful" and "shameful" conduct. The company's share price dropped nearly 40 percent within days, and much of the industry experienced similar declines in recognition of the widespread nature of these practices. An irony of the Marsh story is that one of the larger areas of consulting it offered clients was, yes, risk management.

The second front of the storm erupted in Marsh's Putnam Investments mutual fund subsidiary. Putnam, one of the most recognizable names in personal investing, was cited in a market-timing scandal that spread across much of the mutual fund industry. Certain favored investors were allowed to trade after daily closing prices were known, much to the detriment of its funds' other participants. Putnam ended up paying $108.5 million in restitution to disadvantaged investors. (The industry forfeited over $3 billion.) This came after Putnam had paid $110 million in fines for similar "market-timing" trades of its own portfolio managers. Then, in March 2005, the company paid another $40 million to the SEC for failure to disclose favored relationships with brokers. Even worse for Putnam, investors pulled $94 billion out of the fund's total $204 billion under management.

The final element of this story connects Marsh & McLennan to the extraordinary compensation given to New York Stock Exchange chairman Richard Grasso, who was forced to resign after the details of his $187.5 million pay package became public. Although the NYSE board charged with setting Grasso's compensation included some of the most experienced names on Wall Street, what the board actually knew of the package it approved has never become clear. Spitzer filed suit against Grasso for the return of at least $100 million. Grasso, having a solid contract, eventually won the case. But funds that *were* returned included the nearly half-million-dollar fee paid to Marsh & McLennan subsidiary Mercer, which had served as the board's compensation consultant. Charged with advising the board on customary standards of pay, Mercer returned its fee on the basis of having failed its mandate.

When opportunities to create innovative strategies present themselves, it's crucial to understand their implied risk scenario. Marsh's troubles resulted from decisions taken according to normal business protocols. They received full discussion, review, and vetting by responsible executive groups. Their implementations were integral parts of company business plans. Given the stiff competition in virtually every industry, and the enormous rewards available to those who succeed, senior managers can *expect* to face such crossroads in the course of their careers where a small number of decisions profoundly affect a company's ultimate sustainability. The success those executives achieve, and the rewards their careers generate, can easily hang on the decisions made in such moments.

Nothing happens in a vacuum. If a company is considering activities that may be ethically marginal, it is likely that the company is not alone. Though management may not be aware of it, it is most likely following these strategies because the zeitgeist of the moment seems to allow it, or even promote it. And the fact that others are pursuing similar kinds of activities will create a critical mass of wrongdoing. Attorney General Spitzer could more easily go after Marsh and others because popular opinion, fed up with the general tenor of corporate behavior, supported his doing so.

Reputation concerns seemed to be absent from Marsh's corporate vocabulary. The company's lack of candor in initial communications with Spitzer's office led to the departure of CEO Greenberg, as well as to that of Marsh's corporate counsel, who had told Spitzer immediately prior to the filing of the complaint that he was not aware of any wrongdoing. The expected drop in revenues from the loss of contingent commissions led Marsh's board to fire 3,000 people, about 5 percent of its worldwide workforce. According to one close observer of the insurance industry, the downsizing was due less to an expected drop in revenues than to a panicky board that had little perspective and was, therefore, desperate to demonstrate it had done everything possible to avoid culpability. Because Marsh had not adequately considered reputation issues prior to the crisis, it had no idea how to contend with them as the drama unfolded.

"Gee, Mom—Everybody Does It"

Corporate leaders face such choices in the most normal of circumstances. In fact, there can hardly be a CEO anywhere who isn't conscious of having to operate in an environment fraught with conflicts of interest. Virtually every CEO must therefore answer this question: Why should we make investments and sacrifices for reputation when so many others do extremely well without ever considering such matters? This book is largely devoted to offering a response to that question. And it would be a hollow conversation if we didn't describe some of the obstacles leaders face in committing themselves to build companies around strong reputation principles.

Perhaps the most sensitive place to start would be the field of executive compensation, which has become a source of heated contention for being wildly out of proportion with the pay of others in the workforce. In 2005, average CEO pay was up 298 percent over the prior ten years, the average worker's only 4.3 percent.

Average CEO pay was 821 times the minimum wage. Excessive compensation levels don't present much of a problem for those CEOs whose philosophy is to get rich and get out. But for leaders who are builders, the manner in which executive compensation is established across the business landscape can exert a pernicious effect on the atmosphere in which they work.

The ascendance of compensation consultants has added a significant layer of potential corruption to the process of establishing CEO pay levels. Boards, who must answer to their shareholders over executive pay, generally retain these specialized consultants to render opinions. Doing so enables a board to show that it has impartially vetted the CEO's awards and that those awards reflect the norm. The twist is that the various other services the consultant delivers to the company may dwarf the fees it receives in advising on executive pay. For example, the consultant may offer actuarial services used by human resource departments; it may also develop and administer pension plans and other employee benefits programs. These are highly lucrative propositions, often involving the company's purchase of expensive expertise and sophisticated software.

The second twist comes with the recognition that, while it is the board that retains the consultant for advice on pay, it is the CEO and management team—whose pay is the subject of that advice—that hire him for those other highly profitable activities. U.S. Representative Henry Waxman issued a report to a congressional committee saying that, in 2006, 113 *Fortune* 250 companies employed consultants who had conflicts of interest in their service to the company.

So what the CEO sees in such a compensation consultant is a business entity whom he or she is paying, whom the board is also paying, and whose business plan contains an embedded, institutionalized conflict of interest. To invest in a socially responsible business culture, a CEO must recognize such improper practices for what they are and resist them, no matter how widespread they've become. Experience shows that it's only a matter of time before he is held responsible for ethical violations, no matter how many years they may have been overlooked.

The CEO faces similarly compromised consulting arrangements among his corporate auditors and the credit rating agencies who analyze the company's debt. As pay consultants do, auditors provide management advice, information technology systems, and a host of other support resources. All of these services generate considerable revenue from corporations on whose books the auditor is charged with rendering an impartial judgment.

The most extreme case of a compromised auditor lies, of course, in the shocking measures Arthur Andersen took to protect its client, Enron, as the latter collapsed amid its own monumental fraud. Much of the world gawked at the spectacle of Andersen employees lined up at paper shredders in Enron's accounting department as investigators closed in. But the most interesting piece of the Arthur Andersen story is the way it revealed how an aptitude for gross illegality can lie dormant in a company's culture until a triggering event flushes it out. The ease with which Andersen moved to destroy evidence in protecting a prized client strongly suggests that the willingness to do so did not appear overnight. The overturning of Andersen's criminal conviction on a technicality involving a judge's jury instruction did nothing to remove that impression.

When auditors compromise professional standards, companies often fail. In the case of Andersen, the auditing firm itself went out of business. Eighty-five thousand people had worked for Andersen worldwide before it collapsed. But the fall of any single entity, no matter how dire the consequences for families and communities, pales in comparison to the damage that can occur when companies charged with maintaining the foundations of the financial system abandon their charter in pursuit of value for their shareholders.

The Complex World of Profit-making Regulators

Every CEO whose company borrows in the public markets must submit each issue of the company's debt for a risk rating by one of three agencies—Moody's, Standard & Poor's, or Fitch Ratings. Each of these is a private-sector, profit-making organization that rates securities under government charter. Moody's is listed on the New York Stock Exchange, as is S&P's parent, McGraw-Hill. Fitch is a subsidiary of Fimalac, a highly profitable, publicly traded French financial services group.

During the mortgage bubble that preceded the subprime credit crisis, ratings agencies were under great pressure to give investment-grade ratings to packages of mortgages that banks were selling as investments. Such ratings would induce risk-averse investors to buy these highly complex derivative products. The volumes were staggering, and there appeared to be tremendous financial opportunity for anyone involved in this business. Commercial banks and finance companies had given home loans to virtually anybody who wanted one, paying little attention to whether the borrower really would have the means to repay the debt. The lenders then removed these loans from their books by selling them up the financial chain to investment banks that would aggregate large numbers of them into packages they then sold off to investors. But without investment-grade ratings—required by the operating rules of many investment firms who bought the securities—the entire business of selling these packages would have ground to a halt.

So for the banks, getting investment-grade ratings for their loan packages was everything, and they began to exert the considerable leverage they had over credit agencies to squeeze the required ratings out of them. While ratings serve the interests of investors who want to be exact in determining their level of risk, it is the issuing entity—the investment banks, in this case—who chooses the agency and pay for the rating service. It is similar to a situation in which you find yourself exceeding the speed limit as you drive down a highway and have the opportunity to interview three different cops before deciding which one you want to deal with. Similarly, to get the ratings they required, the banks learned to go ratings shopping among the three agencies. If they couldn't get the rating they wanted from one agency, there were two others with whom they could negotiate. They also lobbied the agencies for favored analysts to work on their accounts, undermining any perception of blind impartiality on the part of the agency. Because investors' and regulators' faith in the ratings process is essential if a financial system is to work, it is a fundamental principle that agencies must resist such pressure.

But the agencies caved in as a group, suspending standards and awarding ratings that the industry in mortgage derivatives would need in order to flourish. Of course, this willingness to please required them to ignore the quality of the underlying mortgages. The market in packaged mortgages consequently boomed, based on the belief that the ratings agencies had acted in good faith. Bankers were able to build enormous wealth until it became clear that default rates on mortgages were becoming many times higher than the agencies had forecast. Real estate prices declined, and many mortgage holders who now owed much more on their properties than they were worth simply mailed their house keys back to the banks and moved to cheaper rental properties. The subsequent U.S. recession and diminished economic activity in much of the world is traceable back to the credit agencies' enabling the banks to sell those many thousands of untenable mortgages.

Any corporate leader working in this atmosphere might be forgiven for questioning the advantage of developing reputation-oriented policies. After all, if government-chartered credit agencies can abandon their public mandates and restrict their focus to narrow business interests, why should others refrain from following the same route?

And what might such a leader think when he observes a powerful agency of the U.S. government—an agency involved in regulating one of the most sensitive industries—behave in a similar manner? That's what he would see on examining the Food and Drug Administration's oversight of pharmaceutical companies. In the section that follows, we'll see how subtle agreements to breach accepted modes of conduct can metastasize wildly and, while dominating the front pages, undermine a great company.

When the Risk Is You

Few tasks of government are more important than making sure the medicines people take are safe and effective. The Food and Drug Administration (FDA) is supposed to do this, and rigor in its practices and procedures is therefore essential in supporting the well-being of every individual in the country. So when the FDA shifts its protective powers from the consumers of drugs to their producers, the repercussions that follow should surprise no one. The scandal involving Merck & Co. and its painkiller Vioxx arose against the background of an FDA that had refashioned itself as a pharmaceutical industry trade association instead of a regulator of that industry.

For decades prior to the advent of this unhealthy relationship between the regulator and the regulated, Merck had stood among the world's most admired corporations. Its business in the U.S. went back to 1891, and in Europe to the 17th century. Merck's drugs had addressed fundamental human ills, from heart disease to hypertension to cancer. Millions had benefited; untold lives had been saved. In addition, Merck had achieved recognition as one of those companies that helps define ethical corporate behavior.

In the late 1990s, Merck faced patent expiration on a number of its big-name drugs. In a period of just two years, 2000 and 2001, it was due to lose exclusivity on products that, in aggregate, provided 20 percent of the company's revenue. To maintain growth,

Merck had developed a host of new medicines, among them an anti-inflammatory drug called Vioxx, which brought pain relief to arthritis patients without the stomach upset millions suffered from over-the-counter remedies.

Merck foresaw an immense demand for Vioxx and, in 1999, launched the largest marketing campaign in the history of the drug industry. In its first six months, the company spent $45 million on advertising—aimed both at physicians and their patients. The effort was immensely successful. By 2003, annual Vioxx sales had reached $2.5 billion.

Between 1999 and 2004, more than 20 million Americans took Vioxx. But as early as 2000, Merck knew there might be problems with its safety. Clinical trials had begun to suggest that Vioxx increased patients' risk of heart attack and stroke, and in May of that year Merck executives met to consider authorizing more definitive research into whether Vioxx might pose significant heart risk.

But instead of pursuing further study, Merck began to argue with researchers over the interpretation of their data. Management maintained that more trials would take too long, and Merck's marketing group believed the announcement of such trials would send the message that the company lacked confidence in Vioxx. In what may be one of the more curiously phrased statements on scientific inquiry, an internal memo said: "At present there is no compelling marketing need for such a study. Data would not be available during the critical period. The implied message is not favorable." Apparently the "critical period" was the time of the drug's commercial introduction. Merck, in other words, had delivered scientific inquiry over into the arms of its marketing department. It seemed to say that no news was good news and that knowing the truth about the drug's safety was not necessarily in the company's interest.

Throughout the next four years, medical observers continued to express concerns over links between Vioxx and heart disease and strokes. Finally, in the fall of 2004, Merck withdrew the drug on the basis of cardiovascular-related data that had arisen from a study intended for an entirely different purpose: to broaden the market for Vioxx as a therapy to prevent the recurrence of colon polyps. In trying to develop new markets, the company instead proved the dangers it would have found in the safety studies it had refused to do. The test in fact showed that the risk of heart attack doubled after 18 months of Vioxx use.

The most natural of questions then arose: How many patients' health had been damaged by the time it took to reach this conclusion? While the company made no estimate, a Merck spokesperson said that a thorough study of the matter, had it been undertaken in 2000 when questions first arose, would have returned results at about the same time as those for the colon polyp study in 2004. On this basis, then, Merck claimed that nothing had been lost in its failure to institute such a study four years earlier. However, without reference to the question of whether earlier studies could have saved lives, an FDA researcher estimated that between 88,000 and 140,000 patients had developed coronary disease as a result of using Vioxx.

Within six weeks of Vioxx's withdrawal, Merck's stock had dropped 40 percent, a decline far greater than the financial harm to the company that would have been explained by its simple recall. The rest can be attributed to reputation damage and the effects of the company's reduced credibility in capital markets. No one knew whether Merck faced similar liabilities on other products through equally lax methodology and lack of transparency. The company lost its AAA credit rating, which it had held since 1975. It also advised its shareholders that it was under criminal investigation relating to the marketing of Vioxx.

Advertisements appeared on the Internet, in print, and in the New York subway from lawyers soliciting people whom Vioxx had damaged, or whose family members had suffered or died, for class action suits against Merck. By February 2005, more than 500 lawsuits had been filed. Estimates of the firm's ultimate liability ranged from $4 billion to $18 billion. That May, chairman and CEO Raymond Gilmartin resigned amid the continuing uproar. Then, in September 2005, the first of many civil suits, this one involving a single patient, came in with a multimillion-dollar jury verdict against the company.

Merck succeeded in preventing consolidation of the lawsuits against it and set out upon a legal strategy of contesting every single one in court. It won and lost in about equal numbers. In late 2007 the company announced a global settlement in which it agreed to pay out $4.85 billion. Observers generally regarded this as a triumph of the company's legal strategy in that it involved an amount well under a year's earnings.

Merck's Vioxx troubles took place against a broad background of misconduct that involved its own practices, those of its competitors, and, most prominently, those of the FDA. Merck gave consulting contracts to doctors to induce them to prescribe its medicines and endorse their broader "off-label" use. In this way, the company attempted to induce physicians to exercise their rights to prescribe drugs for conditions that hadn't been part of their FDA approval processes. The company's financial support of academic research became contingent on the researchers' support of Merck products. Merck's staff delivered its own favorable research opinions and convinced respected academics to apply their names as authors. Nor was Merck alone among drug companies in pursuing practices that breached the bounds of acceptable business conduct, scientific honesty, and traditional norms of patient care. Glaxo-SmithKline paid a substantial fine on similar charges relating to its adolescent antidepressant Paxil.

But the most striking enabler and contributor to this atmosphere of deception was the FDA itself, which partnered closely with the drug companies. In fact, even though the FDA is a government agency, the drug companies actually fund its approval process, delivering a strong incentive for the agency's administrators to consider them their clients and to displace the public as the center of their proper interest and concern. Many of the outside consultants that the FDA used to staff advisory committees making recommendations on drug approvals were, at the same time, on the payrolls of the companies whose drugs were under consideration. The FDA routinely granted these consultants waivers on their conflicts, claiming it could find no other competent people to perform this function. In fact, there's possibly some truth here: So deep was the drug industry's reach into the medical and academic communities that it co-opted thousands of physicians and academics with lucrative speaking and advisory fees. When such lures failed, the companies resorted to threats to withdraw research funding and impede careers.

Merck's manipulation of Vioxx research wasn't a renegade action carried out by a few overambitious individuals. It couldn't have occurred without a broad—and unchecked—internal consensus to engage in improper conduct. This behavior arose out of a steady drift in corporate culture made in increments so small as to go almost unnoticed day to day. Merck suffered from the "echo chamber effect," a term that describes what happens when responsible individuals talk only to one another, without reference to outside, contrary, balancing opinions. Merck's own prescribed medicine for this dangerous conformity should have been diversity in its sources of ideas, a subject I will address later in this book. The absence of such diversity, and the atmosphere created by the FDA's abdication of its mission, were equal contributors to the collapse of Merck's reputation.

"The most scientific thing drug companies do is their marketing," says Dr. Drummond Rennie, a professor of medicine at the University of California, San Francisco, and deputy editor of the *Journal of the American Medical Association* (JAMA). Rennie is also a well-known gadfly who urges drug companies toward what he believes are more ethical practices regarding disclosure of medical research. In pursuing this goal, he points out the enormous discrepancy between what is deemed acceptable in corporate and personal behavior.

The ease with which individuals can participate in unethical behavior expands with the size of the group, Dr. Rennie says. To demonstrate the case, he points to his own experience as a mountain climber. He has scaled peaks in the Himalayas, Andes, and a range in Antarctica. "When you make the decision to climb a mountain," he says, "you generally place your trust in another individual who will largely determine whether you survive. You look him in the eye and decide whether you trust him or you don't. You have to be responsible to each other."

But as groups grow, responsibility becomes diffuse. This, to Dr. Rennie, explains how corporate executives can engage in kinds of unethical behavior as a management group that they would never tolerate in their personal lives. "Drug companies, which are run primarily by parents, don't act as parents would act whose children's lives are at stake," he says.

Merck didn't quite cook the books, but the company did squander something none of the more notorious companies of the age—including Enron, Tyco, and WorldCom—had enjoyed for even a moment of their collective existence: a legitimate reputation as one of the world's best-run corporations. This episode highlights one of the most troublesome challenges of all—how difficult it is to manage risk when the risk is you.

The IPO Game: You, Structural Corruption, and Your Broker

The technology boom and bust of the late 1990s offers one of the great examples of excess in corporate life.

Both NASDAQ and the New York Stock Exchange brought hundreds of companies public, sometimes several in a day, in transactions called initial public offerings (IPOs). On big IPO days, the section of Broad Street adjacent to the New York Stock Exchange could take on aspects of a rock concert, complete with live music, giant video screens, and banners heralding the new listing that stretched the entire length of the Exchange's august façade.

Executives of the IPO company *du jour* were generally given the honor of joining NYSE chairman Richard Grasso on the balcony overlooking the trading floor to ring the opening bell. As the trading day began, the financial media beamed images around the world of grinning executives celebrating with bear hugs and waves. They tossed baseball caps bearing the company's logo to the traders below.

While some of this joy was visible on camera, much intense satisfaction occurred behind the scenes among the investment banks and brokerages that had brought the company public. The IPO game made a great deal of money for everybody involved. The executives of the newly public companies were among the big winners, but the companies they ran often were not.

After trading opened, the price of the IPO shares characteristically began to rise. It was not uncommon for stocks, generally issued at prices between $12 and $20, to rise to several multiples of their original prices on the first trading day. A few hit $100. One can only imagine the thoughts of company founders—who had received the original $15 or so (less fees) per share for their life's efforts—watching investors, who may have had little idea what the company actually did, paying and receiving multiples of the original price.

As important as an IPO was for a company going public, it was as big an event for the investment banks and their associated brokerage houses who underwrote the deal. There, a Byzantine game played out. Because each IPO was an advertisement both to companies who were candidates for the next deal and to the investors who would pay commissions to own these buoyant shares, price performance after the stock began trading was critical. In this, the banks left little to chance.

To help assure that the price would rise after issuance, banks and brokerages carefully monitored their order books, which told them who had committed to buy and therefore gave them a forecast of the demand for the shares of each IPO company. They used this information to price shares at issuance. More accurately, they underpriced them so they would rise in open-market trading.

The IPOs brought enormous personal windfalls to the executives of newly public companies, often consummating years of work, so company executives tended to take their bankers' word on the appropriate price of the shares. It was the bankers, after all, who had appeared to make them wealthy. Therefore, company executives were likely to accept what the bankers, whom they saw as benefactors, determined the correct price to be.

An IPO represented an epic moment in the life of a senior executive. As a principal in a nonpublic company, the value of his or her holdings had always been abstract. There had been no trading in the stock, so it was impossible to tell what the company was worth. Then the bankers provided a "liquidity event," meaning they took a large part of management's ownership, registered it as equity, and sold it into the market at a price. Executives immediately received millions in real money they could put in their personal bank accounts. At the same time, they retained shares that were rising in market value as investors and traders continued to bid them up.

Few executives of IPO companies seemed to think that their banks' assurances of a price rise might mean that it was issuing the stock at a value below what the company was actually worth. It was in no one's interest to question this. If the company was being undervalued, its executives were still making a bundle.

Sometimes the underpricing of the shares at issuance was only the beginning of the game. Banks were constrained by the need for some moderation in their underpricing. After all, they could bring out a stock whose fair value was $30 at a $15 issuance price, but not one whose value might be $50 (although investors might end up paying even more for it). So how could the banks make sure that the price shot up no matter what the original price? Aside from promoting the notion of a "new paradigm," in which traditional standards of value no longer applied, they sometimes made trading at higher prices a condition of entry for investors. "Laddering" was the term applied to the practice of extracting commitments from investors to buy shares at ever-higher levels, even before receiving their first allocations at the IPO issuance price. So bankers knew beforehand that buyers would appear at those higher prices, an advantage that has not often occurred in the history of financial markets.

The IPO game was so lucrative that each set of players paid richly for entry. Investors who wanted allocations of shares at the original IPO price paid the banks and brokers unusually high commissions. Sometimes the banks took this too far, and in January 2002, Credit Suisse First Boston (CSFB), a major IPO bank, paid $100 million in a settlement with the National Association of Securities Dealers to resolve a complaint of excess commissions charged to IPO investors.

While the investors paid the banks, any bank who wanted a mandate to underwrite a company's shares had to find innovative ways to win the privilege. It had to make it worthwhile not for the company, but for the executives within the company who decided which bank they would hire. The banks knew, in other words, that serving the personal interests of decision-makers, as distinct from those of the company, was key to winning those mandates.

"Spinning" was the technique of promising IPO shares to executives of companies who wanted to bring their companies to market. These allocations generally consisted of unrestricted shares, which meant executives could resell them immediately, without the usual holding period that forced them to retain the shares for a time to ensure that they would continue to act in the company's interest. An executive could receive shares in the morning at the IPO issuance price and "flip" them—that is, sell them—in the afternoon for a substantial profit. By offering this deal, a bank could provide an executive with a considerable incentive to give it the under-writing mandate. In some cases, it could make his fortune in a day.

One consideration that seldom arose during the IPO boom was the long-term sustainability of the companies involved. When the Internet bubble burst, the share value of many sank below the original issuance price. Notably absent in the great rush to use companies to create trading events was the sober consideration of their value as going concerns. Extended periods of share volatility caused the demise of some. A number should never have been con-sidered for public markets in the first place—they were less com-panies than vehicles for stock sellers to sell stock.

Stock Exchanges: Utilities or Businesses?

Much in the way the subprime crisis less than a decade later would include the implicit collaboration of mortgage companies, investment banks, ratings agencies, and regulators, so too did the technology bubble of 2000 sweep up much of Wall Street in its delusions. As we saw earlier, equity analysts became celebrities and then fell under a tide of revelations that they were lying in pub-lished research about their real opinions of companies. They did this to pump up companies' stock in order to gain their favor and, therefore, their investment banking business.

One can understand how CEOs who benefited from analysts' lies could think themselves "masters of the universe," in Tom Wolfe's phrase. But, as a model of corporate leadership, this was anything but masterful as a basis for guiding companies into an age in which reputation and social responsiveness were becoming significant factors in their ability to survive.

The technology boom and bust also coincided with the evolu-tion of stock exchanges from their traditional roles as facilitators of liquidity to profit-driven enterprises. New York Stock Exchange chairman Richard Grasso's $187-million pay package was only one reflection of this change. As exchanges solidify their positions in what is now a stock-exchange industry, their revenue-driven incentive to increase volume brings new liabilities. There is little reason to believe that the constant creation of new financial instruments to generate fees and commissions will serve the interests of economic stability. The derivative vehicles at the center of the subprime crisis offer strong evidence to the contrary.

What Made Bernie Madoff So Good? (And Why Did No One Want to Know?)

*"In actual life, I help people with their investments
until there's nothing left."*
—Woody Allen, *A Midsummer Night's Sex Comedy*

Bernard Madoff's alleged $50 billion Ponzi scheme, exposed just before Christmas 2008, became the apotheosis of the subprime financial collapse. The world had endured an unmitigated stream of adverse news throughout the year. The outgoing administration of George W. Bush had used hundreds of billions of dollars of taxpayer money to stabilize banks and insurance companies. It had—at least temporarily—bailed out Detroit automakers, two of which had been so spectacularly mismanaged that they were perhaps within weeks of fading to nothing. Yet the picture, bleak as it was, had begun to clarify. People believed that even if the worst wasn't over, they could begin to see what the worst looked like. Many were starting to focus on economists' forecasts of a return to growth in the second half of 2009 or in 2010. Then Bernie Madoff, overnight, became a household word by taking the public mood to new and unforeseen depths.

On December 11 and 12 hundreds of individuals and institutions received calls telling them that they were victims of a fraud. Madoff had appeared to deliver strong, remarkably steady returns of 10 to 15 percent per year. But investors learned from these calls not only that their gains over the years had been fictitious, but that their original investments had been given to people who had redeemed their holdings earlier. In many cases entire fortunes were gone. People who had been wealthy the day before were wiped out.

Many of those who had lost their fortunes with Madoff had never heard of him. They had invested through "feeder funds," which were mostly financial marketing companies that gathered assets from wealthy individuals, foundations, and other investment companies. Some feeder funds represented themselves as money managers but actually handed the investments to Madoff. Many executives who ran these feeder funds also lost substantial personal wealth. But those who had claimed to be managing the money themselves had a difficult time justifying the substantial management fees they had charged investors.

Although few people knew anyone directly affected by the Madoff scandal, it further intensified the general sense that nothing was as it seemed. The financial crisis, begun in the opaque world of mortgage banking and derivative securities, mystified the public. On the evidence of those whom Madoff had taken in, however, it now appeared that some of the smartest people around couldn't tell the difference between what was real and what was not.

Market conditions exposed Bernie Madoff. Steep price declines during the year brought increased redemptions in virtually all funds, not just his. Madoff's problem was that the general decline of wealth among investors made it impossible to raise enough fresh capital to cover those redemptions. There was no new money to pay off the old money.

How did it happen?

Madoff had long been one of the most respected figures on Wall Street. He was a former chairman of NASDAQ, a high-profile philanthropist, and one of the pioneers of electronic trading. His firm included one of the largest broker-dealers on Wall Street, which meant that he made markets for stocks and cleared trades in immense volumes.

He had built his business by making investing with him look like a privilege. He often said his funds were closed to new investors, but he would make a show of granting exceptions to people he said he liked. These tended to be investors with a great deal of wealth who did not ask questions. People were said to spend hundreds of thousands of dollars a year on memberships in the Palm Beach Country Club in Florida on the hope of getting close to one of his operatives who would bring them the opportunity of investing with Madoff. A genius for creating a mystique enabled Bernie Madoff to make deceiving sophisticated investors look easy.

Wealthy individuals not only put in their own money but they also channeled investments of their charitable foundations to Madoff. Within days of the fraud's revelation, a number of non-profit groups announced they were closing their doors because their endowments were gone. Many of those that did not shut down immediately found themselves significantly weakened. In the wake of the scandal, groups from human rights advocates to the owners of the New York Mets felt compelled to offer public assurances that they were still in business.

Madoff had told his clients that he invested money according to a well-known strategy called "split-strike conversion." This involved using options that limited the downside risk of his investments, but also put a cap on the upside. Investors and traders customarily used split-strike conversion in seeking steady, if not spectacular, gains. What struck some of the very few investors who looked under the hood of Madoff's operation was one simple fact: There were not enough such options traded in all the world to support execution of his strategy at the volumes he claimed.

The few firms who applied analytic back-testing to Madoff's trading found that his financial results and his announced investment strategy were an impossible match. And they said so. They said so to their own investors, whom they dissuaded from Madoff funds. And at least one had been saying so to the SEC for nine years. The SEC nevertheless had given Madoff a clean bill of health, and its outgoing chairman admitted the agency had failed in its duty.

Yet it didn't take such sophisticated analysis to see through Madoff. His business structure failed the most basic governance tests involving checks and balances and conflicts of interest. His brother was his chief compliance officer. His brother's daughter was the chief lawyer overseeing compliance. Madoff cleared his trades through his own broker-dealer. And his auditor was a three-person firm operating out of a tiny storefront office in a shopping mall in a suburban New York town. Of the three members of the auditing firm, one was a secretary, and another was 78 years old and living in Florida.

Within days after exposure of the scam, investors were looking to sue accounting firms who audited the feeder companies. It was no use suing Madoff's shopping-center auditors. They didn't look like they had much money. And any liability or malpractice insurance they carried was unlikely to approach the amount Madoff's investors had lost. Their potential targets were wealthy firms such as PricewaterhouseCoopers and KPMG, who worked for some of the feeder funds. But for what should investors hold them liable? Should those firms have noticed that Madoff's virtually clockwork 1 to 1.5 percent monthly growth was a little too perfect? That argument would be hard to make. But should they not have been surprised that one of the largest investment groups on Wall Street used an auditor few had ever heard of? Perhaps the big auditing firms might have asked who these people were. It might have saved the feeder company Fairfield Greenwich Group some of the $7.5 billion or so it reportedly lost with Madoff.

Rather interestingly, one firm that did take notice, and forbade its staff to invest the firm's or clients' funds with Madoff, was Société Générale—the same company whose own lack of internal controls in the Jérôme Kerviel rogue trading case had cost it more than $7 billion. In the aftermath of that episode, the French government had cited SocGen for an institutional history of fraudulent trading. But five years earlier a SocGen due-diligence team visiting Madoff had noticed the apparent conflicts in governance and the obscure auditing company. They went back to the office and tested his investment strategy against his results and found they didn't match up. The problems were there for anyone to see.

One might then ask why such sophisticated investors weren't more curious? A recurrent theme in public comments after revelation of the fraud was that many investors suspected that Madoff was engaged in irregular activities. But they thought they, themselves, were the beneficiaries. None of them sensed a Ponzi scheme that would make their wealth disappear.

One cleaned-out investor described getting the news this way: "The call came at 6 p.m. on Thursday, Dec. 11. I had been waiting for it for five years," wrote Robert Chew. Later in the same essay he said: "I think everyone knew the call would come one day. We all hoped, but we knew deep down it was too good to be true, right? I mean, why wasn't everyone in on this game if it was so strong and steady? We deluded ourselves into thinking we were all smarter than the others."

Some thought Madoff's stature and connections brought him inside information on the companies in which he invested. Many believed that the information on capital flows from his broker-dealer operation allowed him to anticipate market moves and use the information to his advantage. This is called front-running, and it is illegal. In 2004, five New York Stock Exchange specialist firms who pursued similar strategies in which they traded their own capital with the knowledge of, but before the execution of, their clients' trades, paid $242 million to settle SEC complaints.

Shortly after the scandal broke, Union Bancaire Privée of Switzerland, which had directed half the 22 hedge funds it advised to Madoff, costing their investors about $700 million, issued a letter that said, "We were assured that (Madoff) had some visibility as to the momentum of the markets due to his significant volume size as a broker-dealer. . . . The perceived edge was Madoff's ability to gather and process market-order flow information and use this information to time the implementation of the split-strike options strategy."

This is a remarkable statement. It would appear to be an admission by one of the premier Swiss investment firms that it was investing in Madoff because he took a possibly illegal advantage. One wonders if they even realized what they were saying.

In fact, Madoff appeared not to have been guilty of front-running. A Ponzi scheme does not require market manipulation.

Several weeks before the Madoff scandal broke, a revered American writer, Studs Terkel, died at age 96. Studs was a lifelong jazz lover and used a term for a jazz aficionado in ordering up his epitaph. He wanted his tombstone to say: "Curiosity did not kill this cat." It may have been a lack of curiosity that killed those who consciously invested with Madoff. If there was something untoward going on, many simply didn't want to know. They seemed to say: So what if he's a crook? He's our crook.

CHAPTER 4

Building Reputation Across a Global Company

✳

A global company with a history of operating across many different countries will find it natural to approach reputation risk by pursuing practices that have proven themselves over time. In one country, it might have established a history of building factories and staffing them with its own people. In others, it might have partnered with local firms or other multinationals. "If it ain't broke, don't fix it," the saying goes.

The definition of what's "broke" can change rapidly, however, as new environmental and labor standards take hold in places where they've seldom been considered before. Changes in accepted practice have outpaced changes in the law. Adhering to the letter of the law may no longer offer enough protection. A company's legacy can in fact undermine its efforts if that legacy involves traditional ways of doing business that the world no longer accepts. It's quite possible for a management to wake up one morning and realize that the world has passed it by.

The need to protect reputation has led companies increasingly to apply global standards in localities where regulations demand something less. For example, if the country in which an enterprise is drilling for oil doesn't require certain water purification and site-cleanup processes, that doesn't mean the company involved shouldn't be adhering to best practices.

Managements who pursue this line of reasoning do so out of business necessity. Revelations of environmental degradation—whether or not a company is in compliance with local laws—can bring damaging publicity, deeply uncomfortable shareholder meetings, and calls for product boycotts. So companies increasingly understand that the most remote island jungle or Asian steppe is eminently visible to global watchdogs. International financial institutions receive pressure from their own stakeholders not to lend to enterprises that despoil the environment or violate human rights—anywhere. Infrastructure loan agreements increasingly contain covenants requiring environmental and human rights compliance in highly specific terms. Banks finance projects in stages, requiring certification of environmental and social compliance before releasing each new tranche of funding.

Nike broke no U.S. law when, in the mid-1990s, it subcontracted with Asian companies that turned out not only to employ children, but to force them to work under deplorable conditions. Despite its technical adherence to the law, Nike suffered a severely damaged reputation when the realities inside some Asian factories making its goods became public. Its executives probably wished in hindsight that there *had* been an objective legal standard, because implementing the controls for adhering to such a standard might have spared them the public outrage that greeted revelations about child labor. But mere compliance was not nearly enough. The company's reputation as the progressive-minded manufacturer of quality footwear suffered even though it was operating within the letter of the law.

Nike's CEO and management team had failed to realize that world standards in supply-chain ethics were in transformation. They had been focused inward on their business and had missed the changes around them. Few had previously known or cared about the conditions under which its products were made. But globalization, which Nike fully exploited by outsourcing its manufacturing to countries where labor was cheapest, came back to haunt the company. Globalization meant globalization for non-governmental organizations, too, and the NGOs were watching the subcontracted manufacturers, even when the company wasn't. Nike got caught being a global player with a village mindset. Only after an arduous few years in the reputational netherworld did the company manage a turnaround. And when the turnaround came, it was exemplary. Nike established new standards for qualifying its manufacturers, and today it publishes the names and addresses of all its suppliers worldwide. Anyone can go to the company Web site and have a look.

Nike's experience demonstrates that an absence of clear guidelines does not free the CEO from the need to create the conditions for a favorable reputation to develop. It is a subtle, endless process, and managements must recognize those moments when a new approach is needed. In the old days of the fortress corporation, CEOs would say to their lawyers: "Tell me what I have to do." But more and more, corporate leaders are transitioning to a psychology that asks the question that originally eluded Nike: "What is the right thing to do?"

Still, it's not necessarily as simple as doing the right thing. In fact, doing the right thing isn't always consistent with a company's sustainability. Bribery, for example, has been an unavoidable cost of doing business at many times and in many places. Laws covering business practices in Germany did not outlaw bribes paid to foreign officials until 1998. And Siemens AG—Europe's largest engineering company, with $120 billion in revenues and 400,000 employees in 190 countries—would have had a hard time turning off the spigot even if it had wanted to. Such a company works under long-term contracts that are couched in even longer-term relationships with its customers. The foreign officials on the receiving end of the bribes, who determined whether their companies or governments purchased Siemens products, were unlikely to be moved by anything the European Parliament had to say about the tributes they considered their due.

In late 2006, German prosecutors raided Siemens' Munich offices and came away with dozens of names of people suspected of involvement in bribery. As of January 2008, investigators had uncovered €1.3 billion in bribes. By the summer, two former executives had been indicted, but worse than that, the company had lost two successive CEOs. Of the 12 individuals who had made up the management committee before the scandal hit 18 months earlier, all but one had left. The company had already paid €201 million in fines and faced approximately a dozen other investigations, including one by the Securities and Exchange Commission in the U.S., which held the potential for driving up fines substantially.

In its attempt to determine the depths of corruption within the company, Peter Löscher, who took over as CEO in the summer of 2007, offered amnesty to anyone below the top 300 executives who would come forward with information. No fewer than 110 did. The company's investigations revealed that employees funded the bribery by creating a slush fund that collected fees through sham consulting contracts. Executives signed potentially incriminating documents with sticky notes they could easily remove if things got hot.

The law firm of Debevoise & Plimpton, authorized to carry out an independent investigation, concluded that the bribery that had occurred wasn't a rogue operation pursued by individuals who had taken matters into their own hands. It was instead a fundamental business practice spread across several of Siemens' ten business divisions. The German judge who sentenced the first Siemens official convicted in the scandal said, "All control systems and the entire organization were geared to make such behavior possible." In an interview with the *Wall Street Journal*, Siemens' corporate counsel said, "There was a cultural acceptance that this was the way to do business around the world, and we have to change that."

During the investigation, a Siemens employee reported former CEO Heinrich von Pierer's response to a question about a $10-million bribe to be paid in Argentina. Von Pierer is reported to have said those involved should act like "soldiers for Siemens." It appears that a "we'll-look-after-you" culture prevailed in the company. Management asked employees to expose themselves to illegality in the field with the understanding that the center would always protect them. But it turned out that no one was protecting the center.

Löscher acted to transform Siemens' dozens of businesses into three main divisions and relocated their heads to corporate headquarters. Businesses that had been run by boards all over the world now sat together on a single management committee, and accountability became centralized.

But against the uncertainty over what ongoing investigations would bring to light, Löscher refused to delegate authority to people who, nevertheless, remained part of the management team. In fact, the effect of these events on the company's culture became a cause for concern among Siemens' stakeholders. A *Wall Street Journal* reporter quoted the head of a large supplier as saying, "I am deeply worried about Siemens. In the company, everybody seems to mistrust everybody. There is a real danger of this turning into a culture of fear where nobody dares to decide anything."

Concurrent with the bribery investigation, Siemens also faced prosecutorial inquiries into possible violations of the UN oil-for-food program with Iraq. And one board member came under suspicion of participating in a plan to provide secret financial support to an insurgent, company-friendly labor group despite the incumbent union's holding nearly half of Siemens' board seats.

The perception of a company that failed to respond quickly to laws that changed traditional ways of doing business—through bribery—evolved into a panorama of arrogant behavior. In their own ways, both Nike and Siemens failed to recognize the changes around them, and the sufferings of both companies bear witness to the damages that await those who fail to see change, take it seriously, and react. Sprawling global companies must constantly ask themselves who is monitoring their business across the world day to day, and what the company's ultimate responsibility will be for the acts of those who represent it.

In the wake of Siemens' bribery scandals, Peter Solmssen, its U.S.-born general counsel, traveled to many international locations to talk to some of the company's 400,000 employees about culture change. Solmssen reports that at one meeting in Mexico an employee stood up and simply asked who this American guy was to tell them what to do. This anecdote speaks to the difficulty in leading a company that represents diverse backgrounds and worldviews, all of which translate into culturally specific attitudes and ways of doing business.

Siemens' challenges in rooting out corporate bribery are emblematic of the pace at which standards of corporate conduct are changing. German companies had engaged in bribery as a normal practice to stay competitive. It was known as "schmiergeld," or "grease money." Before the EU outlawed bribery in the late 1990s, it was not only legal in Germany, it was tax deductible.

The U.S. Justice Department has dozens of investigations under the Foreign Corrupt Practices Act (FCPA) underway at any time, and a new era of cooperation between law-enforcement bodies in industrialized countries has shown the growing determination of governments to end bribery practices. Monitoring of corporate behavior has increased to the point that the likelihood of indictments and fines for graft has grown substantially, opening companies up to the prospect of severe and potentially damaging embarrassment. The U.S. oil field services company Baker Hughes paid a $44 million fine in 2007 for bribing officials in a number of countries. Inherent in these investigations is the possibility that executives can go to jail and that governments can refuse to do business with specific foreign corporations.

Today, companies monitor the intensity with which government entities—particularly the U.S. Department of Justice—pursue bribery investigations. Managements do this as a direct way of measuring their risk. At the same time, a tectonic shift has begun to emerge in the attitudes of many companies. Instead of trying to convince governments that bribery is necessary in order to compete, managements are beginning to encourage their enforcement of anti-bribery laws as a way of keeping competitors under control.

Variations in anti-bribery enforcement indicates that old habits die hard. Some companies that engage in significant bribery feel they have little to apologize for, and, on occasion, their governments seem to agree with them. While Germany acted vigorously against Siemens, the British have been considerably less forceful in pursuing a similar case against BAE Systems, the giant military contractor. In 2006, Prime Minister Tony Blair shut down an investigation by Britain's Serious Fraud Office into alleged BAE bribes to Saudi Arabian officials. The House of Lords took the same action against attempts to reopen the probe in mid-2008. Both actions may have been responses to Saudi threats to cease cooperation on anti-terrorism efforts if the investigations continued. The relationship between BAE and the Saudis, which had seen the sale of $80 billion in planes and weapons over the prior two decades, may also have been a factor. Retiring BAE chief executive Mike Turner said that the investigations had to stop because they damaged the reputation of BAE, other UK corporations, and the country itself. Meanwhile, in the U.S., where BAE had traditionally derived about half its revenues, the Justice Department was investigating, under the Foreign Corrupt Practices Act, a possible BAE deposit of $2 billion into the Washington bank account of Saudi Prince Bandar. Not in denial, but in defense of the company's right to pursue business as it chose, Turner said that one of the biggest challenges confronting his successor would be to build enough business elsewhere in the world to offset possible lost revenues if the company's legal difficulties in the U.S. became too great.

Earning the Social License to Operate

When a multinational company begins to operate in a foreign locality, what are its obligations to the people who live there? What constitutes fair exchange for its right to use local resources, dump its effluents into the rivers, occupy the land, and for all the human factors that result from what can be a massive and intrusive presence? The company's contract with the government in a far-off capital gives it the legal right to pursue its business. But how does it earn the social license to operate?

First of all, the company cannot help but represent immense change, and many observers of the developing world have noted a power shift from governments to multinational corporations. Governments have not deliberately ceded this power. But their own failures to make life better for their people have led relentlessly to the dissolution of their hold. Among countries that have become independent since World War II, independence has often failed to bring real democracy and the improvements in infant mortality, education, and economic opportunity that could be expected to accompany it. The infrastructure for productivity has yet to arrive in most cases. In some countries, the privatization of state assets has created wealth for some but has failed to reduce the disparity of income between rich and poor. Corruption continues to drain resources in ways that are profoundly damaging to social progress.

The result has been growing instability. Citizens have little reason to engage with governments that are unable to generate development. As central authority becomes more irrelevant, the disenfranchised may become more open to violent political movements and religious fundamentalism. One result is that they are ever more isolated from the solutions that technology offers.

The involvement of multinationals in such countries, usually to extract natural resources, brings pitfalls and opportunities together in an unsettled blend. For the four centuries that private companies of the developed world have operated in poorer countries, things have seldom gone well for the locals. Devastation of the environment, fracture of societies, brutality against workers, the imposition of puppet governments to facilitate macro-theft— all are known and in little need of elaboration here.

Yet something surprising has begun to happen over the past two decades. The social fragmentation caused by loss of faith in government, coupled with new means of communication and the increasing involvement of NGOs, have led to an unanticipated, roiling kind of democracy. Technology has enormous power to democratize. The world changed in 2000 when crowds in Manila brought down Philippine president Joseph Estrada by deftly intercepting government motorcades with protests that were organized moment-to-moment via cell phone text messages. Today, the world's largest corporations must function in this terrain that is full of possibility and, at the same time, constantly shifting.

In many infrastructure projects taking place in less developed countries, for example, private-sector institutions have imposed global social-responsibility standards. Although local governments may require considerably less of companies operating in their territories, consortia of international financial institutions often impose stringent environmental and human rights requirements on large projects as a condition of lending. They may require preservation of natural areas, or the construction of water plants, clinics, or schools in affected communities. They then require certification of compliance before releasing additional tranches of financing.

Such practices, sometimes associated with the term "privatization of compliance," work to the benefit of all interested parties. They tend to protect local populations against the vagaries of their own governments. A corporation's demonstrated ability to complete projects while remaining in compliance makes financial institutions more willing to lend. Adhering to global standards regardless of local regulation therefore lowers the borrower's cost of capital. And the availability of financing in turn improves the corporation's position with governments issuing contracts for such projects.

Just as local regulatory regimes have given way to higher standards imposed by outside lending institutions, governments are ceding some fields of influence to NGOs that have created global codes on labor conditions, environmental practices, human rights, and transparency of conditions on the ground. Such governments aren't generally abandoning areas of responsibility where they have previously been involved. Yet some also know that the less development a country creates, the less faith its people have in it. So a weak government may be inclined to let multinationals with interests in its country build social infrastructure. These governments know that the weaker they are, the less inclined a populace is to engage with them. A population that doesn't have the tools to advance its own interests by conventional means, and thus has nothing to lose, is probably more likely to revolt.

The imposition of global standards in a more or less unregulated environment tends to reduce the chances that corporations will extract hidden exemptions from governments—such as those that might allow them to skirt environmental or labor standards. Some corporations have partnered with NGOs who can help them set protocols for meeting global standards and can also, in some cases, offer valuable certifications of the company's adherence to those standards. Real cooperation with rigorous interest groups offers one of the most powerful means of enhancing a company's reputation.

Extraction Companies: An Irony

Extraction companies engaged in energy and mining offer some of the most dramatic examples of the ways corporations can go about transforming themselves into organizations that find acceptance among those who monitor their effects on the physical and cultural environment. These corporations are among the most hated on earth for the ecological damage they cause, their historic alliances with corrupt governments, and their displacements of communities. Because of such reputationally adverse factors, extraction companies have had to find creative ways to earn the "social license to operate." They have had to undertake actions that make their presence acceptable to governments and communities that demonstrate widely diverse characteristics. Increasingly, they have had to satisfy international advocacy groups that their activities conform to global environmental and human rights standards. Some of the world's largest enterprises have virtually turned themselves inside out to satisfy such groups. In confronting their own significant challenges, they've paved the way with standards and strategies that other companies can follow. But getting there has been an arduous journey for many.

The history of companies entering geographic areas unaware of their histories and social contexts is replete with difficulty. Managements traditionally negotiate with prevailing governments to obtain concessions and licenses that allow them to drill, mine, or conduct other kinds of businesses. Yet their contract documents usually offer them no guidance on the local history and the people who live where they plan to operate. To these managements, extracting resources seems a socially neutral business activity, and their personal experiences generally support this view. They often come and go, for example, through the use of an airstrip inside a secure company compound. While they may see neighboring villages through the window of a plane, the villages hardly seem relevant to the jobs they are there to perform.

Those looking up at the plane from the ground see things differently, however. They know that a new corporate presence brings with it long-term positive or negative implications for the wealth and character of the community, its relationship with the central government, the use of its land, the development and preservation of natural resources, the quality of work available, the ability to continue traditional livelihoods, and the organization of medical care—to name just a few areas of life the presence of multinationals can change in unpredictable ways.

Companies can find it burdensome to encounter skeptical or even hostile local populations, who may appear uneducated, less well off, and less worldly than themselves. But often the locals project an equality with the multinational that they derive from their ability to impede its operations, or even shut it down. This equality can work against the company—or, if allowed to, it can give rise to a highly productive interdependence between the two groups.

Such interdependence can prove crucial to a company in an environment where it has few friends. Globalization means doing business wherever the needed resources or markets appear. This often means interacting with governments whose leaders live by different values than the company attributes to itself. They might be dictatorships or oligarchies, and their characteristics can range from open to murderous. How a company interacts with such authorities, and the degree of support it appears to show them while pursuing its business in their territories, can exert a profound effect on its reputation around the world.

Guilt by association can follow a company for a long time, as it did Shell when that company grew too close to a dictatorship in Nigeria. NGOs and other observers felt that Shell could have pursued its energy operations in the Niger Delta without rejecting relationships with the local population in favor of close ties to the military government. Shell eventually undertook a thorough examination of its policies and became a leader in some areas of corporate social responsibility. But more than 15 years later it still faced organized theft of oil from its pipelines, violence against its operations, and kidnapping of its employees—much of it fueled by resentment against the company's original arrogance toward the communities around its operations.

Behavior of indigenous peoples toward multinationals operating in their home areas—and toward the governments whom they consider to be the companies' partners—has everything to do with those peoples' wish to be heard. Many companies that have operated successfully in such environments have found that the clear communication of their intentions has moderated the communities' demands. If the company doesn't want to talk to the community, the community can be expected to increase its aggressiveness. Generally, a failure of interaction results in acrimony or violence. Blocking the gate to the company facility or blowing up a pipeline may seem to be the only means of attracting attention to issues important to the community—even when the issues have little or nothing to do with the multinational company involved. If the company or the government wait to act until violence occurs, they'll already have lost the game, regardless of their response. It will be violence they end up rewarding.

A precious metals company operating in Papua New Guinea found its power source sabotaged, delaying its production schedule and imposing considerable expense for restoration. The company found a note attached to the toppled transmission tower: "Sorry," it said, "this is not directed against you, but we want health care." Local people believed they had no other way to get their government to listen except to target the company, which had come to a place the government would not. Years ago Peter Drucker suggested the thinking that should lie behind a constructive response to such an incident when he wrote: "Management has a self-interest in a healthy society, even though the cause of society's sickness is none of management's making."

Any management responsible for its financial performance is also responsible for understanding the landscape in which it operates. Often, managers' personal and professional backgrounds leave them unprepared for what they must face. In the absence of good advance intelligence, realities on the ground can take companies utterly by surprise.

In Indonesia's Aceh province during the 1990s ExxonMobil paid the salaries of 13,000 government soldiers to protect its Arun gas field at a time when powerful elements in Aceh were seeking independence. The soldiers undertook missions on behalf of both ExxonMobil and their own government. While assuring ExxonMobil's uninterrupted operations, they also carried out a terror campaign against the local population that, according to an Amnesty International report, included torture, rape, and the extrajudicial killings of civilians.

In 2001, an NGO brought suit against ExxonMobil in a U.S. court on behalf of 11 Aceh villagers, alleging human rights abuses under the Alien Torts Claims Act. This law, which Congress enacted in 1789, allows plaintiffs of any country to bring suit in U.S. courts against American entities whose presence in their home country has caused them damage. While the defendant does not have to be directly responsible for wrongs to be subject to the act, it was reported that the soldiers used ExxonMobil facilities in interrogation and torture and that the company had failed to act against resulting human rights abuses. Both ExxonMobil and the Indonesian government enlisted the help of the U.S. State Department, Indonesia threatening that the suit would imperil U.S. assets in that country. The State Department told the judge that the case would harm relations between the two countries. The case was dismissed, but not without considerable press coverage critical of the company.

ExxonMobil's failure to grasp the reality on the ground in Aceh represented a misstep for a company that has otherwise set the standard for operational excellence among integrated energy companies. On its Web site, ExxonMobil states that its primary social responsibility is to make a profit. "If you run your company well and provide something the public desires," Ken Cohen, the company's head of public affairs, told me, "that in itself is socially responsible."

The paradox of leading operational sophistication coexisting in the same company with an extremely narrow view of its social effect caused ExxonMobil a great deal of unnecessary trouble. It was not a lack of caring, but a kind of social obtuseness that turned the 1989 *Exxon Valdez* environmental disaster into an even bigger reputational one. The failure of top management to fly immediately to the scene of the spill in Alaska was, to many, sufficient proof that the company took it lightly. Though opinions differ, it seems that management simply saw little merit in making a show of concern and focused instead on applying its resources to remediation. While the company's refusal to act for the sake of appearances was consistent with its no-nonsense culture, the outrage over that original reticence was probably one reason ExxonMobil was still fighting the case in court nearly two decades later.

More recently, ExxonMobil has shown a dedication to incorporating social factors into its operations. It designed a pipeline project in Chad that included a financial mechanism to channel some of its revenues into schools and other social assets—a program unfortunately canceled by the Chadian government.

With its initiative in Chad, ExxonMobil showed an interest

in raising its level of accomplishment in the social sphere to approach its operational excellence. BP, on the other hand, had a paradox to resolve in the opposite direction. I described earlier its operational failures that resulted in a deadly Texas explosion and an Alaskan pipeline spill. At the same time, with its immense pipeline project from the Caspian to the Mediterranean, BP was opening new ground in establishing its "social license to operate." Despite BP's other failings, it's worthwhile taking a look at how they did this.

When BP drew up the plans for the 1,000-mile pipeline known as BTC, CEO Browne understood that the company could not address the project purely from an engineering mindset. He took the view that safeguarding the welfare of communities along the way would help ensure the success of the project. Institutional listening drove the entire enterprise as the company interviewed thousands of land tenants in the path of the pipeline to determine the needs and preferences in each locality. By engaging with communities before laying the pipeline, BP was able to determine the project's effect and plot its least disruptive path. The company then contributed $30 million in "social investment" to be allocated by NGOs to communities along the way for health care, education, water supply, and other community needs.

BP made certain that all stakeholders participated in assessing the potential risks. In addition to interviewing the land tenants, it organized independent panels that examined environmental and social effects, and it committed ahead of time to make their results available on the Web without the company's editorial filter. It adopted this vulnerable position as a way of demonstrating a commitment to open dialogue. By making itself transparent and accountable for others' conclusions, even before management knew what they were, BP established a level of trust that helped the project move forward through a sensitive environmental and social landscape.

No one at BP claimed that these social initiatives were altruistic. The company made it clear that, in a world of close over-sight by environmental and human rights activists, as well as by international financial institutions who were monitored by their own watchful stakeholders, BP's business interests required such engagement. The company's actions reflected an understanding that managing its project's disruption to people's lives would be a primary factor to its success.

One essential business result, BP believes, was that the sup-port it managed to generate among stakeholders lowered the com-pany's cost of capital on the project. By reducing opposition, and therefore risks, BP managed to raise confidence among its banks that the pipeline would be completed on time and on budget. In undertaking these initiatives and then explaining them publicly, John Browne and BP opened a new path for companies seeking greater viability in a world where unforeseen and threatening influences could arise from any direction. The subsequent depar-ture of Browne for reasons having to do with factors in other parts of the business shouldn't diminish these accomplishments.

Going Local as a Strategy

Unocal, now part of Chevron, was an energy company that became expert at teaching itself ways to address the need to show corpo-rate social responsibility. It hadn't been as lucky as ExxonMobil when facing its own Alien Torts Claims suit. Unocal paid to settle a case brought by a group of villagers in Myanmar, formerly Burma, because of the appearance that the company knew the Myanmar army was indenturing local villagers to clear bush, construct heli-pads, and act as porters of ammunition and food for those soldiers supporting construction of the Yadana Pipeline. For years, the project's principal—French energy giant Total S.A.—had faced withering criticism from international organizations over the treatment of Burmese workers.

Long before finally settling the suit in 2005, Unocal had undertaken a dramatic response to the threat that public opinion exerted on its ability to pursue its international oil and gas business. In 1996 the company sold off its downstream marketing assets and its Union 76 gas station chain, saying it wanted to concentrate on exploration and production, not on refining and sales. One result of its exit from the retail gasoline business was that it would now be free from the threat of U.S. consumer boycotts over social-responsibility issues involving countries such as Myanmar and Indonesia.

At the same time, Unocal began taking seriously its responsibilities to the places where it was doing business. The company resolved to initiate a vigorous program of engagement with communities around its facilities, particularly in Indonesia. The question it faced, however, was how to develop such a program where there was little or no tradition for it. How do you go about engaging a large and highly complex population on a systematic basis?

Greg Huger, who helped manage Unocal's programs in Indonesia, described to me the importance of building an inherent consistency between the company's business and social agendas. He said the company must develop personnel with talent and knowledge to find the best ideas external stakeholders have to offer, bring them back to the company, and organize the internal conversation so those ideas have the possibility of entering operations policy. The intelligence they bring back may include insights on how the company can accommodate its presence to local customs and address issues of importance to the local people. This requires knowledge of the sources of influence within individual communities, traditions of resource use in those communities, attitudes toward the central government, prior experience with companies both foreign and domestic, and attitudes toward money, wealth, and work.

As Unocal began investigating the effect its presence could have on its areas of operations, the company learned that in the waters off the Indonesian province of East Kalimantan, oil and gas resources coexisted with important ecosystems associated with coral reefs. Prior energy-related activities had brought compromises offshore, reducing the catches of fishermen who had made their livelihoods there practically since the beginning of time, and onshore, where populations of orangutans and other species had begun to disappear. While international extraction companies weren't the only contributors to these trends, they played significant roles.

Unocal recruited and organized teams of indigenous employees to engage with local communities. They joined development councils where the company participated as one of many members. While some groups wanted money from the company, and although it routed contributions through NGOs to assure it was well spent, Unocal also worked with councils in ways that went beyond direct financial contributions. In general, a company with Unocal's resources might supply engineers to explore ways communities could achieve their goals. If the use of certain fertilizers was causing harmful runoff into drinking and fishing waters, for example, a multinational corporation might have access to experience in other parts of the world—and to other technologies—that could improve local practices.

Huger noticed that the need to adapt the company's approach to the local culture sparked a cultural evolution within the company itself. He says companies can create positive consequences externally simply by giving employees the opportunity to become involved. Applying professional skills developed in the energy business to community-development enterprises offers what Huger calls "psychic income." Such personal involvement by employees can, he says, provide one of the most important avenues for introducing the notion of social engagement into the culture of a large corporation.

Pursuing a policy of engagement changes a company's culture in other ways as well. Programs for engagement with local populations often require resources from other parts of the company. Involvement of the greater workforce in providing necessary resources spreads an understanding of the social dimensions of the company's activities and generally reduces the likelihood of reputation-damaging behavior in all of the company's operations.

Unocal also entered into a deliberate process of finding NGO partners. Jeff Gracer, a New York attorney with long experience advising companies on social responsibility, says a company has to gather intelligence on NGOs the same way the NGOs observe the company. As with prospective partners in any other area of business, management must look at their track records. It must know who the players are, identify the difficult ones, and, based on past actions, figure out who is likely to be helpful. Gracer points out that developing such an understanding of the landscape is different from engaging in opposition research on business competitors. Rather than an exercise aimed at tactically impeding your opponents, building relationships with NGOs is about a search for partners.

The way to go about it, Gracer says, is to initiate very quiet and private talks with NGOs who seem most prominent in your industry or in the geographic area where you're working. Ask for their ideas. Draft a plan if the conversation gets far enough. Then test the plan on friend and foe alike to find out if it will ultimately prove supportive of the company, whether it will satisfy opponents, and which parts of it are likely to arouse the greatest resistance. This open approach, Gracer says, offers the best chance that a project will take place with public transparency while diminishing the possibility that it will arouse anger on the part of close observers. It will maximize the company's chances of operating successfully.

Unocal formalized its search for NGO partners by issuing a global "request for proposals" to activist groups who might be interested in working with the company on a multiyear basis. As one of the winning groups, the Nature Conservancy helped Unocal establish practices for protecting the ecosystem while the company developed supplies of gas and other products in Indonesia. The Nature Conservancy comprised one part of Unocal's multifaceted effort to make its presence a reasonable proposition for affected communities as well as for its own shareholders.

Companies must of course make themselves accountable for the results of their activities in the social responsibility arena. They must be able to answer in their own councils whether they've legitimately earned their social license to operate. If they haven't, it won't be a secret very long. There are many ways to measure results. Companies and NGOs monitor trends in the pollution levels of lakes, rivers, and streams; they watch the disappearance or reappearance of fish and animal populations; they count acres of replanted trees; they measure the health of human communities.

Sometimes, though, a company's generous objectives fail to achieve their goals. Good ideas—as conceived at corporate head-quarters—may not work everywhere, no matter how well intentioned. Which brings us to Johnson & Johnson, a company that, since drafting its famous "credo" in 1943—decades before anyone thought of corporate responsibility—has played a fundamental role in the development of ideas about ethical corporate behavior. The credo states that the company exists primarily to serve people, and J&J associates its century of longevity with adherence to that principle.

J&J implements employee-complaint mechanisms in all its plants, and they are utterly consistent with its philosophy. In one of its facilities in northern Mexico, managers told employees over and over about the company's open-door policy, by which it invited any and all employees to walk into the manager's office to make complaints and suggestions. The offer was sincere, but no one ever stepped through the manager's door. The company had failed to understand that no worker who had grown up in that culture was likely to take advantage of such a policy. Even the language of that part of the world still carries the rhetoric of the master-servant relationship dating back to the Spanish conquest.

Being genuinely open had the same effect as not being open at all. Having learned long ago that it must engage, the company, at that plant, had not yet created the conditions under which engagement could occur.

Performance Follows Culture: A Short Story

"Longevity of the enterprise requires alignment of workers' goals with those of management." The young energy-company executive who said this to me had taken over as general manager of a 300-person operation in a major South American oil-producing nation before he was thirty. His employer had sent him to find out why the operation's productivity had been falling—and to set it right.

It didn't take him long to realize that weak morale and resentment against the parent company had permeated all levels of the local workforce. Hard-core union activists organized work stoppages on a regular basis. Local managers, with virtually no freedom to make decisions and no sense of a career path, resembled order-taking field engineers more than the heads of businesses the company had supposed them to be. On the front lines, staff carried out equipment maintenance at a minimal, rule-book level. This culture of neglect not only showed the poor attitudes of personnel responsible for making the machinery run, but it further compromised the morale of those who were supposed to operate it.

The young general manager soon found the reason for the low morale. It was his own company's behavior toward its workforce. He discovered an employee health-care system fraught with incompetence and corruption. Communication of goals and standards from top management was virtually nonexistent. Relations with employees were so bad that it was difficult to find anyone who could pierce his or her personal cloud of resentment to render a clear and unemotional view of the problems.

Assessing the panorama of difficulties, the manager saw his

challenge primarily as a social problem rather than a business problem. "If you want people to perform at a global level, you have to support them appropriately," he told me.

To address the health-care dilemma, he brought in a U.S.-trained physician on a full-time basis to reform and administer the system, placing special emphasis on care for workers' families. English-language education, previously reserved for families of expatriates, became available to all employees and their families. The hiring of an experienced industrial attorney as ombudsman freed the company from having to rely on hostile union delegates for information.

The new boss told his senior people they would no longer be micromanaged. He decentralized decision-making and segmented managers into task-specific teams. Group leaders would run their businesses as they saw fit and take responsibility for their results. He advised anyone not comfortable with this formula to find something else to do.

Having made these changes over a matter of months, he looked for ways to demonstrate a transformed company relationship with employees. Examining health and employee-attrition data, he identified road safety as a primary factor in workers' well-being. He made defensive driving courses mandatory for employees and available to their families. Many private cars lacked seat belts. He bought the belts and had them installed.

But he knew that driving courses and seat belts would go only so far if the roads were dangerous. The surrounding area consisted of hills and rolling savannah, and the roads through it suffered from neglect. Highway signs hadn't been a priority for anyone in government and were inadequate. The manager developed relationships with local transportation authorities, identified danger spots, and upgraded signage along the district's two major highways. The company paid for the sign changes, and the government was happy to let it do so.

At the same time, the manager began to look for allies. He

announced that the company would reward certain kinds of behavior, such as careful maintenance of equipment and promotion of safe procedures, with gifts and family trips. Several union members responded. Then more did. Hostile activists became fewer.

In the three years he ran the operation, these reforms doubled the productivity of each area of the business, increased earnings, and cut work stoppages to a fraction of what they had been. Enhanced quality of life for employees led to increased morale, and business results followed. "Many tactics were involved," the manager told me, "but they were all focused on ensuring that people who walked through the gate in the morning came in wanting to be there."

This is a story about the process by which companies entering new geographic areas become part of the communities around them. Their frames of reference grow to include social and political factors of unforeseen breadth. And they generally learn that getting those factors right is a prerequisite for having any chance to function as a successful business.

Healing a Company and Its Workforce After Disaster

Sometimes the need to engage the workforce as a community comes in like a storm. As Hurricane Katrina descended on New Orleans in August 2005, Schlumberger, the world's largest oil field services company, braced for disaster. The company, with elaborate operations primarily on offshore oil rigs, had drafted detailed preparedness plans to continue operating in just such a hurricane. As the extent of human devastation wreaked by the storm became clear, however, management realized its plan also had to include a way to keep workers' lives intact. Hourly employees who worked the oil rigs in the Gulf were overwhelmingly Louisianan, most with extended families in and around New Orleans. Many of them ended up losing everything. Relocation out of New Orleans, even if viable for the company, was never an option. In this environment, connections among company, workers, and place took on unprecedented importance and clarity.

Bill Coates, president of Schlumberger North America, explained to me that when Hurricane Ivan had hit a year before Katrina, the evacuation was so disorganized that thousands of people became stranded on the highways leading out of town. Many had to sleep beside the road. Remembering that paralysis, Schlumberger prepared for Katrina by closing its offices six hours ahead of the city's evacuation, and it urged employees to leave immediately after it had shut down. Yet memories of congestion at the time of Ivan kept many in their homes.

Management-level personnel did not have that choice. The company ordered them to Houston, 350 miles west. They made the trip by staying off major highways and keeping to back roads, guided by local members of the workforce.

In Houston they awaited the storm's transit of New Orleans. Only when Katrina had passed and top managers began trying to find their people did they realize that this storm had caused unprecedented damage. New Orleans had lost all fixed-line and mobile telecommunications. The city was cut off.

In addition, several dozen managers were still missing. Some, it turned out, had stayed in New Orleans for personal reasons. One had a physician-spouse whose services were desperately needed. As to the workforce, information about their whereabouts was nearly nonexistent.

Through news reports management learned that the levees had failed and much of the city lay underwater. Broadcasts indicated that civil order was breaking down, that there was no security in the city, and that no one was safe.

The rest of the management team checked in one by one over the next two days. Hourly employees began straggling into Houston, and the company reserved hotel space to house anyone who showed up. It began to receive word that others had gotten to Memphis and various points in Louisiana and Mississippi.

The dimensions of the tragedy continued to take shape in the personal stories of workers. Most people had left everything behind, and, as the situation in New Orleans continued to deteriorate, it became clear that no one who had left could go back. Even if they wanted to brave the dangerous streets, government roadblocks kept everybody out.

Over the first two days the company re-established enough of its Louisiana operations in Texas to place people back on the Gulf rigs to assess damage and operability. But, as managers worked to get the company up and running, headquarters became deluged with an increasing sense of loss as each new group arrived from New Orleans. Hysteria among employees grew hourly over the status of homes, possessions, and the extended families they'd left behind. Management heard a single, constant refrain: "We don't know what to do."

Coates realized that before he could get his Gulf operations running again he was going to have to stabilize his employees' personal lives. And it wouldn't be cheap. He asked his bosses what funds he might have to address the emergency. They told him to do whatever he thought necessary, and the company would sort out the expenditures later. He immediately went to work, renting 200 apartments for employee families who had made it to Houston. (Twenty-four hours later it was virtually impossible to rent an apartment in Houston.) The company arranged for employees' children to enter Houston schools. And although two-thirds of the workforce consisted of hourly workers, everyone continued to get paid. Coates realized he needed to get information on the status of homes and possessions employees had left behind, and to do it he would have to organize what amounted to a small private militia.

Control Risks Group supplies sophisticated armed security for companies and governmental entities all over the world, including Iraq. Schlumberger had used the company, known by its initials CRG, in Colombia to protect assets from guerrillas. Coates sent

CRG operatives into New Orleans to photograph every employee's home.

That was only the start of CRG's involvement. Moving the Gulf base of operations to Houston required the transfer of massive pieces of equipment out of New Orleans, which remained sealed. Schlumberger obtained entry permits and sent in a convoy of 45 tractor-trailers with a CRG security escort. The company also dispatched helicopters to survey facilities in areas that were inaccessible by land.

It was a time of exceptional circumstances, Coates told me. Twelve workers showed up at a Schlumberger facility in Belle Chasse, just outside New Orleans, to spend the night awaiting trucks on which they would load drilling equipment at first light. Each of the twelve came fully armed, and management found itself in the unusual position of having to relieve them of their weapons, which it did. The men spent the night in the facility without electricity. In the morning a sheriff's escort accompanied the trucks in, guarded them during loading, and guided them out. This and similar improvised tactics resulted in the arrival in Houston over the next three days of enough equipment for Schlumberger to relaunch all operations required by the oil and gas companies who were its customers.

Because of the breadth of resources the company developed during the crisis, it became involved in actions that went beyond those that simply supported its business. Coates knew a Schlumberger retiree named Tommy Nicholls who had begun working for the company in 1947. In his eighties, he was virtually blind now. A day or so after the hurricane, Nicholls' son called Coates' office to say his dad had gone missing. Coates sent CRG to the house, which they found ransacked and abandoned. Eventually CRG located Nicholls in the company of a neighbor with whom he'd been moving around the Algiers Point section of New Orleans to avoid the marauding gangs. CRG got Nicholls out of the area and reunited him with his family. Coates says the story had a dramatic effect on how employees viewed the company. Sending out an expensive quasi-military patrol to rescue Tommy Nicholls was not among the things they'd expected to see it do.

As employees' personal dramas played out, however, they offered few such happy endings, and there were many things for which the company simply had no answer. One was the discovery of the body of an executive assistant's father in his attic, where he'd taken refuge from rising waters.

When Coates needed critical payroll documents from his New Orleans office, he couldn't send CRG to sort through his files. Two or three weeks after the storm, he and two associates obtained passes and simply drove into the city. "It was a beautiful Sunday afternoon," he says, "but what we found was a ghost town. There was nobody. We were in a major American city, and there wasn't a person around. Not a dog. If someone had come around a corner and wanted to do us harm, we were dead." The only security Coates and his companions found that day were two private guards, in full battle dress and armed, standing in front of the 29-story building that housed Schlumberger's offices. The three Schlumberger managers approached the guards and showed them their company ID. The guards said they'd heard of Schlumberger and asked Coates for jobs.

The three climbed 27 flights of stairs to their offices. They inspected the premises and found only a few windows blown out. Dead cockroaches littering the floor gave them the sensation of walking on popcorn. They found the payroll data and returned with it to Houston. "We must have been crazy," Coates says.

Schlumberger proved during the crisis that it could run its Gulf operations out of Houston. New Orleans showed little prospect of meaningful recovery any time soon. Still, the company left no question about its commitment to return. Schlumberger had well over half a century's history in Louisiana.

To re-establish itself in the ravaged city, the company rented office space on the north shore of Lake Pontchartrain in time for the school opening in surrounding St. Tammany Parish. It rented additional offices as conditions permitted and became the first large company to return to downtown New Orleans. "There was one restaurant," Coates says. "No cafés. No stores. And no one to go and see." But management insisted on demonstrating its faith in the city. "It was important to show the thousand employees who lived there that we were coming back," he told me.

The question of how to stabilize people's lives persisted, and Schlumberger continued to address the human tragedy that played out among its workforce. The company was intensely aware that the situation could get better, or it might get worse, and management continued to act to keep desperation at bay for its employees. After all, how surprised could one be if some, out of hopelessness or anger at their families' plight, resorted to questionable activities? Management worked to give them alternatives. It undertook an engineering analysis of each employee's residence. It evaluated their personal insurance policies. It continued to pay their salaries whether it had work for them or not.

"We were on a campaign," Coates says. "It was about commitment to employees and a place."

Getting Ready for the Future

The future is unknowable, and the real influences on a business environment are seldom clear. So, any company's efforts to understand the landscape in which it operates means its management team must maintain a kind of worldliness that goes beyond its specific market and industry. The markets of any company of size respond to large, extra-market forces. Macroeconomic and monetary factors, philosophical changes associated with the results of elections, and political risk both at home and abroad are but a few of these forces.

In the 1970s, Royal Dutch Shell initiated a program to plan

strategy for the future. Because it had no special information on what the future was going to look like, the company began to explore what it would need to do to respond to several specific, possible futures. It established a group to envision these futures and propose responses, a process it called "scenario planning." In his book on Shell's efforts, *The Art of the Long View*, Peter Schwartz describes the process not as an effort to see the future, but to make several possible future eventualities alive in the present. The primary purpose was to disabuse strategists of a false confidence in their personal perceptions and to force them, through the narratives that described scenarios, to orient their thinking in accordance with the dynamics of the real world.

Few subjects were more compelling to Shell, for example, than the likely price of oil at certain points in the future. Understanding geopolitical forces and other factors that would influence that price was essential to Shell's planners, who had to decide how much money to spend, where to spend it, and in what kinds of projects to invest.

Scenario planning can be a riveting exercise because it forces the planner to see the world as it is and in an unbounded context. The differences in outcomes of various scenarios are not minor, and the great variation among them forces strategists to confront the enormous implications of any decision they make. As an example, underinvestment in exploration and production in the last two decades has unquestionably contributed to the striking instability in the price of oil. If, years ago, some scenario planners had forecast the dramatic emergence of China and India and the consequent rise in demand, this scenario might have become a driving factor in the planning of energy production. Instead, the industry took to heart the expense it had incurred in overbuilding production capacity in response to the oil crunch of the 1970s and resolved not to make that particular mistake again. It may have known how to win the last war, but it failed to plan for what would become the next one.

Scenario planners must consider the entire range of disciplines that affect the flow of events. Construction of scenarios for the energy industry requires, for example, an opinion on the degree and the way politics will penetrate the business. How far will Venezuela go in nationalizing its oil fields, and what will be the role of international energy and service companies in that new reality? Answering the question requires a focus on considerably more than just Venezuela. What effect will that country's policies have on gas production in Bolivia, where, at this writing, a leftist government seems to grow closer to Venezuela by the moment? What does the renationalization of resources in Russia mean? Are Russian energy companies gaining the technology and expertise to recover their own oil and gas if it is the government's will to go it alone? And what effect will Russian thinking have on access to the enormous deposits in former Soviet republics like Kazakhstan, Azerbaijan, and Ukraine? These are political questions with a strong component of military analysis. Ultimately they are make-or-break questions for the inquiring energy company that needs to make assumptions about the future price of oil in order to plan.

A scenario planner for a consumer goods company will take responsibility for having an opinion on the conditions necessary for Asian countries to continue to supply low-cost merchandise to the West and use the profits to buy its branded goods. If the West's buying power declines because of extended economic weakness, what will the game-changing factors be as Asian countries decide whether to continue to absorb Western goods? What conditions will induce some or all Asian countries to turn inward to concentrate on supplying their own needs? The scenario planner trying to gain perspective on this question will have to understand the basis on which leaders in a variety of Asian countries make decisions. This may have to do with the strength of the government, of diverse political parties, and of the opposition. What has the government told its people about the relationship between the economy and the state?

While the scenario planner develops risk assessments and responses to each of several eventualities, the likelihood that any one of them will come to pass exactly as described is virtually zero. But the preparation makes what actually does happen more recognizable, and makes responses more available. The company that narrows its focus, responding to a single specific vision of the future, will need a great deal of luck to prosper. Sustainability of a company's revenue stream depends on its capacity to understand the world it lives in.

CHAPTER 5

Investor Relations and the Language of Value

✳

The investor relations director holds primary responsibility for the company's relationship with investors and analysts. He responds to their inquiries and explains the company's strategy for growth. He does this in both individual conversations and with large groups. He helps his CEO understand the dynamics of investor thinking—essential in making the company's capital markets communications effective. At the same time, he is well served by recognizing how little direct influence he has over the company's stock price. He learns there's little clear causality. And there's little closure in investor relations. Life starts again every fiscal quarter.

Reasons for stock price movements are so diverse, and so often concealed, that one can seldom attribute a change in price to a specific cause—regardless of the statements of market pundits on television and in the newspaper. Their conclusions are generally "backed out" in the sense that the commentators observe the market movement and assume the kind of investor thinking that must lie behind it. In fact, stock price movements of any significant company show the net effect of thinking by shareholders who are so culturally and geographically diverse as to defy connection between news and price. The exception, of course, occurs when the news is sudden and surprising.

There's little question that improving financial performance compared to investment peers is likely to have a positive effect on price over time *all other things being equal.* But it is also true that investors, individually and as a group, react differently to the same news. In particular, they often give emphasis to news that supports decisions they've made for other reasons.

The investor relations director should be affected by none of this. He is an instrument of the company's transparency, and it is the market's perception of that transparency from moment to moment and quarter to quarter that brings long-term value. Only after considerable experience in his job is he able to discern how some of his investors think, and the kinds of information and communication to which they will respond. In this light, the best approach he can take is an attitude that expresses an alignment of interests with the investors and analysts who follow the company.

Managers sometimes talk about having a passion for their companies and businesses. But the last thing an investor wants is an IR executive who tries to sell him on the company. The IR director should strive first of all to break through the investor's skepticism about his motives. This can be challenging because corporations, in general, aren't known for a high degree of truth-telling. And investors and analysts are often skeptics by nature. It takes time to develop trust and a mutual language for looking at the company. The rest of this chapter will address the ways the IR director delivers information legitimately and in the company's interest.

Getting the Internal Buy-in

The IR director is virtually helpless before his external constituency without the support of his internal one. If an investor wants to know how the chief of a particular division sees his prospects for the year, there's little the IR director can do unless that business head sees the investor's need to know as important. Recognition of the value of giving this kind of information isn't necessarily natural to the business head. But it is in the IR director's interest to help him see why he should contribute to the capital markets conversation.

IR Has Moved to the Center of the Corporate Enterprise

No executive role has changed more in the last decade that than that of the investor relations director. Until the merger and acquisitions era of the 1980s and '90s, investor relations was a backwater that primarily involved putting out press releases and answering the phone when investors called. IR executives tried to respond to the requests of a small number of investors to meet with management, who often felt it had better things to do. To most heads of corporate divisions, IR didn't sound like a real part of the business, and they had little idea what an IR officer actually did.

Then, as the great waves of consolidation began and companies started buying other companies—sometimes on a weekly basis— investors became much more demanding. Mergers and acquisitions generally involved an exchange of shares between two companies, and the value of the stock had everything to do with the price companies paid and whether they were able to consummate the transaction at all. Both boards and investors began demanding that managers take actions that would enhance stock price, and executive compensation became closely tied to shareholder value.

The focus on share price is now firmly cemented into the culture of virtually all publicly traded corporations. CEOs want to know who the company's shareholders are, who's buying and selling, and why. Because management sees these factors as crucial to the company's destiny and to their own, the IR executive has become an important voice inside the company.

Now, during each quarter, a CEO is likely to turn a week or two of his schedule over to the IR director, who uses this time to schedule road show visits to institutional investors and analysts. These periods of intense investor contact may also center on conferences sponsored by brokers where the company CEO may make a presentation to hundreds of possible investors.

Information coming into the company is as important as any communication going out, and the IR executive supplies the CEO with investor intelligence that is critical to his efforts to build share value. Today, few CEOs would think of going into a meeting with an institutional investment group without knowing how many shares that particular group holds and how his own company's profile fits with its overall approach to valuation.

The expanded role of investor relations means it has become a marketing function that uses financial language. While communication remains at the core of IR, the job now requires the corporate investor relations executive to be conversant in accounting and finance. If an analyst wants to inquire about the company's method of pension accounting, the IR executive should be in position to respond.

The astute IR executive realizes that his company's investors and analysts are responsible to their own constituencies. An investor, no matter how large an institution he represents, must justify his decisions to his own management, clients, and shareholders. An analyst has his own management and his investment clients who hold him accountable for offering productive advice. So investors' and analysts' opinions of a company rest to a substantial degree on their expectations of its transparency in the future. They're dependent on its clarity for their own credibility. And because their primary source of financial information about the company is the IR director, their perception of him as a professional has a palpable effect on their views of the company.

A fundamental part of the investor relations executive's role is to educate the market to the way he thinks it should analyze his company's value. This has become particularly important as turmoil in the investment world has made the typical analyst's length of experience shorter. Ethics scandals in the early 2000s forced large institutions to separate their research and investment banking operations, resulting in a reduced role for research. And now, with the reduction in the financial sector due to the financial crisis, still fewer analysts are covering more companies. These changes have imposed an ever-greater burden on investor relations executives in their efforts to ensure that analysts understand their companies and industries.

In representing his company to the market, the IR director's first job is to differentiate his company as a financial performer. Knowing one's audience is the first principle of communicating in any context, and the IR executive tailors his message according to the methods by which he knows the market assigns value to his company.

How does he learn what investors think? He listens, first of all. He's sensitive to the questions asked on conference calls and during road shows. He has the freedom, when called by investors or analysts, to inquire more deeply into the details of their views on the company.

He also has available certain tools that enhance his ability to listen to the market. Chapter 7 of this book describes variations of the perception study, which can bring the IR executive a varied panorama of investors' views and the factors they believe will determine his company's fortunes. Perception study interviews conducted by a qualified third party can reveal virtually anything the company would wish to know about investors' attitudes, including their views of management competence. With their anonymity protected by a third party, investors can be remarkably candid.

A number of personal characteristics shared by many institutional investors serve to accentuate this candor: First, they are, almost without exception, very bright. Second, they're articulate. Third, they're emotionally involved with the company if they've committed their client's capital to it. And fourth, many think they can run the company better than its management. All of these traits conspire to offer the company—via a talented perception study practitioner—a vital sense of the psychology and themes affecting investors' decisions.

Using this knowledge, the investor relations executive can identify the legitimate story about the company that may attract the kind of buying that leads to a higher share price. In constructing the company's investment themes, he may determine that highlighting a lead in technological expertise, more efficient production methods, or a product for which the company can charge a premium will move investors. And he must be able to "train" his management to tell the best story consistent with the company's reality. The ability to analyze how a company's investors think is the single factor that has placed investor relations officers in the executive suite, with compensation to match.

The Strength to Take a Stand with Investors

One way the IR executive earns his pay package is by enlisting senior management to take a stand with investors—even when it seems a risky thing to do. One large U.S. industrial company had given its investors quarterly guidance on 12 different points of data covering its production and financial expectations. Then management decided to stop offering guidance on one of the items—units shipped. The reason was simple. Because of variations in pricing and margins, the information on units shipped was misleading in helping investors predict financial performance. While investors attached considerable importance to this information, management believed it to be a poor predictor. In addition, it tended to focus the market's attention on the short term, and management wanted it to consider the company's longer-term prospects.

Suspension of units-shipped guidance represented this company's wish to get rid of its short-term investors. Many of these were hedge funds who would buy and sell the shares based on such superficial measures. And, because they brought share volatility with little or no net gain, the company believed it was better off without their investment dollars.

The quarterly earnings conference call on which the company announced its decision to suspend unit shipment guidance grew more tense as it went along. Analysts on the call repeatedly asked the company the reason they wouldn't be getting this particular piece of data in the future. Management, unable to tell them that it believed the number skewed their valuation of the company, could do nothing but repeat that the suspension reflected its own best judgment. The CEO sounded like a stonewalling politician, and by the end of the call, one participant made a dire comment for all to hear that this was no way to build investor confidence in the company's shares. Yet management stood by its judgment and refused to be drawn into a defense of its decision.

It turned out to be the right decision. Despite the near revolt on the conference call, the subject never came up again. And the company's investors and analysts began to focus on more complex and more revealing factors. Eliminating information that played to the short term opened the way in succeeding quarters to more productive conversations on the company's long-term growth prospects and the factors affecting that growth. The company was now freer than it had been to tell its story through guidance on margins, operating efficiencies, and cash generation. Management found particular improvement in the market's valuation of its international business. Because the economics of its overseas business were somewhat different from its domestic business, management was able to demonstrate its expectation of international growth unencumbered by a misleading unit-shipment number. It had won a small war.

Premiums and Discounts

The investor relations executive owes the CEO an informed opinion that indicates the factors underlying the market's valuation of the shares. The essential question is how the company is valued compared to investment peers—whether the shares are trading at fair value, at a premium, or at a discount. Investors can consider peers to be the company's industry competitors or companies with similar financial profiles. Determinations of relative value generally make use of such measures as price-earnings ratios, cash flows, and others. These can vary widely, but it is essential that the IR director understand the valuation metrics investors favor.

If the company trades at a discount to peers, it's important for the IR executive and his management team to understand the reasons for the discount. Do investors believe the company is too diverse to manage? Or is it not diversified enough to protect against weaknesses in a particular product group? Has the company failed to deliver its value proposition? Has it even explained what its value proposition is? The most difficult story for the investor relations director to address comes up when it seems that negative perceptions of the CEO are the cause of the discount.

An IR director working for a company whose shares trade at a premium will, unfortunately, have no more rest than his counter-part who faces a discount. Premiums are inherently vulnerable. The company must continually prove that it deserves a share price relatively higher than its peers. If the multiple begins to "normalize," the overwhelming likelihood is that the market will see it as the company's loss of competitive position.

In fact, a high share price and a premium often spell trouble for the IR director simply because, once they're established, it is his or her responsibility to maintain the anomaly—and even to increase it. Among the most difficult of all situations is one in which the premium is undeserved. Analysts recommending stocks to their institutional clients can be just as wrong on the upside as on the downside, and when they are, they'll have done the company little good when the inevitable downward adjustment arrives.

Theories of Growth

The IR executive will do everything he can to attract appropriate investors. A large part of his job is to understand how the investment philosophy of any institutional investor who owns or is considering his stock matches the company's characteristics and its likely path to growth. Having the right investors in the stock is crucial. Not only are they easier than others to convince of the company's value, but their period of share ownership will tend to be longer, and their presence will serve to mitigate any weakness caused by the exit of other investors.

Much of the needed information on any significant institutional investor's approach is easily available. Large funds who manage other people's money must publish their general principles of investment as a regulatory matter, and they are bound by what they declare those principles to be. Money managers must tell their clients how they're going to make decisions. Are they going to invest in specific industries or focus on certain areas of the world? Are they going to seek out companies with particular financial characteristics? Are they income investors who will buy companies with strong dividends? Or value investors who will buy stocks that appear cheap? Are they growth investors who will invest in companies with rising revenues or earnings? Or do they combine the last two in the investment philosophy called growth-at-a-reasonable-price (GARP)? Because the philosophy of most investment funds is known, the IR executive has the means to match his company with the most likely sources of investment capital.

In addition, the content of their portfolios is available. The shareholder list of any exchange-traded company becomes public six weeks after the end of every quarter. Simple programs cross-reference that information and can show the IR director the content of any institutional investor's portfolio, giving him a further gauge to judge whether his company and any particular institutional investor are right for each other. He can therefore judge each investor not only by what he says, but also by what he does.

Using a perception study, the IR director can develop intelligence on such matters as whether investors favor a strategy by which the company attempts to grow through organic development of the business, or by acquiring other companies. If investors see acquisitions as part of the company's scenario, do they consider management capable of executing them productively? The IR officer wants to know whether investors think his management can price an acquisition correctly. Is it capable of determining the most efficient means of financing? And (often the diciest piece of an acquisition) does it have the expertise to integrate the two organizations effectively? How well can the newly formed group combine brands? How will it retain talent? How will it keep competitors from cutting in on market share during the transition phase? An IR executive managing financial communications in an acquisition should have responses to all such questions before investors can even ask them.

In many cases, financial communications involve navigating an investor base influenced by the company's competitors, all of whom attempt to shape the message according to their own interests. The IR director, in cooperation with the rest of management, must choose a specific and disciplined approach to competitor-created perceptions. For example, a competitor may have made claims about its own performance that the company knows to be unfounded. While biting his tongue, the IR executive can redouble his efforts to educate investors and analysts as to how he thinks his own company should be valued—and hope the market figures out the truth.

Communication that fails is often gapped communication, a term that describes what happens when a company's story means one thing to the management who tells it and another to the investors and analysts who hear it. Gapped communication is often the problem when management describes its business and assumes the market's conclusions will be the same as its own. For example, a company with industry-leading technology may go to considerable lengths to explain the extraordinary breakthroughs represented by that technology. Inherent in its explanation is management's assumption that having the best technology means the company will gain market share, its margins will improve, and investors will place a higher value on its shares. Management's underlying message may be that showing this technology not only demonstrates the company's design and engineering skills, but it gives evidence of superior abilities that will enable it to dominate its market in the future. To management, the connections are obvious. But investors, while acknowledging the company's unique expertise, will be intent on figuring out what that expertise means in terms of financial performance. They'll need the company's help in determining the financial implications of its technical achievements, which they may not see as self-evident the way management does.

Targeting New Investors

A company's marketing department has to know how its customers make decisions. Investors are the IR executive's customers, and he has to have the same sort of information about them. Building and diversifying the company's investor base is among the IR director's most important functions. And understanding the features about the company that appeal to investors—revenue growth might be one—enables him to target institutions for whom revenue growth is important. There are thousands of them, however. So he breaks down the universe of likely investors by applying additional criteria—for example, by focusing on those investors within the growth group who have the largest volumes of investable capital.

The key to investor targeting lies in identifying the company's investment peers. Determining the qualities in companies that *make* them peers is an art, and it is seldom straightforward. Are the peer companies those who share the same industry? By far the most common field of peers lies among the company's industrial competitors. If the IR director believes that investors who appreciate the story presented by his competitors will also show an interest in his own, the practice of investor targeting leads him to identify and contact them. By having bought the competitor's shares, investors have shown that they're also likely to understand the story the IR director's company has to tell. When he approaches them, it isn't generally construed as an attempt to compromise competitors, but only to contact investors whose behavior in the market has revealed predilections favorable to his company. They're fair game, in other words.

Competitors are not the only peer group. The IR director may look for companies with market or financial profiles similar to his own. If his company has a strong brand, are its peers other companies with strong brands? The same may apply if his company has a strong balance sheet. Or lots of leverage. In any case, if he finds investors whose thinking about other companies suggests a match with his own, he would do well to reach out to them by proposing a road-show visit by his CEO.

Investors and Corporate Social Responsibility

While corporate social responsibility has become a highly visible part of public perceptions of the corporate sector, its presence in the investment dialogue is still limited. Industry estimates generally suggest that 10 to 13 percent of U.S. institutional investors screen companies for social-responsibility factors. The rules governing funds that run such filters might limit their investments to companies that adhere to certain antipollution standards, or prohibit their investment in companies involved in tobacco or alcohol. Before apartheid fell in South Africa, a number of funds had policies against investing in companies that did business there.

These issues rarely touch the investor relations process, though some energy companies make a point of keeping such funds aware of their actions in support of social responsibility. Investors without specific social responsibility mandates still expect companies to manage risk in a way that keeps them out of the kind of trouble that could compromise the price of the stock. They favor managements who appear strong enough to run their companies in ways that treat workers fairly and avoid polluting the environment.

The Investor Relations Career

The individual who makes a career of IR and practices it in a succession of different companies is becoming less common. The profession is now so sophisticated, and management's need to trust the IR executive is so great, that most large companies are cycling some of their more talented business professionals through the IR post. Familiarity with the dynamics of capital markets has become so important that many companies consider it essential training for those who may be headed for higher management positions.

I am familiar with one company that makes a point of giving investor relations experience to executives who may be headed for the top. Those who have had the job in the past include the current chairman and CEO, an individual who holds enormous respect as a corporate leader. The culture of this company is such that every investor relations director entering the position knows which of his predecessors is responsible for attracting each of the large institutional investors who now hold the stock. He is challenged to seek his own such trophies, with which he'll be identified long after he leaves the IR post for more senior ones.

Adventures in Investor Relations: A Story of Emerging Brazil

"Presenting multiple versions of the same concept can be an extremely powerful way to change someone's mind," the Harvard psychologist Howard Gardner has written. In fact, the gift for telling the same story in the languages of widely diverse audiences can be an enormous asset. And sometimes the task at hand requires nothing less.

In the late 1990s, the government of Brazil decided it was time to privatize its national telephone system, which it had nationalized approximately four decades earlier. During that time the country had pursued an isolationist economic policy, sometimes called "import substitution," under which it resolved to supply its own needs from the extraordinary resources that lay within its borders. It developed massive manufacturing power in steel and other industries. The prevailing belief held that utilities such as telephones, electricity, and energy better served the country under government control than in private hands where profits would go to investors instead of to the Brazilian people. Teachers taught this philosophy to generations of schoolchildren, and when some of those children grew up to be politicians, they showed they'd learned their lessons well by continuing to embed isolationist ideas in Brazilian policy and culture.

But Brazil couldn't develop its telecommunications system fast enough to support the country's economic growth. And at about the time the same realization arrived in the Soviet Union, China, and other countries, Brazil awoke to the fact that governments didn't run these businesses very well. In addition, many Brazilians were ready for change. Years of hyperinflation, during which prices could rise 1 to 2 percent per day due to miserable governance, had revealed their enormous sophistication and forbearance. Taxi drivers and housemaids learned to perform complex currency calculations in their heads. Many people, including executives in glass office towers, received salaries as bags of cash so they could change their pay into goods before it lost its value. The need to speed transactions was so great that, by the early 1990s, Brazilian banks had developed data communications technologies so advanced that any bank branch in the far Amazon with a two-way satellite dish on its roof could clear a check through São Paulo in 24 hours.

To get the telecommunications network out of its own hands and into the hands of companies that knew how to develop it, the government decided to sell Telebrás, the phone utility. It held about 93 percent of the telecommunications assets of a country nearly the size of the United States. The government planned to break it into 12 parts and sell them all at auction on a single day.

This privatization presented three prodigious communications challenges. The first was to reverse the government's own 40-year propaganda campaign against private ownership of utilities. Only by convincing the Brazilian people—particularly public-sector workers and others of privilege—that the country's interests had changed, could the government hope to generate sufficient political support to proceed with the privatization. The second challenge was to demonstrate to bidders—including national European carriers, U.S. Baby Bells, and newly formed Brazilian consortia—that the assets for sale deserved their investment. And the third challenge was to attract the support of a worldwide shareholder base that had purchased the minority stake in Telebrás that the government had made available earlier.

I had the good fortune to serve as financial communications advisor to Telebrás and the Ministry of Communications for the two years leading up to the privatization in 1998. One imperative that overhung this massive exercise was that we had to complete it successfully by August 1 of that year, before the reelection campaign of President Fernando Henrique Cardoso began. But we first had to convince the Brazilian people that a communications infrastructure capable of sending the Internet into classrooms and homes from the Atlantic to the western Amazon, and of supporting businesses in the information age, required ownership by global companies with the experience to develop and operate it and the capital to make the needed investments.

The advertising that transmitted this message took many forms. Much of it resembled in spirit a poster the Ministry of Communications had published, a copy of which I hung in my New York office. It showed a smiling boy of about nine, who looked a lot like Pele must have looked at that age, with a plaster cast on one arm and holding a soccer ball in the other. The legend (in Portuguese) described the benefits of redirecting the government's efforts out of the phone business. It said about the boy: "Let's privatize Telebrás to get him the medical care he needs and bring the Internet to his school."

Once the political opportunity emerged, we had to make the sale a success. And the only way to do that was to convince bidders not only to participate in the auction, but to get them to pay a sufficiently high price. This was not only a matter of filling the data rooms that potential bidders visited in order to examine the numbers. It meant making Brazil look like a place where businesses would proceed according to the terms of agreements the government would make with buyers. It meant, most of all, creating the perception of a government that wanted the winning companies to succeed, and that had the means to create the appropriate conditions for them to do so.

The genius behind the Telebrás privatization was Minister of Communications Sergio Motta, who had learned a number of lessons from the sale of smaller government assets such as the Rio de Janeiro electricity distribution system, called Light. The sale of Light had resulted in diminished electrical service for residents of Rio, and they made sure the government heard about it. The contract that governed the operation of the system after privatization failed to specify a level of performance for which the government could hold the operating company accountable. As a result, there was little recourse at times when large parts of the city went dark. I can remember Motta standing before a long table at the Ministry of Communications in Brasilia, dozens of cowed Ministry personnel and advisors seated along its sides, pounding the table and saying that Light proved that the success or failure of *any* privatization lay in the terms of the original contract. If the contract was weak, there was no way to recover.

The question for bidders on telecommunications assets was whether they were buying companies in an environment that would permit them to pursue their businesses according to methods they knew to be effective. When the government had failed to guard its own interests and allowed Light to underperform, it showed it was not in control. And freedom from accountability brought the owners of Light little benefit in a civic atmosphere that had become strongly resistant to their presence. Telecom bidders didn't want such a weak regulatory structure, not even one that left them unaccountable. They wanted a system that worked. Most importantly, the global investors wanted reasons for confidence in a process that would preserve the gains they expected their shares to make as international interest in Brazil rose.

Telebrás' transition from a classic, centrally controlled government bureaucracy to an efficient capital-markets operator offered more drama than one generally expects from financial transactions, even very large ones. The year prior to privatization, Telebrás' depositary receipts were the third most heavily traded of any security on the New York Stock Exchange. In dollar volume, investors bought and sold more Telebrás stock than they did General Electric, General Motors, Coca-Cola, or Exxon. Yet, during one quarter of that year, the company's financial disclosure was so amateurish that it sent investors copies of a speech the CEO had delivered to a financial forum in place of a quarterly earnings announcement. On a 5:00 A.M. ride to the airport I advised the CEO, a brilliant man who had little capital markets experience, and whom I didn't know very well at the time, that the company had to learn the nature of financial reporting. On returning to Brasilia, he restructured the accounting function so quickly that Telebrás somehow delivered a fully professional level of disclosure the following quarter. The swiftness with which Brazil evolved from a postcolonial, inward-looking society to a fully competent global player was breathtaking.

The breakup of the company into twelve parts would require an exchange of existing Telebrás shares for those of the new entities. Although half the big names on Wall Street had been involved at one point or another, someone finally noticed just three months before the auction that the run-up of the stock price would trigger an enormous capital gains tax for U.S. investors who would have no choice but to exchange their existing shares for those of the 12 new companies. While the matter remained private for the moment, Brazilian officials worried that investors would revolt against the company, collapsing the share price. Investment bankers told a ministry meeting that the government would have to delay the auction six months, which sent it into a panic, as it could cost President Cardoso reelection. Adding to the sense of disorganization was the sudden death, reportedly from Legionnaires' disease, of the brilliant Minister Motta.

Telebrás CEO Fernando Xavier Ferreira, who the year before

had turned the entire Telebrás reporting process around in a fiscal heartbeat (one quarter), instructed me to go back to New York and find an answer to the dilemma. Back at the corner of Water Street and Wall, colleagues and I analyzed the interests of each segment of the Telebrás investor base, from mutual funds to pension funds, institutions, hedge funds, and individual investors. We projected the behavior of each and quickly realized the obvious: Nothing was going to happen. Tax-exempt investors didn't care, and the only revolt the others could take would be to sell their shares, which would trigger the same capital gains event they'd be trying to avoid. The fact that the best minds of their generation had missed a fundamental item out of Finance 101 didn't even matter. I flew back to Brazil with the good news.

The Telebrás privatization required careful coordination of a broad-spectrum message. The government had to change the fundamental way by which people valued their national wealth. It also had to show international telecommunications companies that, despite a rocky history that included repeated rounds of hyperinflation and financial mismanagement, Brazil was a country in which they could prosper—and, furthermore, that they should pay well for the chance to do so. Finally, the government had to demonstrate to international investors that one of the world's great national bureaucracies could transform itself to meet global disclosure standards—that in fact transparency was something you could learn.

The auction took place at the São Paulo Stock Exchange on schedule, though not without a rock-throwing protest outside involving the riot police and a number of injuries. Proceeds of the privatization reached approximately $20 billion, the largest such transaction ever in Latin America and one of the largest of any kind up to that time. In his memoir, President Cardoso, who served a second successful term, pointed out that four years later the number of phones per 100 people in Brazil had risen from 8.4 to 30. Eight years later the number of cell phones in Brazil had increased more than a hundredfold to over 80 million.

PART TWO

The Seven Strategies of Reputation Leadership

CHAPTER 6

Strategy 1:
Establish Core Values and Reputation Will Follow

Core Values and the Authentic Leader

The following story is told of Gandhi. A woman and her diabetic son traveled 12 hours by hot, dusty train to see the great man so he could help the woman stop the boy from eating sugar, to which the boy found access in ingenious ways. When they arrived at the poor farm where Gandhi was living, they stood for hours in the hot sun among other supplicants waiting for their moment. When they finally arrived before him, the woman made her request—that Gandhi tell the boy to stop eating sugar. Gandhi answered by telling the woman to go home and return with her son in six weeks.

They took the long, uncomfortable train ride home, then returned at the time they had been instructed. When they stood before him again, the woman reminded Gandhi of their prior visit. Gandhi looked at the boy and shouted, "STOP EATING SUGAR!" He then nodded to the next supplicant in line. "But, Mahatma," said the woman, not moving, "why did you not say that to him six weeks ago? Why did you force us to make this tiring journey twice?"

"Madam," said Gandhi, "six weeks ago I, myself, still ate sugar."

As the story illustrates, a leader must become the change he or she envisions. Like Gandhi, a contemporary leader leads not by control, but by vision and conviction and a willingness to take responsibility for consequences. His or her accountability is a requirement for any claim to authenticity.

Gandhi's mission was to free India from British rule, which required him to move a large and diverse group of thinking individuals to designed and concerted action. Similarly, a CEO who is as ambitious for his company as Gandhi was for India must make ambitious requests of his organization.

It used to be that a CEO could manage more or less by command. But no longer. Today's workers have too much information and too many choices to allow themselves to be manipulated. They may be willing to follow, but their range of choices and mobility make them increasingly able to hold the boss accountable.

To become the change he wants to produce in his organization, a CEO must be personally transparent—and must possess the courage to address his own challenges as well as those of his company. To win over the best of his employees so they identify with his goals, he must engage them in this task. Two of the most powerful words he can utter in the context of an ambitious undertaking are: "Help me."

By framing his vision as a request—or series of requests—the

CEO wraps himself, his aspirations, and the team's participation in a single thought. Defining the challenges in terms of the support he requires leverages all three elements needed for concerted action: a plan, collaborative effort, and demonstration of his openness to personal risk. In addition, he must be honest about the unknowability of the future, since he's as subject to the unforeseeable as any other mortal.

Whether he's a new CEO or an incumbent intent on building identity within the group, the first question to be answered is: "For what should our company be known?" The answer to this question lies in the discovery of the company's core values. Ultimately it delivers the answer to a still larger question: "Who are we?"

*   *   *   *

Everyone in an organization must understand what it wants to be known for. Core values lie at the center of this understanding, but they are not the company's identity. They are, however, the material out of which its identity, and therefore its reputation, are created. And core values, to be worth anything at all, must remain constant regardless of whether a company's circumstances are prosperous or difficult.

It isn't easy to make them so. The day-to-day reality of many leaders is this: It doesn't matter what you've accomplished in terms of establishing groundwork for the company's long-term growth. The CEO who has the misfortune to "miss analysts' expectations" for several quarters in a row will be gone.

Managers' first response to such pressures, and to difficult times in general, is often to cut expenses, which generally means reducing the workforce. Sometimes this is justified; sometimes it isn't. And, depending on how staff reductions are carried out, they may result in jettisoning people who take with them a valuable portion of the company's intellectual capital. The depth of this loss is never quantified and rarely mentioned. But if one of the company's core values is to be an innovator, then management must know what the loss of the people it fires is costing. So, the manager may face two unhappy choices: cutting some of the assets that make the company innovative, or ignoring the short-term demands of the market and running the risk of cutting himself out of the picture.

When a company looks at its possible means of reducing expenses, the companion to staff cuts is shrinking investment in the business. One place short-term investors are happy to see investments slashed is in a company's research and development efforts. And, as it does in so many areas, the energy industry offers a valuable lesson here. In 2008 the value of a barrel of oil rose above $100—and for a time exceeded $140—as the result of an apparent rebalancing of the supply-demand equation in energy. Analyst after analyst cited the rise in demand in China and India as the cause of the price rise.

Absent from the public dialogue, however, were reasons for the failure of international oil companies to adjust their supplies, regardless of how immensely profitable it would have been to do so. They simply couldn't. Easily recoverable oil was disappearing. And, despite a genius demonstrated over nearly a century for finding new ways to exploit more difficult wells, spending on R&D had dwindled over the prior decade in relative terms. It had fallen far below what would have been needed to access crude in partially depleted wells, at greater depths, and offshore.

At the same time, Wall Street was exerting a new kind of influence on the oil companies. Investors and analysts wouldn't put up with companies that failed to generate a certain amount of cash. In addition to steep cuts in expenses, investors wanted oil companies to buy back their shares. Investors' returns increased when the company bought their shares and took them off the market. The stock that remained in circulation generally achieved a higher value because of the reduced number of shares available. When companies like ExxonMobil bought back large amounts of their shares, both outside investors and company employees who held the shares made out extremely well. But for the company itself, such buybacks were acts of small self-liquidation, as cash given to shareholders was no longer available for the company's use. Buying back shares may express the belief in a higher future share price, since the company would be unlikely to buy the stock unless it thought it was cheap. But any gains were achieved partially by using cash that could have gone into R&D—into finding new ways to produce more energy.

The allocation of a company's capital for buybacks may have generated a payout to investors and raised the stock price, but it didn't speak well for the company's future as a vibrant enterprise. Demand from China and India clearly had something to do with it, but the dramatic rise in world oil prices was also related to the internal value priorities within the oil companies and their decisions to subordinate their long-term ability to produce in favor of shorter-term financial gains for shareholders. These results reflected the bases on which they made decisions. In other words: on the core values they held.

*　　*　　*　　*

Managers intent on establishing core values for their companies must understand, first of all, that there is magic in consistency. As a management interprets new events according to values it has established, those values become substantive in people's minds. Management's responses to events become predictable to its employees. A company that prizes its authenticity runs more on consensus than on compliance. If its values are to serve it, everyone must understand those values on a visceral level. In fact, people are connected, to a large extent, by the values they share. This is true not only in the corporation; it's also the force that creates national identity, political parties, and the cohesion of ethnicity. It is that kind of shared, mutual identity that the visionary CEO seeks for his or her company.

Corporate leaders often face a challenge in inducing a management team and employees to buy into the organization's values. Later in this chapter I'll explain how Citigroup and Chiquita Brands took two different routes to getting employees onboard. In all cases, however, the essential principle in gaining their agreement is the same: The CEO must make employees coauthors of the company's values.

Management can approach establishment of core reputation values along two distinct lines. The first consists of structured internal dialogues carried out in a way that creates fundamental definitions: If the company were to have a strong reputation, what would it look like? For what qualities would it be known? What words would the world use to describe it? Most important to the principle of authenticity, the company must answer the question: "With what descriptions are we most comfortable?"

Dialogues that yield answers to these questions generally occur in workshops whose participants cut across the entire spectrum of the business. Some groups consist of members of a single business team who know one another well, others of disparate employees who have never met. The value of this diverse collaboration lies in its result—a contribution to core reputation values derived from discovery of the company's fundamental beliefs about itself.

Part two of the methodology for determining core reputation values ignores the internal culture, focusing instead on external stakeholders' views of the company. The mechanism for learning these views are the perception study and reputation audit, which we'll describe in later chapters. One of their essential contributions lies in exposing the differences between stakeholders' opinions of the company and the company's view of itself.

Corporate leadership then creates a unified list that is informed by internal as well as external expressions of values. The final list must represent the views of both the company and its stakeholders, since both make up a single sphere of interest. A significant element of this art lies in matching the two sets of concepts of the company while staying true to each.

* * * *

Gathering employees into the values creation process requires a fluid system of communications. While the manner of communicating can vary, it must enable the corporate center to transmit its message and receive back responses, suggestions, complaints, and candid reports on realities throughout the company. Such a communications system, having facilitated the development of the company's values, can then enable the kind of permanent companywide interchange that keeps those values alive in corporate operations. In a way, the values and the communications system on which they rely become inseparable.

One significant feature of an overtly expressed value system is that it attracts to the company those individuals capable of understanding and supporting it. The values-driven conversation will capture the imaginations of some people and repel others. It is, therefore, a self-selecting mechanism by which people choose to enter the organization, choose to remain, and choose to leave. Those who are there only for the salary won't have the necessary patience, nor will they be able to fake adherence to a set of alien values for very long.

A strong connection exists, then, between a company's value system and the nature of the individuals who populate its ranks. Schlumberger Limited, the world's largest oil field services company, years ago made the decision to create an employee base that reflected the many countries in which it operated. This was a business decision. The company began with initiatives that included the donation of computers to schools in those countries and the support of local university engineering programs. Today, individuals of diverse nationalities run Schlumberger's businesses, while its competitors, who also work every place there is oil, still look very much like indigenous U.S. companies. Schlumberger's shares historically trade at a premium compared to its peers. Some observers point to the ease with which the company operates throughout the world as one of the reasons for that premium.

Diversity of Points of View

Diversity is an idea we hear a great deal about. It generally refers to race, ethnicity, gender, age, and other characteristics that are demographic in nature. Diversity is often associated with a company's compliance with standards that are either legal in nature or implied by guidelines that can originate in industry associations, NGOs, and other influential sources. But compliance aside, the most important aspect of diversity for a company's well-being and vibrancy is its diversity of viewpoint. As Schlumberger did, companies should consider whether their workforces resemble the broader spectrum of their stakeholders.

Increasingly they do. One attribute of the globalized environment is that the workforce—in its ethnicity, national origin, and worldview—begins to reflect the world outside the company. That's the good news. The irony is that management may still resemble that of a traditional American company 50 years ago. But such management is at no disadvantage in interacting with its stakeholders and customers as long as it knows how to harness the human assets of the corporation and learn from them.

Diversity is one of the greatest sources of protection against irrationality in an organization. Because it forces management to communicate in reasonable language, it tends to impose a balance on ideas and discourse that is often absent from organizations where a sense of implicit understanding can allow business to be done with a wink. The curse of homogenous organizations, where internal agreement is too easily reached, is that managers and strategists can talk each other into an identical blindness that leads the company outside the bounds of acceptable conduct before any of them take notice.

So, building a management team and employee base that reflects the world around it is one of the greatest sources of protection a company can provide itself. Yet that diversity is of little use unless the knowledge offered by that employee base is accessible. A productive question a management team might ask itself is: "What part of our employees' understanding of the world enters with them through the front door every morning and is available to us?" And its corollary: "What part of their potential contribution do they leave outside?"

One of the greatest dangers lurking in executive decision-making is the natural tendency to focus on the rewards of a strategy without giving sufficient thought to its social implications. A diversity of voices forces management into 360-degree consideration of any important matter, protecting it from the lures and traps of its own wishful thinking.

What any truly aware management must recognize is that diversity is essential not only for the way the company is seen, but also for the way it *sees*. The variation of opinion within its walls can be one of a company's great, untapped assets. But the cultural challenge to harnessing diversity requires recognition that there's no diversity without dissent.

The message of diversity is about more than demographics. It also has to do with a company's ability to leverage the whole employee—both the part of him or her that works in the company and the part that lives in the world. The Harvard economist Joseph L. Bower describes the person who plays an involved role in the company while maintaining independent points of reference as an "inside outsider." Bower's focus is succession planning, but the concept of the inside outsider is of great use in considering employees at many levels who exert an influence on the company's character. Bower describes inside outsiders as "people from the inside of the company who somehow have maintained enough detachment from the local traditions, ideology, and shibboleths that they have retained the objectivity of an outsider." Letting the company's job description define these people rather than allowing them to help redefine the company in individual ways qualifies as a wasted opportunity.

The Corporate and the Personal

More than a few corporate scandals (and many of those considered here) have resulted from choices by executives and employees that they would consider unthinkable in their private lives. The question reduces to this: Why should different standards apply to corporations and individuals? The chasm between personal and organizational values led Merck down a deeply damaging path in its marketing of Vioxx. I doubt that those people who decided to withhold scientific research that failed to serve the company's marketing purpose would have accepted such deception in their personal lives. (And they probably wouldn't have gained employment at such a historically reputable firm as Merck if they had.)

If organizational values prevail over the personal, why can't the dynamic be reversed? Siemens, while it was spending a billion or so on bribes, would certainly have benefited if someone had asked management to take a deep breath and see if they couldn't discover a better way. It's not been reported that anyone did. Would the bosses have listened? Possibly they would have, as these were truly superior managers. I know one CEO who values transparency in his organization for a number of reasons, not the least of which is, as he explains, "It keeps me honest."

Codes of Ethics

Value systems and codes of conduct stand on foundations of ethics. The potential damage from unethical conduct is enormous. A company can build its market share, clean up lakes and rivers, and shock analysts with its dynamic performance. But if a suspicion arises—from any quarter, regardless of its legitimacy—that the company has defrauded a customer or improperly booked revenues, there is little question which story, the positive or the negative, will come to the public's mind on mention of the company's name. Such is the general opinion of corporate ethics and expectations of corporate behavior.

Most sizable companies have developed codes of ethics, and some have done the work to make theirs comprehensive and clear. Even when great effort has been put into the code, however, development of the guidelines is probably the easiest part of the process. Explaining the use of expense accounts, telling employees not to steal, exhorting them to abide by regulations and tell the truth are not difficult exercises. A code of ethics is worth little, however, without an infrastructure that continually educates, monitors, and enforces its compliance. Any company operating in the absence of such structures is driving without a seat belt. Even a small accident can become a disaster because the defense of malfeasance before regulators and prosecutors often hinges on whether management can demonstrate having taken adequate precautions before the supposed offenses took place.

How better to examine the process of creating values and developing structures to assure their relevance throughout the organization than to follow what is perhaps the greatest and most public such campaign on record—that of Citigroup in the aftermath of the scandals it suffered in the early 2000s. Earlier we examined how Chuck Prince and Citigroup mounted an energetic and imaginative campaign to build reputation values—only to experience erosion of the reputation once its restoration had seemed assured. But, as in the case of John Browne and BP, troubles that confronted the organization later on should not erase the lessons that a successful values-building campaign can teach us.

As we saw earlier, Prince's response to the ejection of Citi's private bank from Japan was to travel there. He famously bowed his head at a press conference to express his remorse at the actions Citi had taken. Though this gesture may have begun to restore Citi's stature in Japan, the sheer number of problems with the bank's reputation told Prince that he had to build a new value system from the ground up.

Up to that time, Citi's businesses had existed in silos that had little or no contact with—or even consciousness of—one another. Sandy Weill had ingeniously executed the mergers that created the institution, but he undertook little integration. His mandate to the various business groups was that managers had only to hit their numbers and he would leave them alone.

Prince, on the other hand, believed that the failure to provide better guidance to Citi's diverse business groups contributed to the company's problems, and he aimed to change the system. He saw the absence of a mutual set of values as the root of the problem. To determine what Citi's values should be, he initiated an exhaustive consultative process that included internal panels and employee surveys. He visited other CEOs to get their views, including William Weldon of Johnson & Johnson and Michael Dell.

And he traveled the world to talk to Citi employees virtually everywhere, asking them what they thought the company had to do to get back on track. A crucial element in this dialogue was the explicit acknowledgment that the company was in trouble. Everybody knew it, but Prince's unequivocal admission of the problems, and his refusal to seek shelter in denial, brought enough confidence to the employees to induce them to contribute their ideas. Michael Schlein, who served as one of Prince's internal advisors, observes that the spectacle of a bow by the leader of one of the world's great financial institutions had been a stunning moment, perhaps unique in business history. People who saw the picture remember it. For employees, it confirmed beyond any doubt that their environment was changing.

The set of values that resulted from Citi's companywide conversations turned out to be remarkably simple. They consisted of three "Shared Responsibilities," each considering a distinct set of stakeholders:

- *Clients*: Superior advice, products, and services delivered with integrity;
- *Colleagues:* Opportunity to realize personal potential, respect, diversity, sharing success, and accepting accountability for failures;
- *The Bank's Franchise:* Primacy of the company's interests over those of the individual business units, superior results for shareholders, respect for local cultures and communities, and extending the company's longstanding legacy.

Prince also introduced a five-point plan to assure that employees had the tools and framework to implement the shared values. They were:

- Expanded training
- Enhanced focus on talent and development
- Performance appraisals that include shared responsibilities
- Improved communications
- Strengthened controls

The shared responsibilities and five-point plan came alive in many different forms. Citigroup translated them into 20 languages. They appeared on posters, office walls, and mouse pads by the thousands.

During this period, Prince went personally to report to Japanese regulators every three months until they told him he didn't have to come back anymore. Members of the management team traveled to see regulators around the world on a monthly basis. At the same time, they visited Citi offices to explain the five-point plan and the shared responsibilities. They carried with them the video that Prince had mandated to dramatize Citi's venerable history.

The deeper changes at Citigroup included a complete overhaul of employee evaluations. Performance on shared responsibilities assumed a prominent place in the personnel reviews that influenced compensation. This, perhaps more than any other feature of the program, made values a part of everyday life at Citigroup and substantially changed the mode of expression within the organization. "It used to be," says Schlein, "that someone might complain about his boss and manage to call him an idiot in the process. Now, in registering a complaint, the employee, in order to be heard, might describe how the boss wasn't living up to his shared responsibilities." In this way, the company began to run on a mutual vocabulary of values.

In addition, everyone now underwent 360-degree reviews. This meant they were judged by associates at levels both more junior and more senior to themselves, as well as by their peers.

Coaching became a regular part of management life. Making it mandatory quickly removed the stigma coaching had always carried. In former times, if an executive had experienced problems, you secretly got him a coach on the side. Now everybody had one, and the subject was out in the open. Even Prince began to refer to discussions with his coach on companywide conference calls.

When the Bad Drives Out the Good

Darwin's theory of natural selection asserts that an individual organism that is particularly suited to its environment is more likely to survive and reproduce than a less fit organism in the same environment. It's every individual for itself, with its descendants as beneficiaries. But Harvard biologist Edward O. Wilson says his research on ant colonies shows that survival of the individual organism is not the only focus of the natural selection process. This research has begun to persuade some scientists that selection can also occur at the level of the group. Wilson's theory says groups of organisms with a superiority in fitness tend to survive at the expense of other groups, and a surviving group tends to be made of individuals that support it with some degree of selflessness. So, to some extent, sacrificing yourself for the group can be an individual survival trait.

If valid, this would be good news for corporate leaders, who must work continuously to see that employees identify their personal success with the success of the organization. If a predisposition toward group-oriented behavior is a factor in individual survival, it offers reason for optimism.

Such symbiosis between the organization and the individual prevails when the company is relatively free of stress, when business is good, and when competitive pressures are manageable. But because of the nonstop evolution of markets, companies generally find themselves in states of transition. At those times, the strain on the organization becomes evident in its internal life. During periods of leadership upheaval or uncertainty about the organization, managers and employees tend to see their individual interests as distinct from those of the group, and the results can be severely destructive toward the company's culture and economic health.

Consider a scenario in which two different ideas that employees hold about their personal paths to advancement go head-to-head.

It is a conflict that can arise at any time, but occurs most frequently at moments of high anxiety within an organization.

One view of personal advancement holds that building competence in one's work and finding ways to contribute to the business will find their proper rewards. People who hold this view not only do their jobs, they improve and refine the domains in which they operate, offering greater support to the company as a whole. They don't rule out for themselves the opportunity to lead the organization one day, but they believe any such recognition will be conferred on the basis of contribution. Let's call these people the competence tribe.

Now, let's look at a category of people who see their way forward in a different light. Members of this group view the power they manage to collect as their primary mechanism for advancement. Although they appreciate the importance of competence, the linkage between power and competence is not something they spend a lot of time thinking about. Power is its own subject to them. Let's call these folks the power tribe.

The competence tribe is the primary repository of the company's values. Management has few strategic options without the R&D and execution capabilities it delivers, and the competence tribe can provide the crucial sustaining anchor during times of management turmoil. In 2007–2008, Siemens AG achieved record earnings while losing virtually its entire management team in a bribery scandal. An enormously competent Siemens workforce probably deserves the credit for carrying the company forward while a new management regime gained its footing.

For members of the power tribe, power is its own reward, and they do not confuse it with merit. They believe that having power is identical to deserving it. Such people are generally able to make decisions without a great fear of being wrong, and sometimes even a wrong decision benefits the company more than no decision at all.

These two very different groups generally coexist. When

conflict arises between them, it comes at times that deviate from the norm. Such times might be characterized by dramatically improving business prospects—when new geographies or product areas are opening, for example, so an increased level of influence could potentially bring substantial rewards. But most often these conflicts appear under more difficult conditions, such as those that descend on a business when growth opportunities are diminishing, or a new competitor is on the rise. At such times, increased influence could provide a greater chance for personal survival. So, members of the power tribe begin to push the competence tribe aside.

The competence tribe takes notice when a trusted manager leaves for no apparent reason, when value created is ascribed to parts of the organization that are not its source, or when reporting structures become scrambled without discernible purpose. It's critical that the CEO and other senior managers recognize these changes when they occur, as they mark the moment when a focus on power begins to drive competence from the organization.

Can senior managers foretell the departures of the competent before they occur? They generally can, but doing so requires a careful listening that reveals the indicators of trouble. Early warning signals include internal communications that become cloudy and negative. Such communications are generally written to hide their purposes rather than to express them. A corporate leader may notice the change when business managers' workdays become occupied with defending internal domains, a misuse of time that forces the company deeper into a vulnerable state.

The biggest threat in power-oriented behaviors lies in the ease with which they spread. Everyone down to the receptionist can begin to see self-protection as the road to survival. The sharing of intellectual capital can grind nearly to a halt. People begin to hoard assets such as technical methodologies or lists of clients and potential clients. They value these assets not only for use in struggles for position within the company, but to take with them in securing and prospering in their next job. The likelihood that this is industry-specific information increases the chances that their next job will be with a competitor.

Once this stealth dissolution begins to occur, there's no way of knowing where it will lead. Management is in danger of losing control of the culture primarily because the perceived avenue to success has been altered. People have changed their attitudes toward the company, which has essentially lost its reputation with its own employees.

If management doesn't take steps to reverse the devaluation of competence, it may find that customers and clients begin to notice. Disruptions in personnel may mean that customer contacts within the company change, and external business partners find themselves talking to unfamiliar people. Any negative effect on financial performance will draw investors' attention, inviting skepticism and reducing interest in the shares.

Reversing this process while it's still reversible requires a management with exceptional qualities. They include the character and awareness not only to understand dissonant elements, but to do so at exactly the time when it is most difficult—when management is keeping the lights on late anyway, trying to resolve the challenges that created the friction in the first place.

Values and Corporate Responsibility

Inside outsiders, as described by Professor Bower, present a significant asset to corporate leaders who recognize the need for an expanded notion of the company. This becomes important as societal factors force the pursuit of actions that may at first seem unrelated to financial performance. Earlier we described why companies operating in delicate ecological and social environments should take seriously their "social license to operate"—why, in other words, they are wise to act in accordance with the interests of the communities around them. Their success in this is inseparable from their ability to develop a set of corporate values, or principles, that form the basis of their decisions.

In the early 1990s, the management of Chiquita Brands saw the world changing around it and realized its traditional way of doing business would no longer serve its interests. The company had been reviled as a neocolonial predator and was subject to repeated organized protests by activist groups. Chiquita's predecessor company, United Fruit, had notoriously created the conditions that gave rise to the term "banana republic." Through much of the 20th century, the company held monopolistic control over banana and pineapple production in large parts of Central America and the Caribbean. In support of its business, United Fruit bribed heads of state, built its own railroads and ports, ran national telegraph and postal systems, and conspired with governments to restrict land use by local peasant farmers who might be considered competitors. The company also participated in the CIA overthrow of a legally elected Guatemalan president in the 1950s, and in the U.S. Bay of Pigs invasion of Cuba in 1961.

In 1991 Chiquita's management embarked on a transformation that proved truly remarkable. As in most such cases, it was business necessity rather than a suddenly discovered altruism that moved the company toward corporate responsibility. In Chiquita's case, changes in the world supply of bananas made labor strikes suddenly unprofitable. Previously, strikes had enabled the company to increase prices because of reduced supply. While strikes cut production at Chiquita farms, the company always had access to a considerable volume of produce on which it could immediately raise prices. It could also draw new supplies from alternative sources.

Then the development of new farms in Ecuador changed the banana supply-demand equation. Chiquita could no longer use strikes as a pretext for price rises, and so it resolved to increase competitiveness by raising worker productivity. To do this, it had to begin improving compensation, benefits, and working conditions.

Chiquita teamed up with the Rainforest Alliance, an NGO that had established operating standards covering deforestation, pesticides, wildlife protection, water and soil conservation, worker pay, labor conditions, and unions' rights to organize. Over eight years, with the guidance of the Rainforest Alliance, Chiquita reorganized its farms and practices until 100 percent of its operations in Latin America had received the NGO's certified seal. By 2000 it had subscribed to the Social Accountability International SA8000 protocols. These were the toughest social-responsibility standards in existence for which compliance could be reliably verified. Chiquita also entered into a labor-framework agreement with regional and international unions, making it the most unionized company in the industry. These measures brought an incalculable improvement to workers' lives, raising them up to international standards from virtual peonage.

Chiquita's $20 million investment in these reforms placed it among the global standard setters in corporate social responsibility; at the same time, the company cut its production costs by more than $100 million. But only when Chiquita had seen these results did it begin deliberately to develop an internal set of values.

During the first year of this program, CEO Steve Warshaw and his management team devoted half a day each month to defining and seeking agreement on company values. The outside consultant who ran these meetings inquired of all group members what values mattered most to them. Everyone made lists.

The management team then looked for consensus and settled first on the value of trust. All agreed, for example, that standing behind commitments the company had made to employees was an unshakable matter of trust. But how might the team approach trust when it came to suppliers' violations of laws of their own countries? Was this simply other people's business? If the company facilitated a supplier in this way without cost to its own shareholders, whose trust, if anyone's, did it violate?

After their year of concentrating on these discussions, the team generated a list of core values that centered on Integrity, Respect, Opportunity, and Responsibility.

It was a different approach than the one taken by Citigroup, which first queried its employee base as a means of generating core values. Chiquita CEO Warshaw believed he had to begin by establishing the management team's own commitment. He also felt that, before asking employees to take management's initiative seriously, he would have to demonstrate that management had begun to reverse its record of poor execution on social responsibility matters. He hoped that offering a set of values in which the company had already invested would be more likely to arouse such confidence.

This judgment proved correct, and the project inspired an unprecedented dialogue about values with Chiquita's workers. When responses from the plantations of Central America reached corporate headquarters in Cincinnati, those who had drafted the original values recognized a substantial expansion on their initial work. One value that moved the managers, but which had completely evaded them the first time around, involved primacy of the family. It took a thousand field workers from Guatemala to Colombia—people whose culture overtly centered around families—to remind management of their own. Recognition of the importance of the family became part of Respect, one of the company's core values.

In addition to sweeping changes in living and working conditions, and in environmental standards, the company became a meritocracy for the very first time. One of the most notable transformations arose in its hiring and promotion practices. Throughout Chiquita's history, each plantation manager's authority had crossed the boundary fences of the farms and covered the surrounding communities as well. As *caudillos* (strongmen), they influenced local government and participated in decisions on schools, hospitals, and law enforcement. In their capacities as general managers, they hired and promoted employees according to their personal wishes, relationships, and ethnic preferences. They were, in short, beyond accountability.

With the advent of Chiquita's code of conduct, any of these men who failed to adapt were dismissed. Sexual harassment was the area of conduct most immediately in need of reform, and the company's decisive enforcement in this matter changed the lives of many workers. By taking these measures, the company cemented the perception among the workforce of its commitment to operating in a new way. This helped substantially in making acceptance of further change possible.

*　　*　　*　　*

A corporation needs friends wherever it can find them. One of the greatest protections a company can provide for itself is to embed its employees—from the CEO down—in the community. This is equally important in its home market and abroad. Some companies make involvement in community organizations a component of each employee's performance review. Most sizeable firms have community investment programs, and those who take this facet of corporate life seriously know how to target their contributions for greatest value.

Some focus contributions in institutions, such as hospitals, at sufficient levels to merit a seat on the board. If the company makes the right choice of an employee to occupy that seat, it's quite likely that, over time, he or she will become its chairman. Through its financial contributions and the personal involvement of its employees, the company will have made itself part of the solution to the hospital's needs.

The internal corporate argument about return on investment for society-based initiatives should always retain clarity on the fact that they have nothing to do with altruism. They pertain to business. All the better if external observers, commentators, and constituents see the company as one that cares. But, to be authentic, the company shouldn't say too much about its good works. Let others discover them. Taking care of the society that supports the corporation is simply the new business-as-usual.

Management's challenge in the social and environmental arena is to convert the perception of the company from a possible threat to a clear solution. The leader's personal point of view should be one that sees the company and its social environment in a symbiotic relationship, and he or she should propagate this view throughout the company. Neither the company nor its external constituencies can prosper without the other. From the point of view of an individual within a company, social responsibility and responsibility to the organization grow from the same root. You clean up the river if you've polluted it, and you keep it clean—because in *this* world, failing to do so will cost you much more on the social side than any savings you may have realized from cutting corners on the operational side.

The attorney Siemens hired to implement its companywide program to eradicate systemic bribery practices summed up the challenge this way: "Healthy compliance cultures depend on a more values-based leadership where people don't need to look at the rule book, where they know intuitively what the right thing to do is."

The Company in a Grain of Sand

I asked a senior officer of a U.S. multinational (one of the 30 Dow Industrial components) about the company's vertical communications structure. Its 80,000 employees were spread over more than 100 countries. I wanted to know how management helped its workforce understand the nature of the company above and beyond its identity as a developer and marketer of high-tech products. How did leadership communicate to employees the ways it wanted them to represent it in Paris, Tokyo, and Timbuktu?

"We don't need any such structure," the officer told me. "Our management is the strongest in the world, and they lead by example. If you want to know how you should conduct yourself, all you have to do is watch what they do."

Within a year the board had fired the CEO, who had been with the company more than three decades. It fired him for two reasons: The first was his arrogance with shareholders, who complained about the company's lack of transparency and the poor access to management it offered. The second was his arrogance with employees, who had compiled a mounting body of complaints about the absence of a consultative culture, which became known as "management by command." Against this backdrop and a long-stagnant share price, the board simply stopped listening to the chief executive. His departure bore an air of disgrace that fell just short of that which would have prevailed had fraud been involved. But there was no fraud. Just a toxic atmosphere.

My conversation with the corporate official took place in a well-appointed office, with awards on the walls. In my experience, however, you don't have to go to an executive suite to understand a company's attitude toward its employees and its social and natural environment. A management's character displays itself in any part of an organization, in any part of the world. The poet William Blake said you can see the world in a grain of sand. Similarly, you can come to understand the core ethos of a company from a forklift operator in a facility an ocean away from headquarters.

When an employee makes a statement such as, "We take our cues from watching how management reacts to events," he is offering an observation about what his management is and is not. He is acknowledging the control authority of the boss. But he is not describing an environment in which processes follow an established set of principles. When you hear such a statement, you can be sure that the inhabitants of the executive suite do not feel bound by any overriding set of guidelines. And you do not have to go to headquarters to make this observation. That's why any approach to a value system has to take into account two basic points: It has to get to everybody, and its results will be observable everywhere.

Got a Problem? It's the Culture

The notion that companies in trouble have been victimized by ill-intentioned employees is an idea that managements can overuse in attempting to distance themselves from offensive acts that take place within their walls. Certainly, employees misbehave. But seldom does malfeasance great enough to cause the company or its shareholders real harm occur in a vacuum. Almost always there is a preexisting context that facilitates such acts.

Jérôme Kerviel, the employee who cost Société Générale $7.6 billion in supposedly unauthorized securities trading over two years, used fake transactions to cover his gigantic losses. After the discovery of his fraud in early 2008, French investigating authorities learned that fake trades were no unusual occurrence at Société Générale. It turned out that employees entered "virtual transactions" for all kinds of reasons, including the booking of trades before proper hedges were in place or counterparties were known. These practices were, of course, illegal in all instances.

"It is incomprehensible that there were no internal controls that would catch this," one highly experienced U.S. trader said to me in commenting on the Kerviel case. But as facts emerged, it became clear that the commonness of these acts created an environment that enabled Kerviel, in taking his own illegal practices just a step or two beyond those of his colleagues, to operate with relative freedom. Pity the poor internal risk manager trying to assess whether Kerviel's actions represented the usual kind of improper trade booking at Société Générale, or something new.

Two *Financial Times* reporters attempted to get to the bottom of SocGen's Orwellian distinctions between real fake trades and fake fake trades. They wrote, "[SocGen] has claimed Mr. Kerviel concealed his unhedged transactions using lies. Vincent Guyot, one of SocGen's controllers, told the police that anomalies discovered in March 2007 indicated that some of Mr. Kerviel's operations amounted to 'real fake trades which had no economic significance.'" SocGen seemed inclined to distinguish one kind of lying from another. One was with the bank's permission, the other without.

Kerviel, at one point, faced the dilemma of how to reveal enormous gains to his bosses. By then, he'd made far more money than was possible with the relatively modest amounts he'd been authorized to risk. This potential for gains may explain why management, on a number of occasions, happily accepted Kerviel's lame explanations of discrepancies in his paperwork.

Just a little less easy to understand was the enormous popularity Kerviel achieved in the streets of Paris. Young women walked down the Champs-Élysées wearing T-shirts that proclaimed "I am Jérôme Kerviel's girlfriend." The question some research psychologist from the Sorbonne should investigate is: Did they think he was stealing or not?

CHAPTER 7

Strategy 2:
See Yourself through Stakeholders' Eyes

Market Intelligence and the Art of the Perception Study

We live in a world of wildly diverse stakeholder interests. Any company lacking a thorough understanding of its various audiences—their prejudices, perceptions, and attitudes—navigates in darkness. Before you can hope to convince the world of your merit, and investors of your value, you must first know how they think. Without such market intelligence, all communications are guesswork.

A strong reputation among investors and analysts requires

systematic listening that allows managers to become personally sensitized to their thinking. Such listening offers management a potent influence over the investment conversation about the company. It helps protect the company from its own excessive tendencies by maintaining a continuous outside reference by which management can judge its actions. It helps the company identify those actions that will make friends of enemies and buy critical time and support when future crises occur.

The Value Paradox

A company's most important external constituency is its investors. The gulf that lies between many companies and their investors can be summed up in what I call the value paradox. This term describes the dynamic by which management builds its company according to specific ideas of value that relate to production, innovation, operations, logistics, and so on. Yet its ultimate goal is to create share value, which is assigned by the market according to models that may bear little resemblance to management's own idea of value creation. So, although a corporate leader works every day to build a more valuable company, the company's market value is determined largely by outsiders operating according to their own independent principles. Management's failure to reconcile the two means that much of the value the company has built goes unrecognized and unrewarded.

The company's ability to encompass both its own internal theory of value and the market's is essential to achievement of a higher share price. Much of this effort boils down to investor communications. Is the company disclosing the information investors need in order to value its shares? Is management accessible and responsive? The company must learn to communicate on the basis of what the market wants to know rather than the internal story with which management may have fallen in love.

So before you communicate, you must know your investors' valuation methodologies as well as their opinions of management, its strategy, its competence to execute that strategy, its level of transparency, and how it compares to the competition. The good news is that all of these things are knowable. And the mechanism by which they can become known is the perception study.

The Perception Study and Its Variations

The perception study involves a consultant who, on behalf of the company, interviews influential investors and other stakeholders, then reports their opinions back to management. A trusted third-party interviewer can guarantee anonymity to respondents and therefore enhance the candor of their commentary.

While heavily used in investor relations, the perception study is adaptable to a company's entire range of stakeholders. When applied to the nonfinancial arena, it can uncover opinions of the company's standing in civil society—an asset of growing importance in the age of the Internet and universal scrutiny. The expansion of perception work into the social arena creates an opportunity for corporate leaders to engage NGOs that are focused on environmental and labor issues, for example, well in advance of the emergence of any public opposition to the company. Such engagement develops information and identifies the external conversations that, if pursued, will promote the smooth running of the company in its social environment.

Perception study methodologies fall into two categories: quantitative and qualitative.

Quantitative Perception Studies

With the increasing attention paid to issues of corporate reputation, new approaches have been developed to help companies understand how to improve their images. These methodologies leverage technology to analyze the beliefs consumers and other stakeholders harbor about a company in dozens of different dimensions. They measure customer opinion of brands and levels of worker satisfaction. They dissect newspaper and magazine articles by the thousands. Determining numerical values in each of these areas should enable a company to identify many of its objective deficits. If you get a low score on employee satisfaction, for example, you know to invest there.

Quantitative studies have their roots in consumer research. Dozens of respondents are asked narrowly focused questions to which they can give yes or no answers, or answers that reflect the respondent's relative judgment in values typically ranging from 1 to 5. Data gathered by aggregating large numbers of quantitative interviews lends itself easily to charts and graphs and plays well to a PowerPoint culture. Management may learn, for example, the relative percentages of investors who do and do not think its financial disclosure is adequate. It may find out that performance of the investor relations director has gone from a 3 last year to a 4 this year. Like virtually all information, this is useful. But it can hardly deliver the nuance to tell management how investors value its shares.

Qualitative Perception Studies

Qualitative studies also involve an interviewer who asks questions, but the answers are recorded in the form of commentary. These results are more textured and have the advantage of communicating nuance. Qualitative responses can be idiosyncratic, subjective, and highly opinionated. In other words, they have the possibility of rendering a rounded and comprehensive picture of investors' views about the company.

The qualitative perception study is limited only by the finite nature of the questionnaire. This is no minor limitation, however, because the value of the result derives directly from the questions asked. So the source of the questions is a determining factor in the quality of the intelligence the study ultimately delivers. If your questions are prompted by your prior conversations with the market—the last conference call or road show, for example—you'll find that the answers to those questions are predictable. Often companies believe their ability to predict the answers they get from a perception study proves they have a sound grasp of the market's thinking. "We got confirmation of what we already knew," they often say. Delusional may be too strong a word, but such an interpretation often represents a false sense of security. This illusion of predictability arises not from a sound grasp of investor sentiment, but from the fact that answers they get to specific questions match the prior conversations that put the question on their agenda in the first place. The results of the perception study, in other words, are limited by the questions the company knows to ask.

The Open Perception Study

A perception study restricted by a set of questions—*any* set of questions—fails to do justice to the depth, variety, and intelligence of institutional opinion on any significant company. The challenge is to break the self-reinforcing cycle and find out what investors are thinking regardless of the questions the company has thought to ask them. Management can access this depth of intelligence through open-ended, curious discussions with investors conducted by a qualified third party. Such conversations, carried out through a methodology I've developed and named the Open Perception Study™, reveal not only what investors think, but why they think it. While a questionnaire can be useful in launching such a conversation, only intelligence derived from discussions that go beyond the questionnaire gives management access to investor sentiment that is free of its own prejudgments. Such an open-ended conversation delivers predictive intelligence that provides a valuable indicator of the issues that will arise among investors in the future.

Narrative-based Research

The effectiveness of the Open Perception Study derives from a methodology called narrative-based research. Unlike a quantitative perception study, little if any of the open-form commentary can be represented in a bar chart. An Open Perception Study will never tell management, for example, that 43 percent of the company's growth-oriented investors think it should divest a certain division. What it *may* tell management, however, is what investors think of that division, how it fits (or doesn't fit) the overall business, and whether it supports the company's greatest business potential. Moreover, the company will receive a wealth of varying ideas on this division rather than a reduction of all responses to a single point. Such market intelligence generally makes life more complex for management, not simpler, but complexity is the commodity you buy when you decide to run a large business. The benefit you receive from narrative-based research is simply the best ideas that those who are committed to the company, and who understand it, are thinking at a given time. Those are precisely the people who decide the value of the company through their decisions to buy and sell its shares.

Such open narrative with investors offers an extra bonus: emotion. Neither the company nor the perception study practitioner should ever forget that investors consider themselves dependent on the credibility of the company for their livelihoods. Every portfolio manager has his own management and his own investors looking over his shoulder. He knows that at some point they'll require him to justify his investment decisions. So it's hardly an infrequent occurrence in the practice of the perception study to hear comments made with emphasis and, certainly at times, with emotion. In referring to one of my clients, whom many considered to be on a profligate acquisition binge, a portfolio manager once told me: "I'm no longer going to support his Napoleonic complex." Combined with other comments that arose during the same inquiry, this gave me the conviction to advise the client unequivocally that his explanation of the economic benefits of acquisitions had to become much clearer and more complete. The company's presentations to investors underwent something of a transformation after that, and life with its investors eventually sailed into calmer waters.

Demand-driven Communications

In discussing the value paradox above, I described the chasm between ideas of value creation held by management and those held by investors. A parallel distinction can be made with regard to the company's market communications. Does management frame its conversation with the market in terms that interest investors? Or has it fallen into the habit of delivering its story the way its executives have grown accustomed to telling it to one another? Positive change in investor attitudes, and therefore in share price, can best be achieved when management speaks its investors' language. That becomes demand-driven communications, and it's very different from the all-too-customary communications model in which management attempts to mold market opinion by spoonfeeding it information.

Intelligence developed through an open methodology enables a company to practice demand-driven communications. The following examples suggest some types of intelligence companies can distill from the process:

- Do investors believe we've done what we said we would do? Any discrepancy here presents a credibility problem. What gaps do we have to close?
- Do we and our investors interpret our results the same way? If we're succeeding in increasing margins, for example, do they see it the way we do—as proof of improving performance—or as underinvestment in the business that will come back to haunt us?
- Do they think we're disclosing all we should? Or do they think we're withholding as much as we can get away with, perhaps while claiming to be protecting competitive intelligence?
- Are we meeting competitors' technology challenges better than investors think we are? Would adding clarity on this point strengthen the argument for buying our shares?
- Have we proven the investment case for the acquisitions we've made? If not, what backing and filling must we do to remove investors' possible doubts about our discipline and strategy?
- Have we taken full advantage of our credibility with investors? If our perspective on our market will enable them to make better decisions, should we not let them benefit from our close-up view?

Educating Management Instincts

The kind of intelligence management derives from answers to the above questions delivers more than information. The nuanced commentary it carries can play a fundamental role in developing management's sensitivity to the subtleties of market thinking about the company. This "education of management instinct" goes far beyond the necessities of communication. It helps corporate leadership make informed judgments and anticipate critical issues. If building shareholder value constitutes the company's primary operating principle, and if value depends on market perceptions, then intelligence about those perceptions is central to enabling management to design strategies for desired outcomes.

M&A: How to Get the Answer Without Asking the Question

Management instinct, informed by the predictive value of an Open Perception Study, places the company in position to forecast how the market will react to future events it hasn't even announced yet. By indicating the market's probable response, such intelligence can inform management's thinking about many kinds of strategy.

One area where management instinct can make or break a company lies in decisions regarding mergers and acquisitions. In a world where companies are often rewarded only for growth, buying it in the form of an established enterprise may seem the quickest and easiest way to please investors. Acquisitions, however, are generally so hard to price, so difficult to integrate into the existing company, and so generally unpredictable that investors' response to them is often to sell the stock while they wait to see what happens.

There's a great deal on the line when a company is considering an acquisition, but the last thing in the world management can do is ask investors what they think about it. Competitors would be all over the target company, its price would rise, and the acquiring company's own investors would kill the deal by talking it to death.

There are two different approaches to resolving this challenge, and they can be used in tandem. Both leverage the open methodology's capacity to get answers to questions without ever asking them.

First, a company—with the help of a sophisticated market intelligence practitioner—can structure a conversation with investors that identifies their attitudes toward the attributes of a transaction without ever mentioning the deal itself. Let's say the contemplated acquisition would add assets along a certain product line. General questions about that part of the business would reveal investors' opinions about strengths, weaknesses, and possible market opportunities. If the interviewer were to pursue the subject by asking how the investor thinks management should address its challenges in this area (as he would have done for other parts of the business, as well), the answer might involve developing strength in certain markets and reducing commitment to others. This might well indicate how the investor would view the acquisition under consideration. There's also more than a small chance the investor will suggest an acquisition strategy outright, perhaps even mentioning a target. The interviewer would then capture this intelligence without ever having raised the subject.

A second line of questioning that's particularly fruitful in uncovering investor attitudes toward specific potential acquisitions involves probing the subject of cash allocation. If you ask a series of investors an open-ended question about what they think of a company's cash allocation strategy, you're bound to receive a rich spectrum of answers. Respondents will suggest that the company buy back its stock, or raise the dividend, or issue a special dividend. They may say the company should invest in organic growth, targeting specific business lines. Or they may raise the issue of acquisitions. Because the subject of acquisitions is introduced by the respondent, it opens the door for a line of questioning by the interviewer that is potentially revealing of attitudes toward acquisitions without giving anything away. In fact, the interviewer need not know anything about acquisition options the company may be considering in order to deliver valuable intelligence on investor attitudes on the subject.

The Perception Study in Real Life

Every substantial publicly traded company is the focus of concentrated investor analysis and judgment. The investment community is populated by some of the world's more intelligent people, and each of them is paid to be sharper and more observant than the others. Capital flows into and out of stocks are swift and massive, which, for corporations, means their fundamental value can vary dramatically with investors' perceptions of their results and the contours of their businesses.

Every company is unique, and perception studies, even when conducted for the same company a year apart, present distinctive, compelling stories. The following brief sketches of a few studies indicate the variety, and perhaps a bit of the drama, involved in managements' efforts to run their companies and tell their stories in a landscape that never stops changing:

- A company with a world-famous brand feels imprisoned because its customers—and therefore its investors—hold such loyalty for the brand that the company can't diversify for growth without alienating its base. Conducting a perception study identifies the flexibility that exists within the brand, indicating the areas where diversification may be accepted, and where it won't.

- An industrial company is the undisputed technology leader among its peers. It's known for hiring the best and the brightest engineers, and its shares trade at a significant premium to its competitors. It faces the challenge of inducing investors to continue to pay the premium, or to increase it, at a time when its technology is reaching a degree of complexity that few financial players can assess. A perception study tells this company that flaunting the sophistication of its technology will do little to increase its share price unless it shows investors the added value each major piece of that technology brings to its customers and how it compares to competitors who are working feverishly to close the gap.

- A highly esteemed investment bank encounters pressure on its market share because competitors are growing through acquisitions. Its own acquisition record isn't good, and management is searching for a strategic way forward. A perception study tells this bank that investors value it for its wealth management and fixed-income origination businesses, and more than a few will sell its shares if it starts buying other banks. They don't believe it has the expertise to acquire or price well. And they don't think it has the ability to integrate operations. They believe in its ability to grow its businesses organically, and they value it because it's been—so far—mistake free.

- A spectacularly successful global conglomerate that has grown through what appears to be an indiscriminate buying spree has alienated its investors by failing to stick to an announced discipline of adding assets only in underrepresented geographies and disciplines. A perception study shows that investors still see its CEO as buying everything that comes up for sale, and they're starting to rebel. In response, the company remakes its disclosure strategy and begins to offer significantly greater detail on the economic underpinnings of each acquisition it makes.

The Perception Study as Communication

Companies often find that the act of conducting a perception study creates, in itself, a new kind of engagement with investors and other influencers. Through hundreds of perception-study interviews conducted for corporate clients, I've often received such comments about the company as, "I've been waiting for them to make this call for five years." In addition to the market intelligence a perception study offers, the company's simple demonstration of interest in investors' opinions can change attitudes toward its transparency and its capacity to adapt.

The overriding message that perception studies deliver to company managements is that the elements of investor psychology are knowable. The dissonance that managements experience in their relationships with investors is generally rooted in investor mis-trust of management intentions. Yet investors are always looking for reasons to buy, and a robust perception study is likely to show management the specific path to building trust—in terms both of communication and operation of the business.

One would assume, then, that there's strong interest in market intelligence among companies that are undervalued and trailing in their industries. But as a consultant working in this field over many years, I've found that those companies are generally not the ones who are curious about what their investors think. Companies that mandate in-depth perception work generally turn out to be industry leaders. Getting in-depth market intelligence is just one of the hundreds of things they naturally do to stay on top. They seem to understand intuitively that if you want to know what the market thinks, you have to ask.

CHAPTER 8

Strategy 3:
Define Your Company's Landscape

The Power of Stakeholder Mapping

All the market intelligence in the world will prove worthless without a plan to leverage that intelligence in interacting with stakeholders. The path to clarity in this effort lies in making the intelligence concrete and its contents evident to the entire executive staff.

This chapter addresses every company's need to organize its relationships with stakeholders as a fundamental approach to managing risk. Companies' businesses generally revolve around development and supply of goods and services. Contending with the expectations of investors, as well as diverse groups who have no formal connection to the company such as NGOs and the press, often seems peripheral to the business. But it is not.

Because relationships with such groups would appear to lie outside normal business discipline, the approach most companies take with them is ambivalent at best. Undecided about the importance of stakeholder interaction, they act in a passive manner and miss their best chance to protect and advance the company's reputation. Although managements attempt to address stakeholder questions when they arise, they usually pay too little attention to building a formalized strategy.

Such companies fail to appreciate their own power. A relatively healthy corporation contains, within its own resources, all the attributes needed to maintain vibrant stakeholder relationships. The company's inherent stature gives it enormous accessibility to stakeholders. Unfortunately, it too seldom uses that accessibility. Companies that devote millions of dollars to sophisticated marketing techniques and market analysis often lack the basic talent for picking up the phone and calling those who influence their ability to pursue their businesses. I'm not aware of any NGO ever refusing a call from a company in which it had taken an interest. But too few companies take advantage of the power they have to gain such access. Part of the reason is that there's little precedent for doing so. Such contact requires individuals with a broader view of their business domain than the traditional concept of a company as a purely economic entity.

Having the Relationship Before the Issue Arises

Effective public affairs executives regularly reach out to stakeholders on a proactive basis *before* issues arise. This is much more efficient than trying to get to know someone after they've studied

you, found you wanting, and said so publicly. The purpose of proactive communication is to find common ground at a time when
the company and the external group can cooperate in the effort.

And it pays off later—when problems arise. When, for example,
an interest group raises questions about the environmental effects
of certain product packaging, a preexisting relationship with that
NGO and its principals will help assure a balanced dialogue before
extreme views appear in the press. And, if the company has gone
to the NGO and generated that dialogue, it's likely that the company will be the NGO's first stop when raising the issue, not the
hometown newspaper.

If the company is truly the instrument of its own sustainability,
then leveraging its power starts with an understanding of who its
relevant stakeholders are. Perhaps the most difficult part of developing such an understanding is the admission that these groups
are a permanent part of the company's universe. They may have
appeared on the scene in a gradual manner—first as anomalies and
then, perhaps, as annoyances. But, as a group, they're not going
away, and the company must accept this fact.

So if such groups are going to be around, it makes sense to
analyze them the way management would analyze any part of its
business that exerts an effect on results. And the process starts
with the identification of key stakeholders.

Stakeholder lists are specific to each company, but anyone
attempting to construct one might consider the following as a core
from which to begin.

- Employees
- Potential employees
- Customers
- Shareholders
- Analysts
- Communities
- Regulators

- Ratings agencies
- Suppliers
- Investment advisors
- Banks
- The press
- Trade groups
- Insurance companies
- NGOs

Mapping the Company's Universe

Senior executives' contact with stakeholders is generally sporadic, so management has a tendency to think of these relationships in anecdotal terms—subject to the randomness of memory. Without systematic analysis and grouping of themes, the company's real effectiveness in addressing stakeholders may be reduced nearly to zero. A more disciplined approach can, however, yield significant benefits.

One resourceful way to organize themes lies in creating visual displays called Stakeholder Maps. These are diagrams, or series of diagrams, that aggregate the company's constituencies in a single view. There are many ways of organizing a map, but the most effective displays cluster stakeholders according to issues of shared interest. This clustering helps companies leverage the power of their intelligence. If, for example, a specific concern arises among a number of diverse constituencies, the company receives a strong indication that *this* is a theme requiring the investment of resources. The map therefore helps the company spot problem areas and assess the relative importance of competing stakeholder interests. It also suggests groupings of stakeholders who might be candidates for active engagement in future conferences or other forums.

Figure 1 (p. 168) shows the role mapping can play as an engine that drives reputation strategy. The mapping process absorbs information from varied sources, including internal intelligence, industry forums, executives' private contacts, systematic perception studies, and public media. The map becomes a kind of portable stakeholder "situation room," with all the players and issues brought together in one easily accessible spot and updated with continuous new feedback. In this way, the map becomes the foundation for informed executive decision-making and communication as they relate to stakeholder issues.

This diagram describes a perpetual loop in which intelligence gathered from a company's universe of stakeholders continually informs management about those stakeholders' views of the company. The map captures current information and suggests new ways to approach stakeholders in the future. Those new encounters will, in turn, produce their own fresh information and insights. Information is power, and through ongoing use of a

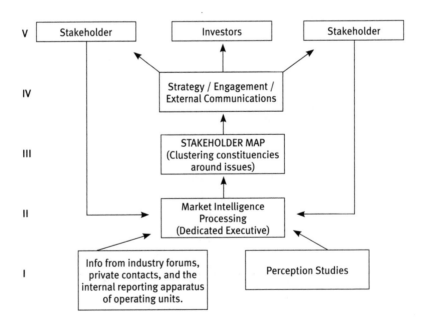

FIGURE 1. Reputation management strategies driven by stakeholder map.

Stakeholder Map, a management team can transform intelligence into strategy.

The bottom of the diagram (Levels I and II) indicates how a company might start this process from scratch. It gathers information on stakeholder attitudes from perception studies and industry forums, as well as from people inside the company who may have had substantive contacts with useful external sources.

Then a market intelligence/reputation officer, designated by and reporting to the CEO, assembles the information and arranges it in a physical or electronic display (Level III) indicating each stakeholder's position toward the company and a summary of specific attitudes. This executive also keeps more detailed information than the map can accommodate and distributes it as needed. He or she delivers intelligence summaries to other principals of the corporation in ways that inform strategy development and external communication (Level IV). That communication carries all the advantages of systematic intelligence gathering by providing support to the CEO and directors of investor relations, PR, public affairs, and others when they address their external constituencies (Level V).

On those occasions, when the dialogue runs in both directions, the company's external communicators bring back the intelligence they've gained and turn it over to the organization's market intelligence officer (Level II). He or she then processes it back into the map in a continuing cycle. In this way, the corporation keeps constant tabs on what its stakeholders are thinking. By watching its watchers, the company changes its posture toward stakeholders from passive to active.

The following diagram (Figure 2) represents information that might appear on a real stakeholder map, breaking out the first diagram at Level III. Its most powerful characteristic is that it organizes stakeholders by theme. The theme taken here—one that's often a source of dissatisfaction to companies—is transparency. (Note that this is but one theme among many that would appear on the stakeholder map of a complex company.)

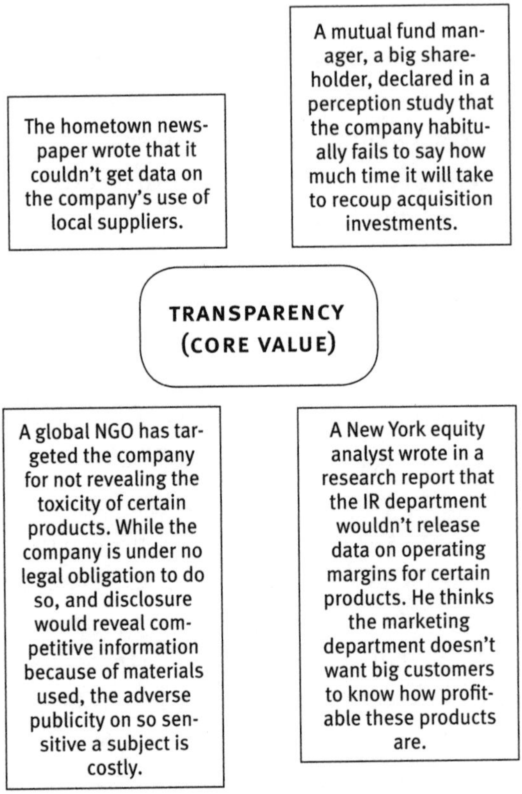

The hometown newspaper wrote that it couldn't get data on the company's use of local suppliers.

A mutual fund manager, a big shareholder, declared in a perception study that the company habitually fails to say how much time it will take to recoup acquisition investments.

TRANSPARENCY
(CORE VALUE)

A global NGO has targeted the company for not revealing the toxicity of certain products. While the company is under no legal obligation to do so, and disclosure would reveal competitive information because of materials used, the adverse publicity on so sensitive a subject is costly.

A New York equity analyst wrote in a research report that the IR department wouldn't release data on operating margins for certain products. He thinks the marketing department doesn't want big customers to know how profitable these products are.

FIGURE 2. Sample of Stakeholder Map Detail
Clustering Constituencies around Issues
Selected Issue: "Transparency" (Core Reputation Principle)

Which stakeholders care about this company's transparency? Apparently a number of them do, all for their own reasons. An NGO wants to know product contents for the protection of customers. An influential equity analyst is concerned that the company is at cross-purposes internally, inhibiting its transparency. A newspaper reporter can't get the information he needs for a piece on the company's local economic impact. And a heavy-hitting institutional investor is having trouble building an economic model because of the company's apparent refusal to provide pertinent information.

So let's look at how the company might use the information contained in this map. First of all, bringing all these reports together in one place helps management actually see the effects of its transparency practices. By showing that at least four significant influencers are displeased for different reasons, the map helps reinforce the importance of decisions regarding transparency. It also points to the specific changes in the company's transparency practices that will gain it the most mileage. In fact, some failures of transparency may be simple oversights, which could be corrected without cost.

It's possible, for example, that the PR or public information officer to whom the reporter spoke simply didn't have the information requested on local suppliers, and either didn't know how to get it or didn't feel authorized to do so. On the other hand, maybe he just isn't very good at his job. In any case, the company's interest in favorable newspaper coverage makes a discreet internal inquiry worth the effort, and the presence of this information on the map dramatically increases the likelihood that such an inquiry will take place.

The NGO's objection to insufficient toxicity labeling may prompt a discussion involving the public affairs director, the executive responsible for reputation, and the CEO. Such an issue has the power to focus a company's attention on distinctions between, on one hand, incomplete labeling that it can get away with, and, on the other, the simple question of what's the right thing to do. This could mark one of those "evolutionary moments" in a company's approach to its own conduct. Such a heart-to-heart talk is more apt to take place when the stakeholder map has so clearly defined the issue.

What of the equity analyst? On balance, perhaps the company's decision to withhold margin information for competitive reasons is reasonable. But the appearance of the item on the map might prompt the CFO and the investor relations director to explore various other ways in which the company could satisfy this analyst. For example, they might decide to release certain information that could partially close the gap for him—information on market share growth, product growth, or growth in certain geographical areas that would provide the analyst with a more complete and satisfying picture of the company.

The fund manager who isn't getting the information he wants about the time the company needs to recoup acquisition investments probably has two questions—the one he's overtly asking and another that is just as important but remains in the background. The question he plainly states involves objective information he needs to "plug in" to his valuation model. His second—subjective—question will be answered by the promptness, clarity, and completeness of the response he gets. This will give him an idea of the degree to which he can trust the company to offer information *in general*. This impression of the company's *willingness* to help him justify investment decisions will likely have a significant bearing on his decisions in the future.

What does it mean that management isn't giving him this particular piece of information? Are they being cagey, which would cast a shadow over his fundamental trust, or is the information legitimately withheld? Perhaps the company hasn't thought about it carefully enough even to have the answer. Or perhaps it's appropriately withheld because some of the company's acquisitions have been made for reasons that aren't primarily financial—for example, the acquisition of technologies, supply-chain assets, or any one of dozens of other strategies for which huge payoffs might be expected, but only over an extended period of time. And management may feel that revealing this thinking could inappropriately skew the emphasis the investor places on various factors of valuation analysis.

When the company considers this important fund manager's complaint, it knows it has a problem. And the problem may center more on the second consideration—basic trust—than on the objective one the investor gave. As in the case of the unhappy analyst, management must understand what the investor really wants and must find a way to give him information of equivalent value.

Or—surprise—they may find that they can give him exactly what he asked for. Questions arising on the stakeholder map may lead management to a more careful definition of the policy under which it withholds information for competitive reasons. When they actually consider this question, many managers find they actually have no such policy. Instead, they've scratched out a wide moat around information they consider sensitive, but have thought no more about it than that.

They may well discover that investors and analysts understand their need to withhold certain information. At the same time, managers may also come to realize that the market sees through any unnecessary withholding. If forced to ponder the matter, managers often come to believe that the cost of protecting some information is greater than the value of keeping it private.

This insight might also lead them to a new approach on the entire question of withholding competitive intelligence. They might decide to undertake a serious review of information to determine its real sensitivity. By all means, information of true competitive value should be protected. But managers might find that it would benefit the company greatly to define for themselves the disclosure-nondisclosure boundary for each kind of information. That which doesn't carry competitive risk should be "liberated." They may even see enough value in this approach that they systematically review the question on a monthly basis. But no company will start down this path until some experience or mechanism, such as a Stakeholder Map, crystallizes the degree of dissatisfaction among investors and analysts—and therefore the cost of failing to respond.

*   *   *   *

The map fragment that appears in Figure 3 uses the same form as the previous map but organizes the information in reverse by associating a cluster of issues with a specific constituent. The intelligence it holds can prove invaluable in creating substantive encounters with any stakeholder—in this case, a major NGO.

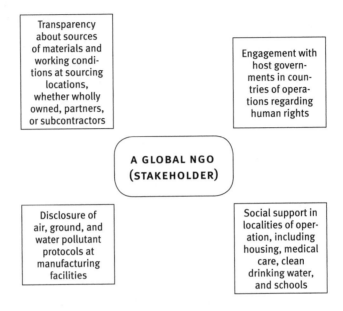

FIGURE 3. Sample of Stakeholder Map Detail
Clustering Issues of Concern to a Single Stakeholder

Internal stakeholder maps can be highly productive. We saw earlier how Unocal leveraged internal resources in helping to develop communities affected by its operations in Indonesia. The company recognized that earning a social license to operate in places where its activities affected land use, water quality, working conditions, and local economic development meant taking some responsibility to see that these factors showed progress. The company devised a practice of internal mapping to identify which of its own resources it could apply toward these efforts. If the external need required engineers to improve a village's water system, the mapping process identified where in the organization those engineers might be found. The map could, in addition, determine who among the company's indigenous work-force might have the social and educational background to pursue relations with local communities.

*   *   *   *

Stakeholder maps lend specific and objective characteristics to intelligence that business professionals have traditionally treated as subjective, incidental, and anecdotal. The good news they bring is that attitudes about the company held by significant influencers are subject to the same kinds of disciplines as the rest of business. They can be made concrete, and so they can become subject to analysis and systematic action.

CHAPTER 9

Strategy 4:
Build Your Reputation from the Inside Out

Become the Company You Want the World to See

Shakespeare's King Lear, in his attempts to negotiate palace intrigue and survive his lightning-struck exile on the moors, could rely only on a fool to tell him the truth. The fool had no possessions and, therefore, nothing to lose. He was without a stake in the outcome, and so no overriding personal interests clouded his vision.

Keeping a fool around, particularly one without a stake, is no longer practical. (Fools these days are not fools and demand options packages.) So a CEO must create the means for getting the information he needs to understand his company's risks. To do this, he must communicate to trusted advisors that it's their responsibility to bring him material information and, further, that they are particularly obligated to deliver news that he might find painful to hear. The reputation-support structure is broken if an advisor doesn't have the confidence to deliver unpleasant news— or argue a point—and know that he or she will still be welcomed back to the CEO's table tomorrow. Employees from senior managers to floor sweepers must be sure their views are welcome. This isn't always the case, however.

On September 15, 1896, in a gently sloping valley north of Waco, Texas, two steam locomotives on the same track accelerated toward each other at high speeds. They crashed head-on before 40,000 spectators whom the Katy Railroad had transported there from all over the state to witness the event. Known as the Great Crush Collision—named not for what happened to the superheated boilers, but for its organizer, a passenger agent named William George Crush—this event would have been a publicity stunt for the ages had the unexpected explosion not killed three people and injured many more. A piece of hot metal shot through the eye of the event's official photographer.

The explosion was, to put it mildly, a surprise to those who had organized the event. The Katy bosses had asked their mechanics if the collision would be safe and received the answer that these locomotives were so well designed that their boilers could survive any likely occurrence intact. The one dissenter was a certain Hanrahan, whose first name is lost to history but who correctly predicted the explosion. When Hanrahan uttered his warning, preparations for the spectacle had already gathered steam, and his dissent about the wisdom of the stunt was consigned to the dustheap of crank forebodings. Temporarily. The railroad fired Crush the day after the explosion. What happened to Hanrahan is unrecorded, but Crush was rehired within the week and ultimately put in 57 years of service with the Katy Railroad. This chapter, however, is dedicated to Hanrahan.

One of Hanrahan's spiritual heirs is another Texan, Sherron Watkins, a midlevel executive at Enron who attempted to tell her bosses that there was something rotten in the way they were accounting for off-balance-sheet partnerships. She wasn't alone. Before Enron's fall, no fewer than 35 people tried to warn senior management about the vulnerabilities its financial tactics were bringing on. Ms. Watkins, who became the most visible of them through her congressional testimony, described how chairman Kenneth Lay dismissed her concerns about these financial maneuvers. She quotes him as telling her, "Everyone has signed off." In *The Smartest Guys in the Room*, Bethany McLean and Peter Elkind show how Enron's auditors and attorneys all approved the company's fraudulent finances. "Beware of law firms telling you what you want to hear," the chief ethics officer at one major U.S. corporation told me in discussing a similar case.

For a more recent example, let's place ourselves in the shoes of David Andrukonis, a former chief risk management officer at Freddie Mac, the gigantic congressionally chartered mortgage finance company that would have failed but for a taxpayer bailout in mid-2008. During the U.S. housing fever that preceded the subprime crisis in which Freddie Mac collapsed, Andrukonis warned his CEO, Richard Syron, that the company's growing portfolio of risky housing loans was pushing Freddie Mac toward instability. He advised Syron that bad loans "would likely pose an enormous financial and reputational risk to the company and the country," because taxpayers would almost inevitably be forced to cover the deficit to keep the institution from sinking. Other Freddie Mac insiders expressed similar opinions, but Syron heightened the company's vulnerability to the subprime crisis by ignoring repeated warnings that a crisis was on the way.

In one muddled response quoted by the *New York Times*, Syron said, "If I had better foresight, maybe I could have improved things a little bit. But frankly, if I had perfect foresight, I would never have taken this job in the first place." The job he would have rejected paid him $38 million between 2003 and 2008.

In 2007, U.S. Secretary of the Treasury Henry Paulson and Federal Reserve chairman Ben Bernanke both urged Syron to raise funds to cushion Freddie Mac's reserves, Bernanke even threatening public criticism if Syron failed to comply. The CEO responded, "This company will bow to no one."

By August 2008, Freddie Mac had suffered four straight quarterly losses, billions in write-downs and credit provisions, and a 90 percent drop in its share price. Yet, in the prior quarter, it had found nearly $2.3 million to spend on lobbying against greater regulation before Congress, which had direct oversight of the company.

As losses and criticism mounted, Syron told the *Times*, "I've had four other jobs as CEO, and I came out of them all pretty well. What I'm working for right now is to save my reputation."

Perhaps to save his own, Andrukonis, who'd tried to warn Syron, had already left to become a teacher.

*   *   *   *

On a grassy expanse somewhere in the middle of America there should be a small museum dedicated to truth tellers, where schoolchildren can come on yellow buses to learn the stories of Watkins, Andrukonis, and Hanrahan. Perhaps those who grow up to be CEOs will ask themselves whether they would listen in similar circumstances—and, even if they were open to hearing such warnings, would they structure their organizations so that the warnings would reach them?

With the preceding three strategies, I've addressed core values, understanding perceptions of the company, and identifying its primary constituencies. This chapter focuses on how the CEO can use those assets to translate values into action. He or she accomplishes this, first of all, by structuring the company's internal processes so they can give support to its reputation.

For a CEO, creating a desirable reputation means building the company he wants the world to see. PR and branding are powerful forces in the corporate world, and image is always important. But no matter how professional and sophisticated these disciplines are, they play to surface perceptions. While you can't do without marketing, advertising, and PR, at bottom they indicate little about the company's inherent character. Any real security of reputation requires a carefully built corporate structure that supports it.

Creating a structure that supports reputation offers management a precious source of confidence that the company will not, somewhere in the world, break through the cosmetic cocoon of its branding with self-destructive behavior. We can think of this idea as *building reputation from the inside out.*

Vertical Communications

One of the most productive initiatives a company can undertake is to build a communications democracy. To call the practice of communications within a company democratic is to say that intellectual assets originating anywhere in the company are accessible everywhere else in the company. Because corporations generally have hierarchical structures, we can think of this as vertical communications. A company with vertical communications is one in which ideas can travel in both directions between top and bottom. Such a culture of unimpeded communication offers a company enormous leverage in exploiting the value it contains, but which may otherwise remain hidden.

Earlier, in discussing diversity of point of view, we considered the availability to the company of the intellectual capital each employee has gathered throughout his or her life. In a similar vein, ideas and understanding developed within the company must become available wherever they will be most productive. A company whose culture facilitates this flow of ideas fundamentally increases its competitiveness and creativity.

Such an open culture also helps assure that management will have the best view of its options on any subject, and that it will find it easier to identify risk wherever it appears. It also provides a channel for teaching the corporation's values and ethical standards, as well as for auditing its own success in applying them. In this way, the process is self-reinforcing.

Formal and Informal Communication Structures

Every organization contains both formal and informal communications structures. "Formal communication" describes the classic ways management interacts with employees. It provides the means by which management distributes all the details of corporate life—from HR forms to advice of management changes—as well as the means by which it puts employees on notice of its expectations.

Informal communication generally takes place within a closed group of individuals who share a specific domain of activity and the concerns that relate to that activity. The content of informal communication can be exceedingly valuable because its sole purpose is to enable interested parties to share candid observations. Water-cooler griping aside, informal communication is insightful because it arises out of the personal concerns of people who know their subject best. It is therefore unlikely to be filtered or edited for political reasons. So it is worth the trouble for any corporate leadership to attempt to harness its value.

A culture that promotes open (vertical) communication also allows the currents of dissatisfaction and disapproval that often move beneath the surface to see the light of day. Such a culture not only offers access to the intelligence that passes through its informal communications, it also reduces the friction created by failures to address matters employees see as important. So it offers a potent mechanism for addressing issues that erode morale.

Management's challenge is to induce those informal groups, as well as individuals, to contribute their unvarnished observations to the formal communications process. To do this, employees must have reason for faith in the system. And they must know that management invites their participation. The CEO takes ownership of the process—as he or she always must—by mandating its development, initiating its use, and openly declaring its importance.

One good way to do this, beyond stating its purpose clearly, is to disseminate a request for suggestions on the solution to a specific challenge. The form such communication takes will always be particular to the organization, whether it becomes a cycle of group conversations, a wiki, an intranet, or a combination of these or other media. The medium matters little as long as it is used. Its character, however, must be established as a clear part of the organization's processes with overt sponsorship from the leader.

One can judge success by the degree to which this communications mechanism changes the corporation's internal conversation. Are voices being heard for the first time? Are the issues under consideration coming from diverse business units as well as from the center? Are insights and new questions being elicited from still more sources? Are challenges drawing a greater diversity of solutions? And is management responding?

The Cost of Waiting for Certainty

The difficulty the traditional business mind experiences in grappling with reputation issues is a subject that has come up frequently in this book. The fact is that doing nothing often seems a lot easier. And one of the reasons for this is that a good reputation is never truly achieved, which every executive instinctively recognizes. A company may receive awards, see its name on a business magazine's most-admired list, and find itself the subject of positive news features. But these phenomena are meaningful only until something happens that, whether it's the company's responsibility or not, casts a public shadow over all the accolades.

The reality is that you can't prepare for everything. You can't offer your management team or your employees a guidebook for every possible situation that might arise. And this becomes even more difficult because there are few currents that flow through the business mind stronger than the desire for certainty. While corporate managers and business gurus get paid for showing cause and effect, equations and objective principles seldom translate one-to-one from the page into real life (even this page).

There are a multitude of business books touting diverse, sometimes warring management concepts, usually derived from research. One basic truth about research results is that they are restricted to what is measurable, notwithstanding all the eventualities the real world is likely to yield up. At the same time, the decision to measure anything is driven by whether or not it has seemed important in the past. The certainty with which researchers-cum-advisors offer the results of their studies assumes the coming to pass of the one specific future—among all possible futures—they've decided to bet on.

For example, as the preconditions for the financial crisis that began in 2007 gathered, risk managers failed to anticipate the looming disaster because their models didn't foresee the collapse in home prices. It wasn't among the futures they recognized as possible. (This fault is endemic to the world of research when it is driven not by a search for truth but by a need to justify financial strategies.) Even the SEC, whose oversight in the long prelude to the crisis was undistinguished, requires companies to explain on their securities filings that past performance does not predict future results. So, in the absence of hard data, executives who take the necessities of building reputation with great seriousness may still have trouble finding a clear platform on which to stand with confidence in setting strategy. And this often stops them.

This is not to claim that we shouldn't perform research, or observe carefully, or strive to reach reasonable conclusions. But we should be modest about it. Few people want to admit the complex dynamics that underlie their results. In business you seldom get paid for telling the truth if there's no measurable value to it. What you get paid for is being *sure*. The appearance of certainty is the currency of business. But it can sometimes divert from the need to see.

Reputation Training

The CEO of a reputationally sound company works to align every part of that company with its core values. More than any other corporate function, training communicates the values that bind a company together. Training techniques and resources continually evolve, shaped by experience in an ever-changing business environment. The design of a training program is one of most critical enterprises any management can undertake. Allowing training to become a mechanistic afterthought to the business opens a company to the fissures in corporate behavior that can lead to public embarrassment. Staff training isn't only a means of transmitting information, it is a signal—and often the first signal—of management's seriousness about its moral identity.

Management must decide what its program should train employees to do. There's a big difference, for example, between training them in procedures and helping them learn to respond to the unexpected. Training in procedures doesn't require much philosophical foundation. But if a CEO wants his employees to identify with the organization, they must understand how they fit into the company's strategy.

Understanding strategy increases flexibility and helps employees adapt when strategies change. Employees who understand, and have internalized, the company's strategy are more apt to act both efficiently and effectively when management shifts directions in response to market changes. They may even have some ideas of their own. If the company's strategy in gaining a competitive advantage is to streamline the supply chain, for example, those individuals who participate in the supply chain must understand in their bones *why* it has been the way it has and why it needs to change.

Training can be a tool management uses to make employees its partners. In doing so, management has to ask itself this question: How do we train people to have good judgment? No training can preprogram employees for every possible situation, so management must instead try to use training programs to educate their employees' instincts—just as their contact with stakeholders educates their own. Such programs require more than a well-filled loose-leaf binder, no matter how well prepared and comprehensive.

An effective program begins with the selection—and training—of the trainers themselves. An employee's belief in the organization and its values starts with the person standing at the front of the room. Truly productive training involves the discussion of varied scenarios with a constant focus on practical situations. So a successful training program requires leaders who are also humanists, who are marked by a lifelong curiosity about the challenges that others face. This includes, and goes beyond, the ability to listen. It requires empathy.

This concept of partnership creates a condition in which leadership can emerge from any part of the company. The more employees know about the company's strategies for accomplishing its goals, the more they'll be able to contribute to its achievement.

In W.C. Fields' 1935 film *The Man on the Flying Trapeze*, the meek desk clerk played by Fields loses his job. Soon, however, the boss recalls him to the office because no one can locate a certain document. Standing before a desk piled high with disorganized papers, Fields, his back turned, gently moves his hand into the pile, feels around for a moment, and withdraws the precious item. While this may overstate the dependence of an organization on a single worker, the shared expertise and memory of an employee group far exceeds any set of data that might record and store it for future use. Such data would begin its obsolescence within days anyway, and can't be compared to the reservoir of knowledge that constantly renews itself in the shared understanding of workers through the daily conduct of business. You can't train workers to do this, but using training to involve them in the internal strategy conversation provides the best means of securing the company's access to its own intellectual capital.

The Executive–Employee Dialogue

The company makes a clear statement about inclusion when it sends a senior executive to talk to employees about strategy and values and to solicit opinions. The executive's acquired insights then translate into a contribution at high-level seminars where senior staff draw conclusions and design policy on the basis of many such discussions. The company uses this collaborative approach as a means of educating the workforce on its own intentions, building consensus around values, and gaining intelligence on the business. One of the most important features of such discussions is that they develop employees' sense of ownership. The effect is heightened by the return of the executive every year or so to renew the discussion, reinforce principles, and offer a reminder of the company's commitment to its employees.

All these pieces of the inclusion strategy strengthen employees' connections to the center, which opens the way for harnessing the company's hidden intellectual assets. One of the most important points a CEO can make is that he welcomes unconventional ideas. Dynamic managers know they don't succeed against the competition by merely following popular trends. CEOs who take this view therefore welcome contributions from the far reaches of the company, and they especially encourage creativity. "Send us your ideas, including the wilder ones," becomes part of the message.

*　　*　　*　　*

Once established, this communication system developed for values-and-strategy training finds a multitude of applications. An organization that has developed a facility for internal communication—and has the infrastructure to support it—is one that has given itself the best chance to benefit from its experience and resolve the ambiguities that will inevitably arise in its business.

To Andrea Bonime-Blanc, an attorney who has served as chief ethics officer for several companies, I owe the term "risk brainstorming." Groups similar to the seminars described above examine their local risk profiles in areas that range from antitrust issues to discrimination to intellectual property. The company institutes training based on what it has learned from those discussions, then monitors progress—all in a continuous cycle. While nobody can prove that the funding of these practices is worth the investment—it's impossible to assess the cost of missteps that *didn't* occur—the communications mechanism they help create remains an essential component of reputation risk management. It gives the company its best chance of avoiding costly events. If such events should occur, it documents for regulators and others, including prosecutors and plaintiffs' attorneys, that the company has taken every reasonable step to assure adherence to appropriate standards.

Demonstrating that a company has undertaken such measures can prove crucial when prosecutors or regulators—or the press— bring allegations of impropriety. The organization and its key employees should understand the principles and actions for which they'll be held responsible if things go wrong, and adopting this approach offers one of the better ways to make sure they do. Secondarily, it helps in establishing a demonstrable record of strong controls and probity.

Some companies have found an interesting—and perhaps ironic—way to protect themselves and build strong internal structures. They have adopted as training tools the U.S. Justice Department's sentencing guidelines for individuals convicted of corporate crimes. The Holder Memorandum and the Thompson Memorandum define the kinds of conduct for which the government holds corporations accountable. They set forth the principles U.S. Attorneys are likely to use in deciding whether to proceed with specific prosecutions and in making sentencing recommendations to judges post-conviction. Criteria include the company's history of misconduct, whether it has been forthcoming with information and has voluntarily reported wrongdoing, and whether it had adequate systems in place before the misconduct occurred or has implemented them to prevent the recurrence of violations.

Knowing how regulators and prosecutors judge corporate behavior offers an unquestionable advantage. When translated for corporate training use, the principles embodied in the sentencing guidelines offer some of the clearest and most widely applicable "best practices" available in building a solid corporate culture. Along with a system of controls that monitors internal compliance, they afford a foundation for reputation while creating a record that provides built-in legal protections.

Internal control systems that monitor adherence to codes of conduct and demonstrate intent to comply with the law can literally save a company. The government based its aggressive pursuit of Arthur Andersen for fraudulent accounting and auditing practices, mentioned earlier, on the systematic nature of its violations. The real damage arose not out of the simple act of destroying Enron documents, but from strong evidence that the destruction reflected a firmwide policy. The same policy also characterized the payment of fines simply as part of the cost of doing business, which contributed to the perception of enterprise involvement in criminal behavior.

Tracking Progress: Surveys as Part of the Dialogue

Training in values and strategy not only teaches, but carries with it the impression of an entire organization engaged in a coherent effort. Values and strategy, after all, pertain to the organization, not the individual—even when the individual is the chief executive. Internal surveys carry the message of engagement further by bringing management useful intelligence on employee attitudes. At the same time, the conduct of surveys demonstrates that management finds group attitudes important.

Surveys should be detailed and quantifiable. One large U.S. company inquires regularly about attitudes and experiences relating to the implementation of its values in the day-to-day conduct of business. It queries employees for their views on the success of management's approach to teaching and implementing the values in the company's business. It asks questions on the degree to which employees feel valued by their direct managers, on the clarity of their roles, and on dozens of other positions from which to examine their standing in workgroups and in the company at large.

Other survey protocols pose specific questions and ask for degrees of agreement and disagreement with each. They may inquire into opinions about the company's ethics, confidence in management, whether employees have a sense of pride in working for the company, whether they believe management authentically adheres to the values it espouses, and whether employees feel safe in expressing their true opinions.

One key feature of such studies is that their results are easy to tabulate. Survey practitioners can derive numeric values for each subject considered and then track changes over time. As we observed in the difference between rigid and open perception studies, however, the results are limited by the questions asked. The questions, in turn, reflect the study practitioner's presurvey prejudices about the relative importance of issues. In comparison, open surveys, which involve conversations that go beyond questionnaires, elicit the responses people want to offer, whether or not the survey directors have anticipated them. But those results aren't quantifiable. A combination of the two types generally renders the most complete information.

Making Ethics and Compliance Work

Training programs and their supporting communications structures can double by serving ethics and compliance efforts as well. The ethics and compliance officer stands as the firewall between the corporation and employee behavior that might bring it down, divert its business, or poison its culture. In a large organization, it's close to inevitable that one or another employee will steal a computer off a loading dock, an executive will expense activities that have nothing to do with the business, a purchasing manager will accept graft, or a country manager will pay a bribe to a local official.

The person who holds the ethics and compliance position must be a deliberate, resourceful individual. He or she implements systems to educate the workforce in business ethics, monitor its behavior, respond to specific instances of misconduct, discover new risks, and report on measurements of compliance to the CEO and the board.

A company says a great deal about the importance it places on ethics by how it positions the ethics and compliance group within its organizational structure. Companies who make ethics a function of human resources or the general counsel's office are telling employees that it's part of the company's adherence to "best practices" and to normal compliance procedures. On the other hand, a company whose chief ethics officer reports directly to the CEO and the audit committee of the board signals to employees that it considers ethics a fundamental component of its business franchise. Such a company may further emphasize this perception by requiring that all strategic and operational decisions be vetted for ethics compliance.

The initiatives that a strong ethics officer can undertake in protecting his or her company are virtually without limit. If you have thousands of people working in different countries across the world, you can't be too surprised if, over time, you find yourself confronted with challenges relating to, for example, the Foreign Corrupt Practices Act (FCPA) mentioned earlier. No matter how strong you've made your ethics education program, someone may take it upon himself to bribe one of the highly bribable officials with whom he comes in contact, and to do it in the company's name. Knowing there's no way categorically to prevent this, some leading ethics officers generate a matrix of responses that anticipate specific potential events. They categorize and code them to prepare legal and PR responses.

Foreign corrupt practices issues constitute one area of exposure that qualifies for referral to the board. The ethics officer generally works with the corporate security group on such matters, and together they take facts to the board's audit committee or to its advisory panel. Other areas for board consideration might involve systematic environmental violations or compliance failures with regard to working conditions.

A CEO who is intent on insulating his or her company from reputation risks that arise out of ethics violations will establish a reporting structure that enables the ethics officer to keep the CEO and the board informed on trends and emergent problems. Cross-disciplinary standing committees can be tasked to identify risks and solutions associated with elements of the business environment that may threaten reputation. These may be specific to the company, its industry, or the geographies where the company does business. The CEO empowers these committees to present and defend their solutions; then he monitors their progress as they follow the approved actions through to completion.

Such programs keep an ethics consciousness near the center of the internal corporate conversation. The more a company concentrates on education and training, the fewer compliance issues it is likely to face. The ethics and compliance group at Xerox collaborates with virtually all parts of the organization to embed ethics messages in communications on general business topics. It keeps ethics a constant presence in employees' awareness through companywide newsletters and Web sites that offer guidelines on specific business situations and case studies. It publishes summaries of real ethics cases with their resolutions, altering details for anonymity where needed. In a dedicated corner of the company's intranet home page, the ethics group posts weekly reinforcements of specific ethical points as well as ethics questions that, if answered correctly, may win the respondent a prize. Bertelsmann produced, under the direction of Andrea Bonime-Blanc, a video takeoff on the game show *Family Feud* in which teams of contestants competed against one another to give the right answers to ethical questions.

Companies that make their ethics programs a priority frequently maintain telephone hotlines offering clarifications on ethical issues and the opportunity for anonymous reporting of possible violations. They generally provide distinct hotlines to ethics and legal departments.

David Frishkorn, when he was ethics director at Xerox, fought the view that the ethics structure is a matter of enforcement and compliance. "I'm not the local cop," he said. Instead, he presented his group as a facilitator for pursuing business in the most efficient and effective way. "It's a business resource," he said. In a message he drafted for dissemination by his CEO, Frishkorn said that Xerox's assumption is that most employees come to work wanting to do the right thing. The challenge is that there are issues and decisions they have to think about in a consistent and ethical manner. And sometimes they need help in clarifying how to do that. He said his approach was to help employees do the right things because they wanted to.

Accountability Means Accepting the Facts

In examining how business structure supports reputation, it's worthwhile to look in greater detail at how BP approached development of its enormous BTC pipeline. One of the largest infrastructure projects in the world during its construction between 2003 and 2005, the environmentally and socially sensitive pipeline now winds its way more than a thousand miles from Baku, on the Caspian Sea in Azerbaijan, through the Georgian capital of Tblisi, to Ceyhan on Turkey's south Mediterranean coast. In approaching the project, BP took as fact the idea that open dialogue brings access to the most productive people and the cheapest capital. The need to maintain support for the enterprise led the company into extensive engagement with local communities and regional bodies. Those discussions yielded an action plan and a map of the environmental and social issues associated with a project. "All of it," says David Bickerton, who is now BP's director of communications, "was in service to the business strategy." Attacking a project exclusively from an engineering mindset solves technical challenges, he says, but an exclusive focus on engineering can expose the company to environmental and social risks for which it will have no answer.

To demonstrate its seriousness about including the voices of all affected parties, BP assembled respected outside authorities to lead a diverse and independent advisory panel. The company believed that establishment of this panel would promote confidence in the company's neutrality, which it viewed as especially important in light of its position at the nexus of many competing interests. These included local communities, governments at all levels, and international activist observers. The panel identified crucial issues, including those relating to safety, security, and the environment. BP published the results of the panel's deliberations in a special section of its Web site. The critical aspect of this process lay in BP's making itself accountable for reputation issues it could not predict.

BTC became the first project to apply the Equator Principles, which set a benchmark in managing social and ethical issues as a condition for project finance. The extensive measures BP took to build consensus around BTC set the stage for further refinement to its conduct of environmentally and socially sensitive projects, a process that has continued to evolve. Today BP has implemented an "Environmental Requirements for New Projects" regime that categorizes, screens and aids in the management of new developments. Persistent updating has created a full-life-cycle assessment process that sets each new project on a social responsibility platform. BP believes such a rigorous management approach to issues affecting society around its projects makes them more likely to add to the company's reputation than to compromise it.

*   *   *   *

I alluded earlier to some of the personal risks inherent in steering companies toward behavior that supports reputation. Telling the boss what's wrong has seldom provided a path to riches and job security. (It's hard to get paid for delivering bad news.) Auditors and law firms know that the client can go elsewhere if the relationship gets too difficult. So they often find themselves walking a razor's edge in trying to adhere to the codes of their professions on the one hand while holding onto the business with the other.

Ethics officers, risk managers, and other internal corporate players live in a similar bind. Our earlier stories of Hanrahan, Watkins, and Andrukonis demonstrate that individuals can face difficult personal challenges in bringing problems to management's attention. It's particularly so for ethics officers. Unlike Lear's fool, who had nothing to lose, they depend on the boss's pleasure for their wealth and career longevity. So the ethics officer's formula for personal survival is generally to manage down, concentrating on lapses in the far-flung workforce—not in the executive suite. In fact, his or her job is usually structured to do exactly that.

Who, then, is going to deliver the message when the CEO has shown an aversion to receiving any kind of uncomfortable news— or, worse yet, when the CEO happens to be the problem?

It may help at such times to remember the boss's fundamental humanity. The following exchange between Ben Blue and Jimmy Durante in the 1944 movie *Two Girls and a Sailor* offers such a reminder:

Blue: I thought you were a comedian.
Durante: I'm an executive.
Blue: You're a dope.
Durante: Can't you be both?

The ethics officer has to be free to say when you're either—or both.

CHAPTER 10

Strategy 5:
Tell Your Corporate Story

Engagement and the Communications of Convergence

Communication is the heart and soul of business. It can convey, and even enhance, a company's value. It can heighten credibility with allies, critics, and skeptics. It can, in other words, create the conditions for leadership.

Communication becomes critical in a crisis. When times are good, the public, investors, and regulators have little appetite for questioning how things got that way. But when good times turn bad, the impulse to examine how business is done becomes stronger. And there's nothing like a global economic collapse to arouse intense curiosity about how business and finance actually work.

At some point early in the world financial crisis that began in 2007 it became apparent that an enormous abdication of responsibility had occurred. Over the prior decade, many different parts of the financial sector had willingly assumed an opportune blindness in which everyone assumed that someone else was monitoring how the industry issued mortgages and how it aggregated them into new financial instruments.

Regulators believed that market players understood their own interests and would protect themselves from undue risk. Investment bankers believed that rating agencies had analyzed the complex securities the bankers had concocted and found them to be sound. Each rating agency saw its competition build business by assigning investment-grade ratings to questionable hybrid securities, so each accepted the other's apparent judgment that it was sound practice to do so. Mortgage companies issuing loans to home buyers who could not possibly afford them assured themselves that these nontraditional practices were legal and that ever-rising home prices would assure repayment of the loans. And when they sold the loans up the line to investment banks— who aggregated, redivided, and resold them—they told themselves that they were beneficiaries of a virtuous cycle in which everyone was a winner. Home buyers who took the loans told themselves that the mortgage companies were professional risk managers and wouldn't have lent them money they couldn't pay back. But what the mortgage lenders failed to recognize was that rising house prices were a direct function of the ease of obtaining loans. They lent because prices rose. Prices rose because they lent. It was a game of follow-the-leader that was remarkable for its lack of actual leadership.

The resulting financial meltdown formed a true implosion, beginning at the periphery with homeowners' defaults and collapsing into the center where the packaged mortgage securities lost most or all of their value as a result of those defaults. By the time the dimensions of the disaster became clear, many of those in finance who had created it were gone from the scene. Some had practiced what *New York Times* columnist Thomas Friedman called "Y.B.G. and I.B.G." lending, meaning "you'll be gone and I'll be gone," before the bill comes due.

The former chairman of the Federal Reserve, Alan Greenspan, in Congressional testimony, expressed "shocked disbelief" at such behavior, saying that he expected "the self-interest of lending institutions to protect shareholder's equity." He made no distinction between the self-interest of the lending institutions and that of the executives who ran them. It would be interesting to know if he considered such a distinction to exist—and, if he did, how he viewed it in light of his lifelong interest in the teachings of philosopher-novelist Ayn Rand, who advocated the unimpeded pursuit of self-interest.

Few companies emerged from the crisis unscathed. From the standpoint of individual enterprises, the enormous destruction of value was only partially measurable. You could quantify the loss in revenue, earnings, and share value, but not the loss of business advantages and goodwill that had built up over years. The rout of market confidence turned out to be a leveler of all things, and it became difficult to distinguish the great from the mediocre.

The dangers of this environment were unprecedented in the business experience of anyone living. No one could have been prepared to confront the sudden disappearance of credit and demand for goods and services—the disappearance, in fact, of trust.

Suddenly, an utterly new set of questions dominated business life. If the equity value of the company had been cut in half over just a few months, as happened to many, how did that affect the company's traditional sources of credit? What other sources were available? How did one obtain the advantage needed for survival in an environment where no one was certain of anything?

If a manager was unsure of his company's credit, he could be no more sure of his customers'. Which customers were even still in the picture? Were they telling the truth about their own solvency? And which of his own business lines were still viable? How could the manager adjust the company's internal resources to respond to these new questions and conditions?

Survival and Competitiveness

The challenge virtually every CEO faced was to act in a way that gave the company the best chance of survival and, if possible, the greatest competitive advantage for the time when the business climate revived. These were not the same thing. If you made drastic cutbacks now to increase your survival chances, would you be able to be competitive when the business returned? If you attempted to keep running full speed now to be ready for the future, would you even make it to the future? The crisis therefore augured an inflection point in virtually every manager's career. How would he or she judge the actions taken during this time when looking back at them from the future? Staring each manager in the face was an opportunity to prove a reputation, to build it, or to lose it. And each had to select a concept, perception, or set of data on which to base decisions from a landscape that was anything but clear.

Decisions made now could reach far into the future. Many understood, for example, that when you got rid of a group of skilled individuals—engineers, for example—they would not be easily replaced when the need came. You were not only abandoning the investment you had made in them over the years, but your actions, and similar ones by your industry peers, would likely reduce the number of university graduates in those disciplines who would become available in subsequent years.

Companies proceeded to draft new business plans that looked radically different from those that had prevailed just a few months earlier. So, the question became: How do you communicate the new plan convincingly? Some managers understood that the way they presented it largely determined how successful it would be.

Most new business plans began with workforce reductions. Whether or not to cut—or how much to cut—during periods of market weakness can be one of the most excruciating decisions management faces. Such decisions have a profound effect on whether employees can keep their homes, stay in their communities, and where a family's next generation is able to go to school.

How a company communicates the rationale of its response to events determines in large part whether or not it can maintain the confidence of its workforce. That's because employees will always deduce both the viewpoint and the character of management from its actions. If you cut jobs in favor of maintaining the compensation levels of those who remain, you are making a strong statement of support to them. While the firing of a considerable portion of the workforce confirms that the company is experiencing dire circumstances, it also says to those selected to stay that management is betting the company on their abilities and commitment.

Managers navigating the financial crisis confronted such questions as: How do you deliver bad news? What is the most humane way to tell employees that a division, or the entire enterprise, is being sold? Or that you are firing a specific group of employees? Or that a single employee who has done nothing but give his or her all to the company will no longer be needed?

The Language of Layoffs

Management speaks to two different audiences when it communicates about layoffs. The simplest communication takes place with its most important external constituents: investors and analysts. In that conversation, management generally refers to the firing of workers in language that allows it to take credit for reducing corporate expenses. It projects an image of its own discipline in keeping costs under control.

Management discipline is also a subject of considerable interest to employees. The kind of discipline that interests them, however, relates less to the expense line of the income statement than to the way management utilizes resources within the company. Are group leaders and business heads adequate to their positions? Or have they been placed there by senior managers more interested in securing a power base than for their competence? Are those selected to stay with the company chosen on merit, or have they been able to save themselves through superior political positioning? Is the bad driving out the good, or are the good even being recognized?

If management's response to the drying up of credit and its customers' inability to spend money is to fire a fifth of its workforce, for example, it must make that action appear rational to those who remain, and retain their confidence in how the company is being led. Depending on how it communicates such an action, management can appear weak or strong.

If the message is "We are forced to take drastic measures in the face of circumstances that are not our fault," management could well be viewed as having panicked. It chooses to project the theme that it is driven by some larger power for which it wishes not to be held responsible. In framing the problem this way it has failed to declare the nature of its *own* responsibility. This management is communicating only what it needs to do to stay afloat for now. It conveys no sense of the company's future. It steers clear of the mention of any values that can drive the company forward.

If, on the other hand, it undertakes the same action (firing a fifth of the workforce) and colors it as a drastic and difficult measure designed to ensure the company's future, the absence of recrimination and the forward-looking statement of strength may provide the company's first step toward greater stability.

Firing people isn't the only way to reduce expenses. A

management in similarly difficult circumstances sends a different message when it foregoes significant layoffs but keeps the workforce at reduced pay. (It must be said that the first pay cuts should be management's own.) The message this strategy delivers, and which management should stress in its communications, is that the company expects to need its full staff cohort when business improves, and it anticipates that will occur within a reasonable time.

A company that makes this call on its workers' loyalty is generally one with some confidence that it can inspire their belief. It demonstrates in the way it asks for that loyalty that it is not broken and that it sees a future.

Communications Won't Fix Anything

Credibility rests on consistency among communications, actions, and results. There is no stronger message to investors and other stakeholders than positive news embedded in a statement that says "This is what we said we were going to do, and this is what we did."

But if used improperly, communication can provide unmistakable evidence of management cynicism and ineptitude. Poor communication can lay waste to an executive's authenticity.

At times corporate leaders may be tempted to use communications as part of a manipulative strategy. Investors and analysts, whose livelihoods depend on their ability to follow a company, can smell the difference. The dirty little secret about communication is that, by itself, it can't fix anything. It cannot make the leader look successful when a strategy or execution is ineffective. Nor can companies use it to convince their investors to focus just on the metrics that make them look good. Communication can only convey what is so. And while attempts to use it for other purposes can deliver the appearance of a benefit in the near term, such shortcuts always carry the seeds of their own destruction. We have only to look at the earlier story of Perrier and its fatal struggle with a fixable problem of benzene pollution to observe how a belief that you can say whatever serves you will eventually turn against you. Perrier's management made the mistake of thinking it was born credible.

When communication fails, management may believe that communication itself is to blame. Rather than respond to challenges inherent in the business or in the company's governance, such managements often frame dissonance with stakeholders as a matter of being misunderstood. And the problems continue.

There's a simple way of saying this: The way you communicate shows who you are. And the manner of communication can become most revealing at times when a company is most vulnerable—when, for example, it must maneuver around a difficult set of choices involving many divergent interests.

Prior to the 2008 Beijing Olympics, the Chinese government and the games' corporate sponsors faced opposition from a galaxy of activist groups. These groups used the event as a pretext for highlighting their opposition to China's government over issues that included its occupation of Tibet, its violation of basic human rights among its domestic population, and its association with the government of Sudan.

Sudan had become a focus of humanitarian attention because of the central government's repression of the people in its Darfur region. Groups in many parts of the world who focused on Darfur variously characterized the government's campaign, which included military action and neglect of basic human needs, as genocide or ethnic cleansing designed to rid the region of its traditional inhabitants. A month prior to the games, the International Criminal Court indicted Sudan's chief of state for committing genocide in Darfur. At the same time, China's close ties to the Sudanese government remained unaffected, driven primarily by China's interest in Sudan's oil and Sudan's need for Chinese investment, technical expertise, and weapons.

Among the tactics adopted by activists to induce China to

influence Sudan was to confront those large corporations who bought Olympic sponsorships—costing about $70 million each—and demand that they urge China to change its policy on Tibet and Sudan.

Coca-Cola was one company on the receiving end of such pressure, and it responded. In an op-ed piece that appeared in the *Financial Times,* Coke's chairman and CEO Neville Isdell said the company was already doing everything it should. He cited the work Coke had already undertaken to improve conditions in Darfur, including its support of the Red Cross in Sudan and its participation in forums aimed at improving conditions there.

Isdell claimed that the "lack of clean water in Sudan" had been an important factor in starting the Darfur conflict, which, he said, the international community had missed. Coke, however, had taken the initiative to address the problem with a commitment of $5 million. Coke's sensitivity to Sudan's water problem may have been enhanced by the severe criticism the company had recently endured in India for its (legal) use of water in its beverage plants that would otherwise have been used in local towns and villages. While no one would assert that the purpose of the clean-water investment was to manufacture Coke in Darfur anytime soon, one view of the donation might characterize it as a particularly intelligent use of funds that could be of value in helping the company deflect future criticism such as it had faced in India.

It's impossible to judge Isdell's op-ed performance without walking in his shoes. Consider for a moment the powerful influences that must have come to bear on his drafting of the text. First, there were the shareholders of Coca-Cola, one of the most widely held companies in the world, who were indirectly footing the bill for the company's Olympic sponsorship. Then there was the government of China—arguably the most dynamic country in the world at the time, and one whose favor Coke would require in order to realize the benefits of its enormous investments there. And there were, of course, the activists who had prompted his writing the piece and who could be expected to provide the company with more rough sledding in the future.

Isdell intended to show the lengths to which Coke had gone in Darfur, and, in doing so, to demonstrate that the company was responsive to the catastrophe there. At the same time, he tilted toward China and his view of his shareholders' interests. And who could blame him? Failure of Coke's China strategy would have angered more shareholders more deeply than any chagrin some might have felt seeing their company sidestep social issues for which it had no direct responsibility.

Isdell's real view of the matter came out in an interview several weeks later, and it was definitive in showing how little influence social activists would have on Coke under his leadership. Referring to those who agitated publicly against Coke, he said: "It's the 3 to 4 percent who try to influence the 96 percent by utilizing a symbol."

Isdell has been known as a reputation builder with an inclusive approach to management. He customarily solicited opinions both inside and outside the organization. In addition, Coke has collaborated with NGOs in many areas of the world. And it is possible that demands for the company to engage China on Darfur fell outside the bounds of reasonableness. But by publicly dismissing as insignificant those who appealed for Coke's further engagement on Darfur, and stating that the company had predetermined its exact level of involvement, Isdell on this occasion allowed his opponents to define the limits of his openness.

Greenwashing

Many companies have recognized the need to highlight their environmental initiatives, but some have allowed their communications to get ahead of their actions. The tendency to guide public perceptions on environmental matters through overstatement has given rise to the term "greenwashing." Aware that communications don't always reflect reality, interest groups monitoring corporate environmental responsibility have become watchful for companies who exaggerate the case for their "greenness." Allegations of greenwashing can call a company's general credibility into question.

Florida Power & Light, an electric utility, ran a program called Sunshine Energy that allowed customers to help the company preserve the environment by making a monthly contribution of $9.75 for the purchase of renewable power. The company Web site told its customers that each one of them could reduce atmospheric carbon dioxide emissions equal to those a car would produce in 12,000 miles of use.

But an investigation sparked by staff questions about the program revealed that only 20 percent of the $9.6 million that customers contributed went to emissions reduction. Management had applied the rest to the company's general marketing and administrative expenses. A public service commissioner responded to the revelation by characterizing customers' contributions as having fallen "into a black hole where there is no transparency." The regulator ended the program because Florida Power & Light had deceived its customers under a false promise of helping a cause in which they believed: a cleaner environment. When the company defended itself by claiming that commission guidelines failed to specify the percentage of contributions required for emissions reduction, it ran the serious risk of appearing disingenuous. It offered no reason for assuming all contributions should not go for their stated purpose.

Communicate a Plan: Three Auto CEOs Go to Washington

In November 2008, as the full force of the financial crisis took hold, the Big Three Detroit automakers faced an apocalypse. Dramatic cost-cutting across the industry had failed to keep pace with an even more precipitous drop in sales. The highest gasoline prices in history had rendered Detroit's predominantly large-size product line uneconomical. The absence of credit made it virtually impossible for buyers to finance the purchase of a car, truck, or SUV. General Motors and Chrysler said they had enough available cash to continue operations for only a matter of weeks, and press coverage of GM openly considered the possibility of a workout through bankruptcy. But no one seemed to know who would buy a car from a bankrupt company. Ford seemed in somewhat better shape, but it was doubtful Ford could support the industry's vast parts-supply infrastructure on its own. If any one of the companies failed, the others would likely follow.

Against the specter of losing the industry that most symbolized American industrial strength, chief executives of the three companies went to Washington to petition Congress for what they called a "bridge loan" of $25 billion simply to stay in business. It was notable that only one of the three, Rick Wagoner of GM, had even been in the auto business three years before. Alan Mulally of Ford had been at Boeing and Chrysler's Robert Nardelli at Home Depot.

In their prepared statements before the Congressional committee, the CEOs emphasized the enormous constituencies that depended on their survival. They cited employees and pensioners who supported families and relied on their health plans. They referred to the thousands of businesses in surrounding communities whom plant closures would irreparably damage. They then went on to explain the profound transformations they had undergone in recent years. They described their cost cutting and the conversion of portions of their product lines to more efficient vehicles that would inflict less harm on the environment and support the nation's need to reduce dependence on fossil fuels.

What escaped mention, however, was any response to the financial crisis that had occasioned their trip to Washington. They seemed to be saying they had been meticulous all along, and all they needed was a cash infusion to get them through to the point where the world around them straightened itself out and started buying cars again. Their narrative was full of their own good behavior. But it lacked a plan.

Nature abhors a vacuum, and it was a vacuum that remained when the CEOs finished making their request. By failing to offer any idea of how they would adapt if given the loan, they left it to the Congressmen seated before them to carry the hearing forward. The conversation quickly migrated to the domain of politics, and the three CEOs found themselves confronted by an absurd and cynical question. Representative Brad Sherman asked the three to indicate by a show of hands, as though they were schoolboys, whether any of them had flown to Washington for the meeting on commercial aircraft. None responded. Each had taken his individual corporate jet, which is what CEOs of large companies do when traveling on important business. A highly unlikely conversation on their means of conveyance soon engulfed the hearing as legislators feigned disbelief that companies trying to save money would allow their leaders to travel in private airplanes.

"There's a delicious irony of seeing private luxury jets flying into DC and people coming off them with tin cups in their hands, saying that they're going to be trimming down and streamlining their businesses," said Representative Gary Ackerman. "It's almost like seeing a guy show up at the soup kitchen in high hat and tuxedo . . . Couldn't you all have downgraded to first class or jet-pooled to get here?"

Business jets are little more than a raindrop in the ocean of corporate expense structures. If the three men responsible for resuscitating an industry considered to be one of the foundations of American capitalism can't save time, enhance their efficiency and the confidentiality of their conversations, as well as their security on such a mission, use of private jets should be restricted to ferrying people to the Cannes Film Festival. But by failing to present a substantive plan, the three CEOs opened themselves to the kind of personal attack whose only purpose was to play to the committee members' home constituencies. With survival of the entire auto industry riding in the balance, they had allowed their means of transportation to become the theme of newspaper headlines across the country the following morning.

By the end of the hearing, the committee seemed to warm to its taste for treating the heads of some of the more prominent corporations in the world like students. It told them to go back to Detroit and return in 12 days with a plan that specified how they would use any money Congress might make available. The legislators were justified in doing this. The CEOs' failure to present such a plan in the first place was inexcusable in terms of respect for the Congress and obligations to all those constituencies they claimed to represent.

They returned to Washington for the second round of hearings in cars they'd driven from Detroit. The General Motors public relations team arranged for news photographers to catch CEO Rick Wagoner as he emerged from a new Chevy hybrid, stressing the company's commitment to green technology.

The Senate Banking Committee's reception was no warmer than the CEOs had experienced in the earlier hearing, and it was clear that their stature had failed to improve. Senator Chuck Schumer summed up the mood of the meeting: "I don't trust the car companies' leadership," he said, "but we can't let the industry fail. Millions of workers [will] lose their jobs."

The three executives conceded to the committee that they'd made mistakes, and they proceeded to offer plans for restructuring their companies. They committed to reduce the number of manufacturing facilities and brands. They said they would make labor costs competitive with foreign manufacturers within four years. And, realizing that lawmakers did not believe they had sufficient expertise, these three individuals who had ascended to the top of the corporate world volunteered to report to a government-appointed authority that would oversee their use of taxpayer funds in running their companies.

None of it worked, and Congress refused to grant their loan

request. Two weeks later President Bush signed an executive authorization for loans of $17.4 billion, considerably less than the $25 billion the automakers had requested.

The ultimate award of a substantial bailout package notwithstanding, the three CEOs failed to reverse their original loss of credibility. They had come to Washington full of the story of their accomplishments, yet they were inexplicably disengaged from the crisis dialogue that prevailed there. It is probable they were better managers than they showed themselves to be. But they had not seemed to grasp what was required of them. At that moment in their lives they happened to find themselves trustees of a critical national asset. They received most of what they wanted not because of the leadership they'd shown, but in spite of it.

Transparency

As management requests the confidence of its stakeholders, so must it reciprocate. To do that, it has no alternative but to opt for transparency, which constitutes an act of faith that the market will fairly interpret the information management provides. Transparency is an essential tool in getting investors and other stakeholders on the company's side, and it distinguishes the company to the extent that its performance in this area exceeds the norm. Transparency requires management to speak publicly about the challenges it faces. It therefore centers on process and the way management makes decisions.

"If you don't come totally clean about your failings, you develop a reputation for not telling the whole truth," says Tom Jurkowsky, Lockheed Martin's chief spokesman. "In essence, you've let people think you're capable of lying. In the end, there's no middle ground. Your integrity is compromised and you've lost credibility—both valuable commodities that are hard, if not impossible, to earn back."

When opponents attack a company on its actions, there's no more disarming response than an attitude that says: "Here are our challenges. If you want to get involved, help us find solutions." Later in this chapter we'll see how Steve Parrish of Altria (Phillip Morris) engaged with antismoking forces to forestall crippling legislation against the tobacco industry.

One of this author's client companies ran into trouble with its investors because of the opacity of its internal processes. Investors liked the company, and they particularly liked the financial results it showed. But they couldn't understand how management made its decisions, and this kept them from making confident judgments on the sustainability of its performance. Because investors couldn't see how management did it, they weren't sure whether it owed its success to genius or luck. The company's interest lay in helping investors who were more or less willing to buy the stock, but who needed the support that better transparency of process would give them. As another client of mine likes to say, "Rather than flaunt your achievements, you invite stakeholders into your process. It gets them involved with you."

As in any case where varying viewpoints must be reconciled, it is in the company's interest to see the issue from the other side. Earlier I pointed out that management must understand that every institutional investor has to justify investment decisions to a boss, clients, and fund shareholders. Those groups don't ask many questions as long as things go well. But when the stock doesn't perform as anticipated, the portfolio manager may have to defend his or her original decision to invest. It's not always the case, of course, that an investment's failure to pay off means the thinking behind it was faulty. But disappointment often leads to a painful re-examination of the original decision. The investor knows even before making the investment that such a review might be necessary, that there's no sure thing. So a careful investor will normally ask himself ahead of time whether there's enough information to justify the decision and defend it later. The company that makes this easy for the investor, and offers confidence that management will be available and candid should things go south, will likely experience more interest in its shares and enjoy a higher value over time.

Accessibility of Management

Like transparency, accessibility is its own message. "Eighty percent of success is showing up," Woody Allen said. For CEOs attempting productive communications with investors the figure may be somewhat lower, but it's still substantial. Through investor road shows, leaders create for themselves the opportunity to make their financial and strategic case to institutional portfolio managers and analysts. At the same time, they demonstrate their own accessibility, a key intangible factor in the decision-making process of most large investors. Failure to travel to see investors makes a statement, signaling remoteness in a company's management and calling into question its willingness to consider investors' interests.

Similarly, when management issues quarterly results, it has the opportunity to do more than merely meet the regulatory imperatives governing disclosure. By expanding the customary limits of the information it conveys, as well as adding color that gives the information context, management also sends an unspoken message about its own quality. This message tends to transmit its belief in the business, its confidence in itself, and trust in the communications process. In sending such a message, management also establishes its belief that investors will understand what it has told them. This is the dynamic by which transparency becomes value.

The degree of trust that institutional investors give management ranges from benefit-of-the-doubt to severe skepticism, and at times it can fall below skepticism to utter dismissal. But belief never gets better than benefit-of-the-doubt. One large investment company hired former FBI personnel to train their analysts to determine whether company managements were telling the truth. "They'd come with off-the-wall questions to test you," an investor relations director told me.

In many ways, stakeholders see a company's management as nothing more nor less than the promises it makes. Some promises are overt: *We expect to earn X dollars per share this year.* Others are implied: *We're making initial investments in a certain product because demographic trends tell us it will be big in three to five years.* The company's share multiple is a measure of how it performs against a constellation of such promises, and managers are mistaken if they believe there's more involved. Neither elegance of communication nor charisma is worth much beyond the manager's ability to offer insights into the company as it is and convey his honest expectations of its future. Jim Collins, in his book *Good to Great*, made a strong case for the noncharismatic CEO as a long-term performer. In my experience speaking with hundreds of institutional investors every year, a leader's performance against his own promises far outstrips in value his performance against competitors. Investors know that the market can change, but corporate leaders, being human, seldom do.

Creating a Communications Strategy

Strong external communication depends on a coordinated strategy that includes all internal players who engage with stakeholders. Management must design and implement a mechanism through which it establishes a communication policy, both broadly and with regard to specific issues. Companies that are good at this generally hold a weekly conference call that includes the CEO, CFO, division heads, and directors of PR, IR, and public affairs.

Instituting such a communications conference call assures that every external communicator grasps the underlying themes prevailing at the time. In reviewing issues that affect the company on that day, the communications group can agree on what they'll say, if asked, on any subject. If the IR director learns through the preparatory meeting that his PR colleague has been getting calls about a strike at one of the company's plants, for example, he'll prepare his own guidance to investors and analysts in a way that's consistent with statements the PR director has made to the press. In addition, he'll be alert for analysts' inquiries on any change in the production outlook due to the strike. The IR director's ability to anticipate such calls is likely to have lasting benefits in supporting analysts' confidence in his future guidance and disclosure.

In the earlier chapter on stakeholder mapping, I discussed the need for a constant review of information considered to have competitive sensitivity. The need for this reassessment acknowledges the ever-shifting distinction between information the company can safely disclose and that which it must withhold for competitive reasons. The communications conference call offers the CEO another opportunity to review the need to withhold specific information and to consider whether some can be released in the interest of candor with investors.

While preparation is always essential, no company should try to program its spokespeople. A reputation for responsiveness and transparency arises from a communicator's ability to make judgments. He should have the same presence of mind as a senior engineer at Lockheed Martin who might discuss sensitive defense systems with a foreign government at one point in his day, while an hour later he may consult with a competitor like Boeing on a joint project. Both conversations are likely to involve complex details of technology, and they are likely to stand on a platform of underlying technologies that he cannot disclose. No amount of rules-making on confidentiality will prepare him to navigate these conversations successfully. Only his constant immersion in all the issues involved will enable him to fulfill the purposes of these conversations while preserving the interests of the U.S. government in the case of the foreign power, and those of his own company in the case of the competitor.

Addressing Diverse Audiences

One of the overriding communications challenges is to find the common terms with which to address diverse audiences. The most frequent advice one hears on this subject is to keep the message simple. Patrick Moore, who was investor relations director at Bell-South a few years ago, would always ask himself one question: "Could my mom in Reform, Alabama, make any sense of what I've just said in this press release?"

The question of content rests ultimately on the nature of the communication. When a company advertises a product, it might focus its message on the product itself—or on the way the product makes life better. And if it makes life better, does it do so by over-coming a fear or inconvenience, or does it serve a quest for personal status? When the company itself is the product—as it is in dealing with investors and other stakeholders—the need for simplicity and clarity remain the same.

For example, if a company is describing its technology to investors, is its purpose to demonstrate that it has beaten its competition in the current market, or that the cleverness of its engineers should induce investors to rely on it for future hypercompetitive technologies, or that it is refocusing its business on new areas? The specific message that management chooses will determine how much it reveals about the nature of the new technologies, their expected economic value, and the applications to which it will deploy them.

If a company describes the strength of its balance sheet, is its purpose to demonstrate that it is expert in financial management, or that it's capable of making a major acquisition, or that it's planning to raise its dividend or buy back millions of shares? The company may be sure that its discussion of the balance sheet will arouse such questions. Will it anticipate those questions by providing the answers as part of the original message about balance sheet strength? Or will it allow the questions to linger in investors' minds—only to appear during a future conference call or analyst meeting? There, those questions will most likely create a diversion from the communications of *that* moment. In doing so, they may cause further diffusion in management's original message, and they will almost certainly raise additional questions. Management would have served itself better by anticipating the questions and answering them before they were asked. This deliberate preemption of expected questions can keep investors listening.

Everyone Is Listening

No management team should forget that its institutional investors, whose primary contact with the company comes through the CFO and the IR director, see the company's consumer advertising as well. If the commercial on the Sunday night TV movie emphasizes the low price of the product, and the IR director has been saying margins will increase, the investor may go to the office Monday morning and take a closer look at the company's expense statement. If the PR director has placed a story with a reporter on the international expansion of the firm's manufacturing capabilities, thereby promoting the theme that a local company is expanding onto the international stage, management should assume that union leaders and local politicians will read the story along with everyone else.

Just as a company never knows the true extent of its risk, neither can it understand the real dimensions of its audience. You never know everyone who's listening. You don't know their various interests or the specific filters through which they hear you. This is the reason manipulative communications nearly always fail. No management team can predict the responses of unseen, unanticipated observers.

The Willingness to Be Influenced

I said earlier that the era of the fortress corporation has ended, and a new era in which organizations must operate with greater public involvement has begun. Most companies, however, have not gone willingly into this "Age of Consensus." The democratization of the corporate sector is an evolutionary process that extends over decades. And it has come into being only because corporate managements see little choice but to respond to pressures that originate with outside groups—most particularly their investors.

In May 2008 a remarkable event occurred during the run-up to ExxonMobil's annual shareholder meeting. The descendants of John D. Rockefeller, founder of Exxon's predecessor Standard Oil, filed a resolution to be considered at the meeting calling for a separation of the CEO and chairmanship posts. In an explanatory letter in the *Financial Times*, the Rockefeller family, still significant Exxon shareholders, said the separation of the CEO and chairman jobs would enable the board to "provide independent oversight of the chief executive and management team." But their purpose was much larger than a change in the governance structure. The letter went on to say that "the company has not articulated a complete, long-term corporate response to the challenges of a rapidly changing energy environment." The Rockefellers claimed that ExxonMobil had failed adequately to address such issues as energy security, carbon dioxide emissions, diversification of supply, shortages of skilled labor, and the challenges of replacing reserves in an increasingly difficult environment.

While the resolution attracted the support of many large institutional investors and received nearly 40 percent of the vote, it failed in the face of heavy lobbying by the company and investors' pleasure with its financial performance. ExxonMobil had explained its position when the Rockefellers announced the resolution weeks before, pointing out that oil and gas would still provide up to 80 percent of the world's energy over the next 30 years. "To abandon that would not be wise," it said. The company did not explain the reason for its reference to abandonment of the oil and gas business rather than the expansion of its concept of energy sources as suggested by the Rockefellers. But its oblique manner of communication apparently helped buy it another year before it might have to face such questions publicly once again.

ExxonMobil management will certainly focus on those exact questions in the future. A shareholder resolution that gets 40 percent of the vote carries a strong message, and management's survival instincts are acutely sensitive to such messages. There is, in fact, a tendency for managements publicly to reject or remain neutral on unsolicited advice while responding to that advice with vigorous internal initiatives. ExxonMobil chairman and CEO Rex Tillerson may have indicated as much immediately after prevailing over the shareholder resolution. "We don't talk a lot about what we're doing until we've got something," he said. "That's our culture."

Tillerson's statement hinted that the company might be working on alternative energy sources. And it might not. He seemed to say, "Even if we were, we still might not tell you." Among the things for which Texas is justly famous are the oil business and poker. Tillerson was employing techniques of the latter in managing a public conversation about the former. Because his company is the largest private-sector energy company in the world, and arguably the most profitable, he could get away with this. Others would find it more difficult.

Most companies are finding it to be in their interests to take shareholder resolutions seriously—even if they don't come from Rockefellers. Some months after ExxonMobil's shareholder meeting, Ceres, the U.S. network of investors and environmentalists that urges corporations to adopt environmentally sustainable practices, offered further evidence that companies respond to well-supported resolutions even when they fail. Ceres announced that investors had filed a record 57 climate-related resolutions with U.S. companies during the 2008 proxy season. Approximately half reached a vote, and those gathered 23.5 percent shareholder support overall, up from 17 percent a year earlier. As an example, investor backing for a resolution submitted to one coal company requesting its response to outside pressures on carbon emissions came in at nearly 40 percent.

While no climate-oriented shareholder resolution has yet achieved a majority, Ceres noted that companies have been implementing practices designed to reduce climate change at an accelerating rate. The real effects of shareholder resolutions seem to arise not from success or failure of the resolutions themselves, but from the pressure their increasing frequency creates on management thinking. Ford, for example, responded to a shareholder resolution with a plan for lowering greenhouse-gas emissions in its vehicles by 30 percent. And in 2008 two major homebuilders agreed to greater transparency on energy-efficient construction.

Even the implied threat that investors will file such resolutions influences decision-making. Wal-Mart has implemented new climate-friendly measures—particularly in its fleet of trucks—on the apparent recognition that such issues will inevitably grow in importance with stakeholders.

Fund managers clearly hear their own clients telling them that they want them to influence companies to take responsibility for their effects on the environment. Those fund managers are no less interested in financial returns than they've ever been, but the influence of their own investors, and the expansion of their funds' influence on companies, means that responding to outside points of view has become a factor in management survivability.

The Communications of Convergence

"I have no more made my book than my book has made me."
—Michel de Montaigne

The reciprocity implied in the great French essayist's comment is, I think, universal. In corporate life, it points to the power of engagement in resolving public conflicts and dissonances. The simple act of engaging with those whose views differ from yours can result in a new (and perhaps unexpected) alignment. Such engagement generally creates a reciprocal openness in stakeholders, leading to a phenomenon I call the communications of convergence, in which participants in a dialogue begin to share a way of speaking about mutual issues.

Whether they agree or not, they start to rely on each other. The company and its constituents establish a common vocabulary in discussing their respective concerns, and eventually the company finds it has gained some influence over the terms stakeholders use to discuss its affairs. Of course, the company can influence only if it agrees to be influenced. But the striking benefit of the communications of convergence lies in its power to create consensus through the evolution of a shared language. All sides arrive at a higher level of trust in the others' intentions, and the investments they've made in the relationship drive the dialogue forward.

In an essay called "The Moral Instinct," the psychologist Steven Pinker writes that when we have a gut instinct about right and wrong, often that "gut" is based in the physiology of our brains. MRI imaging shows that different parts of our brains become active according to the specific moral questions we are considering, and the reasons for this appear to be at least partly genetic. A sense of right and wrong often translates into a belief that those who agree with us are moral, and those who see things differently are less moral. This describes to a significant degree the dissonance on both sides of the question between corporations and those who think those corporations should behave differently. While conceding that there are people in the world with bad motives, Pinker says that "in any conflict in which a meeting of the minds is not completely hopeless, a recognition that the other guy is acting from moral rather than venal reasons can be a first patch of common ground."

Let's say you're a manufacturer of electronics products and that your processes require chemicals whose toxicity calls for delicate handling. Let's say also that some of these chemicals have escaped from one of your plants into an estuary, bypassing approved disposal procedures. And let's say that the employee responsible for this illegal chemical disposal decides he's going to do everyone a favor—including your environmental compliance people, your corporate counsel, and your PR department—and alter records so as to hide the event. But as one might expect, an independent environmental group, an NGO, discovers the leak, and news of it appears on the front page of the local newspaper.

So now you undertake the necessary adjustment of the records, fire the employee and the executives responsible for his supervision, and pay your fine to the Environmental Protection Agency. But then you find that you've become a large blip on the radar screen of the environmental NGO that discovered the violation. You've been caught disguising one illegal environmental discharge, and there's no telling how many times you may have done it in the past without being caught. Your future behavior is now viewed as suspect, at best. Yet your business must go on, of course, and that business must continue to apply for operating licenses in new localities. These require official approvals that involve public hearings, and sophisticated activists associated with the NGO know this. You face the task of convincing them, and any other interested parties, that the chemical spill and its cover-up were one-time events. Although you did it, you're not the *kind* of company that does such things.

Let's say, then, that you've determined that your approach to such a problem is to consult your corporate values for guidance, as they may suggest ways to proceed and to communicate. It also happens that one of your values is "unquestionable ethics." Do you believe you've fulfilled this value by firing those involved, correcting the records, and paying the fine? If so, what have you changed? You've solved your immediate problem, but you're still exactly the same company you were before the problem arose.

It's possible that this significant mishap has presented you with an opportunity. But to identify that opportunity, you have to see that your communication choices have expanded. In applying your ethical values to this clearly ethical problem, you might seize the chance to make a statement about the ethics of environmental stewardship—not only by reaffirming your opposition to what occurred, but by announcing a companywide training program in ethics and the proper handling of dangerous materials, then offering the public (and the NGO) details of the program.

In other words, applying one of your core reputation values to your own violation offers you the chance to make a statement about ethics that you can back up with visible actions. So, the core value goes live. This will make a good story in the local newspaper, and your PR people will take advantage of the opportunity by generating a piece that shows the strides the company has made in internal training and controls in the wake of the chemical spill. But what do you do if the NGO's principals remain unconvinced?

You realize, at this point, that you've got to engage them. You can't have them trailing you around from one county commission and regulatory body to another telling the story of what you did. So let's say that your public affairs director makes an appointment to see the director of the NGO. The director accepts because of the example you've set for others through your ethics and other training programs. This doesn't mean they trust you yet, but they're willing to meet.

At this first meeting, you get acquainted but make no attempt to reach any agreement. Both sides, however, commit to go on talking on a periodic basis. In fact, you get together every couple of months or so. The relations become cordial, but, more important, each side begins to understand the language with which the other expresses its views.

After eight months, there's still no agreement by the NGO not to confront you on new licenses. But its language becomes less aggressive, and its principals acknowledge that your company has begun to build a record of compliance and exemplary staff training.

Without much hoopla, both sides have invested in the dialogue that is characterized by the slow alignment of diverse interests.

The entire process started with a communication strategy based on a clear-and-simple reputation value. Nothing dramatic has happened except that your regulatory hearings now proceed more smoothly. And those looking to make you a negative example have no more recent material than the original violation. In the interim, you've not only corrected that original violation, but have established new standards that other can follow. It's even possible that the NGO might eventually use your solution as a model for other companies.

What has occurred between the company and the NGO is a communication of convergence. The company has solicited a dialogue with the NGO in a scenario that reverses the customary balance of power in which the company's size and resources lead it to assume its own dominance. This sudden equality has created the possibility of dialogue. The essence of the dynamic is that the company, in explaining its challenges and corrective measures to the NGO, draws the NGO into the use of the company's own vocabulary. So while acting out of vulnerability, the company actually influences the terms in which the NGO discusses its affairs.

And as the company influences, so is it influenced. Because of the exposure a good NGO relationship creates, it can lay the groundwork for many such relationships. These become partnerships that can benefit the company. One corporate executive responsible for reputation describes how an informal relationship with an NGO gives him insight into his own company that would otherwise be unavailable, "You can go out to one of your overseas subsidiaries, or a supply-chain partner, and they lead you into a spotless room," he says. "Everything looks impressive—just the way you'd want to see it. If you wander around and open a certain door, though, you can walk right into a Dickensian scene. But you seldom get to open that door." The NGO, he says, is able to make inquiries and conduct research that would be risky for the company to undertake with its subsidiaries and business partners. Such a strong relationship creates a condition, he says, in which the NGO makes the company its first stop on discovery of violations rather than the regulators, courts, or media.

Many individuals involved in protecting their companies' reputations see stakeholder engagement as one of the most cost-effective forms of reputation risk management. Maintaining a dialogue with opponents builds mutual trust, while helping those who may confront the company at some point understand its case. If the corporation is an automaker, say, a relationship with activists advocating pollution controls may give those activists an appreciation of the economic challenges the company faces in making cleaner-burning cars. A dialogue that occurs before arguments come to a head may give credibility to the company's expressed wish to manufacture and sell low-pollutant automobiles. It may, in fact, identify any common ground the two sides might share, and from which a constructive dialogue could begin. The cost of pursuing such a strategy is a fraction of the investment needed to send lobbyists to Washington. The advantage of engaging stakeholders in this way is similar to that of conducting perception studies among investors: The company in effect uses those stakeholders as consultants to offer advice on how to address some of its biggest challenges.

A Genius for Thriving in a Nasty Business

Altria, the owner of Phillip Morris and a maker of products that face enormous social resistance, provides what might be the most dramatic example in American corporate history of a company exercising the communications of convergence to influence the public agenda around its business. The forces arrayed against Altria and the other tobacco companies are committed, inventive, and powerful. Yet Altria has generated good returns for investors year in and year out.

There has to be a reason for the remarkable success of a company that virtually everyone despises. It has faced enormous restrictions on its ability to market its products and find consumers. It has been forced to settle a series of lawsuits for more than $200 billion to be paid over two decades. And its products, not to beat about the bush, will kill you. The reason Altria has done so well despite these challenges is that the company tends to attract very bright individuals who like a challenge. When you ask people at Altria why they choose to work in such a stigmatized area of business and society—particularly when they have all the options in the world before them—most say the same thing: They're attracted to the professionalism of the people. If you want to work with the best lawyers, they say, you'll find them at Altria—and the same with marketers and communications practitioners.

One of the more prominent among them is Steve Parrish. We may not like his cause, but there's little question that he's the best at what he does. Over the last two decades, Parrish, who has retired from the company, has engineered an extraordinary dialogue between Phillip Morris and its opponents in the anti-tobacco advocacy world. From the status of pariah, he has developed relationships that evolved into partnerships on designing tobacco regulation, giving the company a voice among groups who previously wouldn't have granted it a seat at the table. The result was that Phillip Morris, whose reason to exist remains deeply questionable, continues to flourish.

Parrish's natural instinct is to make contact with the other side, and he has a particular talent for keeping the conversation going no matter how aggressive his antagonists become. "You have to have empathy," he says. "You have to see what the other side is going through. Ally yourself with your opponents—and disarm them by speaking their language."

Parrish also recognized, and convinced his own management, that there was no way to avoid the real problem with the public conversation about tobacco companies: Smoking kills, which the tobacco companies had denied for years. That was where he started. "We weren't going out of the tobacco business," he says, "but we could begin by admitting the truth." He began to realize that he had to ally himself with his opponents, and he began to believe that "giving new information was better than shutting up in anticipation of lawsuits."

In fact, information was one of the prime assets that his company had to offer, and Parrish began to use it as a tool. He decided that the best way to engage the other side was to become part of their conferences, so he began contacting the leadership of the anti-tobacco forces, saying, "You're having all these conferences about tobacco. Who knows more about making tobacco than we do? Why not invite us?" They did, and Parrish became a familiar face at anti-tobacco meetings. He knew the deal. On panels, as he put forth the company's ideas, he absorbed a stream of hostile, withering criticism. Nevertheless, he kept talking and listening.

Phillip Morris is a thriving concern today partly because of Steve Parrish's ability to prevent closure on the public conversation about tobacco. He did this by continually moving the goalposts of the conversation through the addition of new elements. "Always give them more information," he says. "Always shift the conversation."

In the late 1990s he did a complete about-face, coming out in favor of government regulation of the industry. This naturally shocked industry opponents, who had been calling for the same thing for years. If *Phillip Morris* is for regulation, many thought, shouldn't we be against it? They wondered what the trick was— what subterfuge was the company up to now? In fact, Phillip Morris saw regulation as a long-term asset. They knew there would be rules, and regardless of what those rules turned out to be, they would be the same for everyone. Management believed it could beat its competition regardless of the shape of the playing field. What's more, they believed that real regulation would help guarantee the industry's sustainability, as the government wasn't very likely to ban something it had agreed to regulate. The industry was willing to accept extensive controls over production processes, cigarette contents, advertising, and many other defined restrictions—as long as cigarettes remained legal.

Regulation, however, was not to be. The Congressional debate degenerated into a diffuse argument about how much punishment the opponents of tobacco could exert against the industry, and the entire enterprise ceased to make sense.

For decades, big tobacco denied that there was anything harmful about its product. Parrish sometimes wonders what life in the industry would have been like if it had conceded the truth in earlier years and engaged its opponents. "What if, in '64, when the first Surgeon General's Report came out, we had agreed to cooperate?" He points out that "the more you put things off, the harder it gets." What would have happened if, instead of interminably dragging things out—saying there were open questions, worrying only about litigation—they had tried to live in reality? "You're always going to litigate, settle, and confront the possibilities of legislation and regulation. And you're never going to get legal protection from being sued in the future for the simple reason that you don't deserve it."

* * * *

During the 1990s, the most visible advocate of tobacco industry regulation was David Kessler, the activist Commissioner of the Food and Drug Administration for much of the Clinton administration. Before Phillip Morris decided regulation might be a good idea, Kessler had come close to convincing Congress that cigarettes were a drug and the industry should be subject to the FDA's regulatory control. Kessler, trained as both a physician and an attorney, was highly articulate in making the case against the tobacco industry, and he was Parrish's nemesis. Parrish says he thought frequently of calling Kessler, but colleagues characterized such a call as a sign of weakness and dissuaded him. Then Parrish received a call from Kessler, who had left the FDA to become dean of the Yale Medical School and who wanted to interview Parrish for a book he was writing about his time in government. Parrish immediately accepted, and the two became friends. On hearing of Parrish's frustrated attempts to call him during the congressional wars over tobacco, Kessler confessed to having had the same urge. Sometime after the interview, Kessler arranged for Parrish to speak at a meeting of the National Center on Addiction and Substance Abuse in California.

They flew out together, and during the flight Kessler turned to Parrish and said it would be a wonderful thing if he were to admit that tobacco was a drug. Parrish did as Kessler had asked. The willingness of a few anti-tobacco campaigners to speak with him afterward demonstrated to him that admitting the truth about tobacco's addictive qualities would become his ticket into the conversation about whether tobacco was to be regulated or not. Parrish knew he had to become part of the conversation if others were working toward regulation and additional controls on tobacco. And in order to become part of the conversation, he had to admit the truth: that tobacco was a drug; that it was addictive; that it killed.

* * * *

At a conference, Steve Parrish heard General Colin Powell tell this story: When he was President Reagan's national security advisor, Powell accompanied then-Secretary of State George Schultz to the Kremlin to meet with Soviet president Mikhail Gorbachev. As they waited for the meeting to begin, Gorbachev burst into the room in a state of great agitation. "You've got to tell Reagan to stop demonizing me," Gorbachev said. "You have no idea who in the (Soviet) army is waiting to take over. You don't want them in your life."

Powell said he had to stop and think about this. He reflected on his lifelong dedication to the army. The U.S. military had developed a sophisticated set of strategic choices to apply against any anticipated Soviet action. But if peace came and aggression disappeared from the scenario, all that work and imagination might turn out to be wasted—as well as all the intellectual value that had gone into it. Powell might even be out of a job. So how much did he want to help Gorbachev end the Cold War? He had to ask himself what he wanted, and from a personal point of view, maybe peace wasn't it.

Powell, of course, became an accomplished statesman. And his story of self-examination helped Parrish understand that the best approach to Altria's challenges was to disarm opponents by becoming their allies.

*   *   *   *

One day, as Parrish sat with an Altria executive in the company's Richmond, Virginia, offices, the phone rang with the news that a worker had just been killed in the adjacent manufacturing facility. Parrish and the executive rushed to the immense plant that took in cured tobacco at one end and delivered hundreds of millions of packaged cigarettes per day at the other.

Near the end of the production line, huge robotic cranes lifted cases of cartons onto high shelves for storage to await shipping to the dock. When the imperfect placement of a case caused spillage, an employee had to go in along the track beside the robots to manually rearrange the stacking. When Parrish and his colleague arrived, the body of a worker still lay under a robot, which had crushed him to death.

About two years earlier, internal safety auditors had produced a document recommending a lockout system requiring operators to shut off the crane before such a procedure could take place. The auditors had stipulated that the mechanism should be tagged in a way that involved a series of deliberate procedures to turn them on again. The plant manager had placed this document in his file, and no action had ever taken place. The worker left a wife and two small children.

The Occupational Safety and Health Administration (OSHA) investigation naturally requested documents, but since there was no record that indicated the existence of the internal safety audit, the company could have withheld it. Parrish insisted that they produce the document, and from there the company undertook a complete study of exactly what conditions had made the accident possible. The study report named those who failed to implement safety directives.

Parrish took the document to the widow's house. He described to her what had happened, and he left the report behind. After she'd read it, he asked her what she wanted him to do. She replied that she wanted the information given to everyone in the plant. Meetings took place with each of the three shifts during which management examined the accident in detail, again naming those responsible. The widow attended each meeting. After the last one, she asked Parrish to come back to her house and meet her dead husband's parents, which he did.

Although Virginia law required no consideration for the family beyond workman's compensation, the company made them whole financially. Some time later, when Philip Morris endured one of its episodes of withering criticism in the press and in Congress, the widow contacted the company and offered to come forward and say what kind of company she thought it really was. The company decided it didn't want to ride on her back and declined her offer.

Steve Parrish tells this story, and in view of the immense dislocations associated with Philip Morris in general, it is believable. Philip Morris products kill tens of thousands of people a year with 100 percent predictability. But the company culture has so perfected the psychology of compartmentalization that its behavior away from specific issues of the product is exemplary. What tends to shock the sensibility is that a technique that so perfectly mimics empathy can prove so powerful in the domain of human life and death. The mimicry is so perfect that the mime, himself, appears to experience his own empathy without the slightest irony.

The irresolvable ambiguities involved prove the power of the technique of engagement. You can create acceptance for practically anything as long as you frame the conversation—and the experience others have of you—with your own humanity.

Engaging with Regulators

The most feared of all stakeholders may be the government. No stakeholder has more power, nor appears less susceptible to negotiation. Federal, state, local, and even foreign government organs claim jurisdiction over widely varied areas of corporate activity, including accounting, securities, the environment, labor policies, and the antitrust implications of mergers and acquisitions. And yet, even with so much at stake, many companies fail to realize that preemptive conversations with the right regulators may help avert serious problems.

The Federal Sentencing Guidelines discussed earlier imply that regulatory personnel hold considerable discretion on whether or not to take action against a company. If such discretion exists, then the outcome of an inquiry is subject to legitimate influence. But the company must take action by engaging.

If it has engaged prior to the appearance of problems, so much the better. A dialogue with regulatory staff can establish relationships that frame any future conflict. These conversations can prove crucial in the eventuality of regulatory investigations or charges by creating a record of openness and a familiarity that creates an avenue for communication. A regulator can hardly claim that a company has been evasive if that company has already initiated a conversation, whether to obtain general guidance or to address a specific issue. Such preemptive dialogue also provides the company with a means of eliciting, and coming to understand, the regulator's point of view.

If, for example, a company is contemplating a significant acquisition, its attorneys might note that the Securities and Exchange Commission or the comparable European authority should be open to the question, "If we make the decision to acquire XYZ Corp., would you expect us to have an antitrust problem?" If the answer is yes, the company may have saved itself millions of dollars in fees and other expenses, as well as the needless public exposure of corporate strategy. If the answer is maybe, management might be able to discover measures that can help it realize its goal. And if the answer is that there would be no problem, then those inside the company who favor the transaction have come upon a stronger argument for the acquisition than existed prior to posing the question.

What if a management team discovers, belatedly, that it may have violated the law, even though no one outside the company knows about it (yet)? Even here, a proactive stance before regulators can spare the company considerable misery and expense. Contact with the Department of Justice under its amnesty program might, for example, offer an opportunity to avoid the kind of embarrassment that can bring with it dramatic loss of share value and business franchise (to say nothing of financial penalties).

There's no room for a Pollyannaish anticipation of happy endings, however. Violation of the law, even if the culprit has turned himself in, will involve penalties that are uncertain at the time the offense is disclosed. When Chiquita Brands told the Department of Justice it had made protection payments to Colombian guerrillas, it received no concessions for the voluntary disclosure. On one hand, there were circumstances that could easily have argued for mitigation—the company wanted to keep its people alive. On the other hand, it came at a time the U.S. government was spending billions to support the Colombian government *against* the guerrillas. Chiquita lost the gambit, but was certainly no worse off than it would have been had the violation been exposed by other means.

Sustainability Reports: Disclosure or Diversion?

Many companies issue elaborate sustainability reports. They present statistics that relate to compliance with environmental codes, to emission levels that cover both individual facilities and aggregate data over the company's global operations, to investments in antipollution programs, and to contributions to community causes. While stakeholders recognize the effort that goes into these reports, many also consider them to be a variety of smoke screen behind which companies hide their real policies and intentions.

One large mining company asked stakeholders—including employees, investors, banks, insurance companies, and NGOs—to answer a detailed set of questions about the kinds of information they wanted. Because of the business in which this company was engaged, its questionnaire focused on the environment, health, and safety.

It turned out that stakeholders had little interest in the kinds of technical reporting that generally goes into sustainability reports. While a few wanted some localized data, no one was interested in sweeping technical panoramas. What they wanted to know was what the company had actually done. They wanted demonstrations of its intent. What they really wanted, it turned out, was not data, but stories.

The public affairs officer who related this experience described the challenge he faced in adapting data-centered communication to a more narrative style. Data collection and storytelling require two different skills, he said, and corporations are much better prepared to amass data than to construct narratives. His particular task was to convince county and state regulatory commissions in the western U.S. to grant his company mineral extraction rights. When he now went before these regulatory commissions, he no longer talked much about clean technology, nor did he dwell on his company's carbon footprint. "It's odd," he said, "but the more data you give them, the more abstract the conversation gets."

Instead, he described for these regulators how his company had conducted operations in other places. He used only a few stories, but he told each of them from beginning to end, describing the kinds of preparation his company undertook in each project, the way they hired, the benefits they offered workers, and how they sometimes had to find innovative ways to keep promises.

"There's a difference between telling them what you plan to do, and telling them what you've actually done," he said. "When you tell them a story, you name the place. You give the dates. You tell them how you started, the problems you ran into, and how things are now. You give them someone to call to check it out. It gets you a lot farther than PowerPoint and spreadsheets."

Influencing the Dialogue: Becoming a Thought Leader

In the end, the way to a strong reputation lies in making a contribution. One component of contribution which some companies focus on lies in becoming a source of ideas that lead to the evolution of industry standards and "best practices." Some companies, for example, have elected to sponsor conferences and seminars in specific spheres of stakeholder interest. They do this on their own initiative or through established industry organizations. Their motivations for initiating such events include the belief that the ties they create among a regular circle of stakeholders bring new institutions into the company's orbit, promote specific ideas to inform the general stakeholder dialogue, and demonstrate engagement as a prime value of the company.

HP and IBM were among the companies who took the lead

in establishing the Electronic Industry Code of Conduct, which guides behavior in such areas as labor, health and safety, the environment, management practices, and ethics. Other companies later joined the original group, but not all of the industry's major players signed up. Among the reasons given by those who declined were concerns that the code might later bind them to agreements they hadn't foreseen in such areas as labor and the environment. So those who originated the initiative not only demonstrated ethical leadership and openly assumed a certain risk in doing so, but also differentiated themselves from those nonsignatories who declined.

Such pan-industry organizations as the Conference Board's Global Council on Business Conduct provide opportunities for companies who are otherwise competitors to develop notions of best practices through the sharing of experience.

CHAPTER 11

Strategy 6:
Prepare for Crisis

How the CEO Saves the Company Every Day

The saying that a reputation can take a century to build and a minute to lose—while underscoring the importance of performing appropriately in a crisis—isn't entirely accurate. Reputation is generally lost in all the sins of commission and omission that lead up to a reputation-threatening event. But even when a defective product hits the market or toxic waste finds its way to a river, there's still much a CEO can do to salvage reputation. The public's view of him and his company only becomes irretrievable when he denies responsibility.

When a crisis occurs, observers of the troubled company become its stakeholders. They take an interest in the progress of events, often for deeply personal reasons. They respond to a crisis as a window on hidden truths about corporations in general, not just the one in crisis. They know that all companies are not deceptive. But they harbor a distinct suspicion that there's more misconduct in big business than ever comes to light.

What is the fascination crises hold for us? There is, without question, a good deal of schadenfreude—pleasure at the misfortunes of others. But there's also a desire to know how the world really works. Did those corporate insiders, who belong to a privileged class, get where they are on merit? If not, how did they do it? One gains the opportunity to learn more about them when their excess and their hubris become so great as to reach the public. Then everyone watches. Stories about the company move from a newspaper's business section to the front page, and people who seldom read the business section become absorbed. In addition to contending with its own specific challenges, any company undergoing a public crisis carries a heavy burden in that the public sees its story as shedding light on the nature of business in general.

Yet the reason for the public's fascination with corporate crises lies beyond both schadenfreude and curiosity. Its underlying dynamic is identical to one of this book's central themes: the effect corporations have on people's lives. Crises deepen their audiences' understanding of forces that directly affect them. Those audiences take crises as indicators of what to expect in the future. Crises therefore influence one of the most important aspects of the individual's relationship to the social environment: trust in institutions.

This chapter will describe how the CEO builds immunity to crisis into his company—how he saves the company every day, in other words. It will also provide a guide for managing and communicating when that immunity fails and a real crisis occurs.

The CEO ought to expect crisis. If you run an airline, you may someday have a plane go down. If you run a bank, you may find your organization involved in a scandal at a client company or that you've been sold some rotten assets. Any leadership team that merits the trust of its stakeholders must subscribe to the law of unintended consequences. When a crisis occurs, its sense of shock should last no more than a moment. The responsible executive group must absorb the reality of what has occurred and activate a preexisting response plan.

The CEO must foster a company whose characteristics are such that its influencers assume both its good intentions and its fundamental ethics in all circumstances. Should a crisis occur, that company receives the benefit of the doubt during the crucial time it takes to investigate the oil spill, the factory explosion, or the defective product. It will already have earned the chance to tell its story before the adverse event takes place. That's the most important characteristic of a good reputation.

The history of corporate failings is laden with tales of companies that have arrived completely unprepared at moments of crisis. In *Only the Paranoid Survive*, Intel chairman Andy Grove calls such moments "strategic inflection points"—times in the life of a business "when its fundamentals are about to change. That change can mean an opportunity to rise to new heights," he says, "but it may just as likely signal the beginning of the end."

In 1994, Intel shipped a Pentium chip model with an infinitesimal flaw, one the average user would encounter once every 27,000 years. The company was working on a fix when a story about the problem broke on CNN. Over the next few days, it made most of the newspapers in the country. The press had no idea of the minute nature of the flaw, but because of the adverse publicity, IBM dropped the Pentium chip, sending Intel into an immediate crisis.

Computer users by the thousands began calling the company for replacement parts. Intel's business had been restricted almost exclusively to supplying computer manufacturers, and it had little experience with consumers. Nevertheless, Grove decided to replace any chip that was returned, requiring immense changes in the company. He pulled engineers and managers off their jobs to answer phones. The problem, which consisted almost entirely of a *perception* of a product flaw rather than one that would actually affect users, forced the company into a $475 million write-off.

The CEO must understand that a crisis always leads to a new reality. After Intel's chip crisis, the company's dominance of the microprocessor industry continued its trajectory, but its business had changed forever. It could no longer shape the market through its own innovative products. Grove realized that it was his customers' perceptions of their own needs that now created the market. The most dramatic shift, however, came with the transformation of Intel's image from a pioneering entrepreneur to a mega corporation with all the opposition that such organizations attract. "A strategic inflection point is when the balance of forces shifts from the old structure, from the old ways of doing business and the old ways of competing, to the new," Grove writes.

Grove's story demonstrates a strategic inflection point reached through a change in the company's relationship with its commercial and social environment. Like Nike's embarrassment over revelations of human rights violations in its Asian factories, Intel's ordeal took place in public. Although transformative, such experiences are painful and costly, giving rise to the question: How do you change a company without undergoing the humiliation and business loss of undergoing a strategic inflection point to which the whole world is witness? The answer may be that you create a strategic inflection point internally if that's what's necessary to change the company.

Lou Gerstner's experience upon arriving at IBM in 1993 is instructive. He found in IBM a company that had already undergone a strategic inflection point in its failure to react to new technologies. At the time, it appeared to be succumbing to Grove's second outcome—the beginning of the end—as it prepared to capitulate to its circumstances by selling off units. Gerstner created a counter inflection point by acknowledging the crisis and proclaiming outright that the company wouldn't go on as it had.

This statement by a new CEO caused a drastic change in viewpoint among those who thought they would eventually take control of their own fiefdoms, or find their business units sold into other companies where they could begin to exert leverage. The strategic inflection point Gerstner created was both institutional and personal for everyone who worked at IBM. It was the first chapter of a story, virtually unique in American business, in which a dominant giant that had nearly expired rose from the dead as strong as ever. One looks to the Detroit automakers today for the same kind of miracle born of vision and a willingness to break with the past.

Corporate dramas that end up playing out on the public stage frequently involve the exposure, over time, of a series of problems that may have to do with safety, the environment, or ethics. The company invariably claims they are unrelated aberrations. But as the sequence unfolds, the press, investors, and the public may start to see a broad systemic failure. And when the press and public begin to lead the discussion, the company has lost.

At such times, the CEO must be honest with himself about the potential difficulties at hand. When a leader goes into public denial, two things become apparent—the problems he's denying are far from being fixed, and the depth of the problems that have become known is probably dwarfed by those that haven't. A CEO who thinks he can put the genie back in the bottle when this begins to happen is probably headed for the door.

The purpose of crisis management is to make sure you'll still be in business when the crisis is over. Crisis management is management in a fishbowl. Therefore, it offers extraordinary opportunities to demonstrate competence, skill, and ethics under an unnatural degree of scrutiny. The beginning of true communication may be the first moment the CEO starts to exert control over a crisis.

Own the Story

Capturing the story is key. This is a principle that politicians often understand better than business executives. In an extreme case, New York mayor Rudolph Giuliani's now-legendary performance in the weeks after September 11, 2001, showed how an astute executive could answer not only the public's desire for information, but also its need to see intelligence and responsibility applied to the management of a crisis.

A company under siege has a brief period in which to act before the great external opinion machine—media, blogs, and activists—has a chance to roll against it. The moment in which opportunity presents itself has been called the "golden hour." It is that fleeting moment just after a crisis occurs, and before the media can weave its own narrative, when the CEO and his management team have the chance to present themselves as the solution.

The best crisis-communications practice requires that management immediately come clean with the public about what has occurred. Next, it must openly recognize its own responsibility. Then it must say what it's going to do about it.

If the CEO doesn't take these actions immediately, and if the public receives the news from other sources, the company's communications become reactive and defensive. People remember where they heard the story first, so management loses the authority it would have enjoyed from taking the initiative. If the market and the public receive the news directly from the CEO, then the company has the chance to describe its action plan as part of the original story and express whatever emotions may be appropriate, including empathy for victims. This golden hour presents the company with its one opportunity to define the terms of the story before the air becomes crowded with voices that may be highly selective in the information they convey—and may, in fact, be pursuing their own agendas.

Earlier we discussed the communications of convergence, the process through which management, by engaging stakeholders, builds the opportunity to help establish the terms under which they discuss its affairs. A crisis offers the same kind of opening, except a process that may otherwise involve years is compressed into a very short period. It is a time when all the training and preparation—and, in fact, the leadership team's true character—emerge for all to see. At times, it even presents the possibility of raising the opinion of the company above where it had been before the crisis occurred. This was the result for Johnson & Johnson's reputation after the Tylenol contamination tragedy in the early 1980s. The company's ultimate contribution was substantial; it changed forever the way we open a bottle of medicine.

A crisis only becomes a crisis when it begins to damage people or the things they care about. When people see or feel loss, they become emotional, and a CEO's communication in a crisis must also contain an emotional component—not just facts. Emotional positioning can prove critical to the ultimate result for the simple reason that the world needs to hear that you're sorry, whether you're a celebrity who's been caught in a faux pas or an oil company that's just dumped a tanker load of crude into a pristine wilderness. The world wants to hear about the pain you feel, your regret. It wants to believe you're sick to your stomach for what has occurred. Much of the antagonism toward Exxon in the wake of the Alaska disaster was associated with the general impression that the company didn't care. And if it didn't care, then the oil spill must have been a result of its not caring. Its steps toward remediation would then, almost by definition, be inadequate. As I pointed out earlier, Exxon's mistake lay in failing to dramatize its concern before opinions formed against it.

Planning for Your Next Crisis

Any company with public shareholders, or debt, or suppliers who offer payment terms, or employees whose morale and loyalty are important to the smooth running of the organization, requires a standing crisis-management plan. The plan has two indispensable components—a permanent crisis-training program for executives, and a crisis management handbook with clear protocols covering responsibilities and communications in difficult times.

Through the permanent training program—and "permanent" means crisis or no crisis—executives learn how best to communicate with one another in circumstances when information may be sketchy, fast breaking, and unverifiable. Role-playing through varied scenarios can bring them invaluable experience in assuming authority in sensitive situations.

The company's crisis management handbook must derive from extended planning and consultations, both within the company and among outside experts. It details the preassigned role of each participant in the company's crisis-response system. Every responsible executive has a dedicated phone and e-mail network to be activated at the moment of crisis. The response sequence generally begins with a conference in which the crisis team sets strategy. Then the individual players go into action. The media relations director calls the newspapers; the general counsel calls the regulators; and the investor relations director, having discussed strategy with the CFO, calls analysts and shareholders.

Naming the company spokesperson is the most straightforward piece of crisis-response preparation. That's because the spokesperson can only be the CEO. People don't want to hear from the PR director or the head of media relations. Responsibility must have a face and a voice, and the only person capable of initiating the restoration of faith is the one whose orders can mobilize the company's resources. The CEO must come to work every day ready to play this role.

Respond or Sink: Five Companies Who Looked Fate in the Eye

When a company encounters a crisis—regardless of its nature or cause—management must realize that the dice are in the air. The presence of a crisis means that normal processes have been disrupted. The course of events, and the effects of unforeseen entrants into the conversation as stakeholders assert rights, are as unpredictable as the fall of the dice. The following stories trace five corporate crises, each with its own path to resolution and its own highly specific result.

Huntingdon Life Sciences

Huntingdon Life Sciences was a British contract research company that performed preclinical drug trials on animals—an essential phase in assessing drugs for human use. Its customers included most of the top 50 pharmaceutical companies in the world. In the late 1990s, Huntingdon was the only such company quoted on both the New York and London stock exchanges. Government regulators and clients rigorously monitored its procedures.

Huntingdon had just broken annual revenue records and issued a rights offering that was twice oversubscribed when, in March 1997, a news crew gained entrance to one of its facilities and filmed what appeared to be abuse of a dog. A program that reached British television screens called *It's a Dog's Life* appeared to show lab workers punching a beagle. They also seemed to falsify data.

Outrage was immediate and massive. Calls of indignation swamped the company's switchboard. Crowds of activists appeared outside its gates calling the company murderers. Some of them followed employees home. They burned employees' cars. They entered their homes. They attacked companies who did Huntingdon's laundry and drove its buses, as well as the neighborhood branch banks of its big lenders.

CEO Christopher Cliffe apologized for the misconduct shown on the program, but he insisted that, despite activists' claims, no systematic mistreatment of animals had occurred at Huntingdon. He also carried out an investigation that, he said, disproved any notion that there was general falsifying of data.

In the face of overflowing public outrage, however, Huntingdon faced abandonment by its customers, banks, investors, industry associations, regulators, and the politicians whose support had helped the company play a significant role in maintaining Britain's status as a center of medical research. Many of these groups not only deserted the company, but they condemned it in the press. The universal rejection and consequent decline in business Huntingdon suffered was sudden, extreme, and shocking. The London and New York stock exchanges delisted its shares.

In an extended essay published four years later, Cliffe described in articulate detail the experience of watching his company disintegrate around him. He conceded that the outrages *It's a Dog's Life* showed were real, but he severely faulted the media for failing to solicit his comments before reacting publicly to what they'd seen on the videotape. He described his own disbelief as all the support his company had enjoyed evaporated. He watched many of his key employees depart out of fear for their safety and a diminished view of the company's prospects.

The company moved its operations to the U.S. in an effort to keep its business going against the poisonous atmosphere in Britain. It remained there for several years before managing to reemerge as an international concern with geographically diverse operations. Eventually it managed to return to Britain.

The remarkable characteristic of Cliffe's account of the disaster is his passivity. He condemns the press for not asking the company's viewpoint. He castigates the major industry association for decertifying the company without a hearing, shortly after the association had thanked Huntingdon for its support. He details the betrayals of politicians. But, while railing against the clear injustice of his situation, nowhere does Cliffe describe an attempt to interject the company's viewpoint into the public discussion.

While clearly an intelligent and judicious chief executive, Cliffe appears throughout to be frozen in place by his disbelief at his situation. Only toward the end of his description does he say: "I *now* (italics mine) recommend that at the first whiff of crisis, companies should seek publicity and not secrecy. Communicate from the outset using the media. Rather than concentrate on knocking down the allegations of your accuser, promote your strategies, objectives, and achievements."

Bausch & Lomb

The ability of a company to recognize and respond to crises almost always reflects the nature of its internal culture. Companies whose weak accounting and other financial controls compel them to restate earnings, for example, are likely to be the same ones that find themselves dangerously flat-footed before a crisis. Such companies can go on for years until a single event—one that surer hands could manage—finally pushes them over the edge.

The foot-dragging incrementalism of Bausch & Lomb's response to a product defect tells the story of a company that tried to run but couldn't hide. In late 2004, Bausch & Lomb undertook a worldwide product launch of a contact lens solution called Renu with MoistureLoc. By July of the following year, reports from health professionals in Asia began to link the product with a fungal infection called *Fusarium keratitis* that could cause blindness.

In October, Hong Kong health officials advised the company of this potential link. The company didn't notify the U.S. Food and Drug Administration, as it should have, and when it had also failed to respond to the Hong Kong authorities several weeks later, Hong Kong put the company on formal notice. Two months later, the Malaysia health department started its own investigation. By February 2006, Bausch & Lomb had stopped shipments to Hong Kong and Singapore, where similar outbreaks of the infection were reported. But it left the product on the market everywhere else, even though its potential dangers had become apparent. By May

2006, the U.S. FDA finally caught up with the Asian health agencies, and only then did the company stop shipments in the U.S. and to the rest of the world.

At around the same time, Bausch & Lomb found itself the defendant in a number of class action suits. These suits alleged that B&L had withheld from investors information about the problems with its contact lens solution as well as other facts on accounting problems in its South Korean and Brazilian groups, and that executives had benefited from insider trading on this knowledge while they remained publicly silent.

The failure of Bausch & Lomb's crisis response was rooted in its culture. Its crisis communications clearly was no more advanced or thoughtful than its reporting to industry regulators or adherence to securities rules. This company, which had been in business for a century and a half and was known for its successful development of innovative products, failed to realize that there were times when maintenance of its franchise depended on transparency and responsiveness. In 2007, Bausch & Lomb remained a strong product innovator and marketer, but its share price had descended in response to its lack of transparency and no longer reflected the company's economic value. Bausch & Lomb was cheap and lost its independence in a buyout by private equity group Warburg Pincus.

Hewlett-Packard

Like the Bausch & Lomb case, Hewlett-Packard's boardroom wars of 2005–2006 show there's nothing like a crisis to reveal the true culture of a management group. Sometimes an unanticipated sequence of events entirely outside the company's playbook comes along and exposes cultural and personal traits that would have remained concealed forever had the company's experience not diverged into realms for which it was unprepared.

Early in 2005, a series of earnings disappointments highlighted chairman and CEO Carly Fiorina's remote management style, and the board's dissatisfaction with her became known to the financial media. Fiorina launched an investigation into the source of the leak, and was soon using third-party contract investigators who further subcontracted some of their work to outside informants. The board's increasing loss of confidence in Fiorina, which was unconnected to the investigation, led to her firing before it reached any conclusions.

Patricia Dunn succeeded Fiorina to the chairmanship while Mark Hurd became CEO. Yet the leaks persisted—this time revealing turmoil between Dunn and board member Thomas J. Perkins. The two had cooperated closely in managing the exit of Fiorina, but then they became virulent opponents in a roiling dispute over control of the board and, therefore, the company. Dunn felt Perkins was attempting to take control of the company from his position as head of the board's technology committee. Perkins believed Dunn's adherence to procedure was holding the company back. Their personal animosity became extreme. Interviewing Perkins on *60 Minutes*, Lesley Stahl referred to a statement in which he'd reportedly said he couldn't stand to breathe the same air as Dunn. (Perkins said he couldn't recall making the comment.) Whether he made it or not, the substance of their internal conversations continued to appear in the press, particularly the *Wall Street Journal* and CNET, an online technology news service. As Fiorina had before her, Dunn became obsessed with finding which of her colleagues was betraying these confidences, and she put the head of corporate security to work sniffing out the culprit.

The security chief hired an outside investigator who, in turn, subcontracted part of the work to a firm that engaged in "pretexting," by which its employees impersonated specific customers in calls to the accounts departments at phone companies. In this way, they obtained the phone records of a number of HP board members, as well as the records of reporters and others, enabling them to determine who was calling whom and the dates and times they were calling them. A *Wall Street Journal* reporter later learned that the investigators had obtained her phone records, had explored ways to examine her household garbage, and gathered information on her husband.

HP and its agents also explored the possibility of planting spies in the San Francisco offices of the *Wall Street Journal* and CNET. Investigators considered placing clerical and cleaning employees in the news organizations. One e-mail from none other than HP's chief ethics officer asked his manager of global investigations whether methods employed were "aboveboard." The investigations manager replied that it was probably OK because the company had done it before, to which the ethics officer replied, "I shouldn't have asked." That the ethics officer, of all people, was involved in supporting the company's efforts at subterfuge disposes of any argument that HP's compromises were confined to the boardroom. It argues instead for a systemic ethical failing among senior staff.

Eventually, the investigation identified the leaker as director George A. Keyworth II. Chairman Dunn revealed his identity to the board, which voted to request his resignation. Keyworth refused, but his longtime ally, Perkins, who had been associated with the company for more than 40 years, stood up impetuously, slammed his briefcase closed, and resigned on the spot.

Perkins went public with demands that the board reveal his announced reasons for leaving—the shady investigations that pointed to Keyworth. So, the very private wars of the HP boardroom, which Dunn and Fiorina had worked so hard to keep from the public eye, became front-page news. The next stage of Perkins' vendetta against Dunn involved the delivery of information on HP's pretexting to the SEC and the California state attorney general.

It happened that the latter official, Bill Lockyer, was running for state treasurer at the time. In a Sacramento news conference, he announced the indictment of Dunn and several others on four felony counts covering alleged wire fraud, illegal use of computer data, identity theft, and conspiracy. Dunn resigned the next day. Approximately three months later, Lockyer offered Dunn a plea bargain in which he would drop the four felony charges if she pleaded guilty to one misdemeanor. Public speculation around his reasons for offering this deal included (a) he didn't have a case, (b) he'd already won the race for state treasurer, and (c) sympathy for Dunn, who was suffering from ovarian cancer. In any event, she declined the deal and within a couple of months the judge presiding in the case dismissed the charges "in the interests of justice."

Shortly after Perkins blew the lid off HP's pretexting campaign, both Dunn and Hurd appeared before the House Committee on Energy and Commerce, Dunn to give her version of how the company had come to pursue these investigative methods, Hurd to put the pieces back together. At this he was flawless. Before the television cameras, he delivered a lesson in crisis communications. He admitted that the abuses had taken place, took responsibility for them, and declined to make excuses. He apologized to those whose privacy had been invaded and committed to telling each of them what exactly the company had done against them (the means by which the *Wall Street Journal* reporter would learn of the exposure of her phone records and possible surveillance of her garbage). Hurd also apologized to employees and stated that the investigation had contravened the company's values. ("If Bill Hewlett and David Packard were alive today, they would be appalled," he said.) And he described the measures the company would take to make sure violations of fundamental ethics would not recur.

The entire scenario offers a highly specific and valuable lesson in crisis communications because Hurd, himself, was not above the fray. He attended a meeting that specifically addressed pretexting, though HP said he was present for only part of it. During the internal crisis he specified certain board members to be investigated for leaks. He received at least one memo that outlined in detail the pretexting techniques used. So Hurd was also tainted. He survived this vulnerability because no one was out to get him. Particularly in the humble and comprehensive way he addressed the congressional committee, he succeeded in portraying himself as someone with good intentions who, in trying to manage HP to succeed against Dell, had erred in devoting too little time to how the company addressed its boardroom crisis. Hurd remains CEO at this writing, more than two years later, with his reputation intact as one of the more respected CEOs in America.

Total S.A.

In chapter 4 I discussed the criticism energy group Total S.A. of France encountered for its association with the armed forces of Myanmar (the ruling junta's name for the country of Burma). At issue had been the army's repression of local populations in construction of the Yadana Pipeline during the 1990s. Total offers an example of a company that learned crisis response on the job.

While continuing its involvement with the army (and, it goes without saying, failing to reform the army), Total began to develop social programs within Myanmar. In some villages it made contributions to health, education, economic development, and infrastructure. Although testimonies differ, it's unlikely these efforts came close to balancing the damage the company's presence had caused. Yet they offer evidence of Total's gradual move to acknowledge its social obligations.

Progress, however, can be tempered by uncontrollable events. In December 1999, an oil tanker chartered by Total broke up off France's Atlantic coast in heavy storms, spilling 15,000 tons of oil. Most of it came ashore, and it killed an estimated 120,000 birds. Management, which had been preoccupied by its simultaneous mergers with Petrofina and Elf Aquitaine, did not react with the seriousness the occasion required. It pointed out to the public that the tanker was a chartered ship that belonged to someone else, and the crew had no connection to Total. These comments would haunt the company when the press and public interpreted them as evidence of its desire to avoid responsibility. That Total eventually paid for the cleanup brought no more image improvement than did Exxon's restoration of Prince William Sound in Alaska.

Two years later, an explosion at one of Total's chemical plants in Toulouse, in the south of France, killed 30 people and injured over 2,500. Having learned from tough experience, management's response was immediate and full. The chairman flew from Paris to the site within an hour, making clear the company's pain and its empathy for the victims. The results were startling. Despite damage from the explosion, the company's surveys showed that the public didn't regard this accident as a disaster for the corporation.

Total, however, took this accident with such seriousness that for two years it suspended all nonfinancial communications with external constituencies. While it continued minimal advertising for its retail products and maintained its investor relations program, the company went into a deep silence with regard to any attempts to establish a corporate identity. When the executive committee ended this moratorium in 2003, it began with a simple message that addressed the basic functions of an energy company.

Today, Total is still involved in Myanmar, and it continues to receive criticism. The junta, its partner, is still among the most brutal on earth. And as far as one can tell, the army supporting the pipeline still forces villagers to carry its bullets and food for little or no pay. But through the moral fog that often seems to envelop the energy business, Total's management appears to have learned some important lessons. When given the chance, it has shown itself capable of acknowledging the broad impact the company has on the human life around it. If the relatives of those who died at Toulouse still fill their tanks at Total's stations, indicating their forgiveness, part of the reason would be that management has found an improved way to respond to crisis. It has become another kind of company.

Xerox

When a corporation loses the trust of its stakeholders, it's often the result of a failing in one part of the business. Though the problem may be confined to a single discipline, the loss of trust takes in the entire organization. When the seal of trust is broken, no one knows how far within the company the problem extends, so the entire organization becomes the problem. Where trust is concerned, appearances are everything.

When Anne Mulcahy became CEO of Xerox in 2001, she knew she might be presiding over the demise of one of the great American corporate names. Xerox had developed a unique brand by pioneering technologies that changed the world. But now it carried an enormous debt and, at the same time, had shown a steadily deteriorating financial performance. It had just restated the last three years of its financial statements, and six of its former executives, including two CEOs, faced SEC charges for fraud over their method of booking revenue.

As accounting frauds go, it wasn't the worst. Management hadn't made up revenue; they only accelerated its recognition, taking a disproportionate share of the revenue from extended-term service contracts when the contracts were signed, rather than as they earned the revenue over time. By seizing revenue from the future, they made their current performance look better than it was, which improved their compensation. But as usually happens when companies begin to stretch ethical rules, a first instance necessitated a second. At Xerox, the need for rule bending accelerated as succeeding quarters and years arrived with their revenue already declared.

Exposure of accounting improprieties, as mild as they may have seemed, hurt Xerox's business profoundly. Its suppliers, who had generally accepted payment for components over extended periods of time, and banks, who had financed the company, couldn't be sure whether they'd seen all the problems, or if what they'd seen was only the tip of an iceberg. In addition, harshly adverse stories began to appear in popular business magazines.

Like many large companies—GE, for one—much of Xerox's business depended on its ability to finance its customers' equipment purchases. Xerox's investment-grade debt rating had enabled it to obtain financing from banks at interest rates lower than those it charged customers. This not only made it easier for customers to buy, but it helped the company price its products more competitively. Now Moody's downgraded Xerox's debt to junk, and perceptions of the company's risk increased. Banks ceased lending at low rates, and the company found itself borrowing at higher rates than it was lending. It therefore had to go to its customers and raise prices. At the same time suppliers, who shared the banks' loss of confidence in Xerox, grew concerned about its ability to meet its obligations. They not only stopped accepting deferred payment for parts and other supplies, but some demanded payment in advance. No banker, and no finance manager at a supplier, was going to risk the personal exposure of advancing favorable credit to a company whose accounting was improper in any degree. These events turned Xerox's business model on its head.

If the former executives' actions fell outside the norms of their time, it wasn't by much. It's likely they believed their revenue recognition, while aggressive, fell within the norms of standard business practice. It was, after all, an era when investors demanded that their managements meet analysts' quarterly earnings expectations at all costs.

While the former executives prepared to fight the charges, the employees underwent a profound identity crisis. Working for Xerox had always provided them with a source of pride. Its excellence as both a corporate and a consumer brand had become part of their own identity. Now both were broken.

Mulcahy began her efforts by going public with a candid view of the company's challenges. She declared to employees and to Wall Street that Xerox lacked a viable business model. It also lacked the discipline to compete in its industry. One thing the company had to do was rid itself of the notion that it could run new businesses off older ones that had already established profitability. It had to narrow its ideas of markets where it could compete. And, on top of it all, Xerox no longer had the borrowing power to finance purchases of needed materials.

The first thing Xerox would have to do with its investors was prove that it could survive. To do that, it had to generate cash. And it had to formulate a convincing business model in which Wall Street could see future profitability.

Mulcahy spent much of her first 90 days traveling to Xerox offices and listening to anyone who cared to offer a perspective. She knew that prior efforts to reorganize the company had failed because management had designed them without understanding the reality on the ground. "You can never depend on filtering information up through the company," she said. "You have to talk to frontline employees."

She began to identify the decisions she would have to make: Which businesses should be divested? Which should she simply shut down? How many employees should retire early, and how many should she lay off? Of the businesses that remained, how should she restructure each? Which groups should she consolidate? And how could she reduce manufacturing expenses?

Mulcahy told her team that the company had to speed up new-product development and make better use of its research center. Despite severe cost reductions, she never cut a dime of R&D investment. Even during its worst times, Xerox pursued a research model that generated important intellectual property. But while new ideas were plentiful, the company only had the capacity to leverage intellectual property that fit its current core business. It had to close the gap between its ability to come up with new ideas and its ability to put them to work.

To turn her diverse resources into an integrated financial engine, Mulcahy had to create a new kind of accountability. She said that when she'd taken her post, "I had to bring in ten people to make a business decision." Her solution was to reorganize financial reporting so that profit-and-loss statements were geographically based. This may have seemed an old-fashioned way of doing things, but it offered clarity. "I took out a lot of layers and think it was instrumental in improving performance."

One path Mulcahy used to show employees that Xerox had a new way of doing business was a dramatic strengthening of its ethics and compliance operation. This provided one important way of demonstrating that things would be different now. While the company had had a strong code of conduct, Mulcahy now directed the ethics and compliance message at everyone in the organization through varied media such as glossy printed booklets and the company intranet. The officer in charge continued to repeat the message that Xerox was an ethical company. Employees learned the kinds of behavior that would be tolerated, those that would not, and how management would handle ethical violations. A representative of the ethics and compliance function sat on all strategic and operational decision-making bodies at the corporate level.

Mulcahy saw that executing solutions depended almost entirely on communication and gaining commitment from employees. "When your organization is struggling, you have to give people the sense that you know what's happening and that you have a strategy to fix it," she said later. "Beyond that, you have to tell people what they can do to help." In rising to the level of complete disclosure about the company's problems, Mulcahy requested an equivalent personal risk-taking from her employees. "I gave people a choice to make," she said. "Either roll up your sleeves and go to work, or leave Xerox." She didn't as much throw people overboard, as ask those who should to jump.

Mulcahy put a systematic internal communications strategy into action. Throughout the company, she published detailed explanations of how she planned to execute the turnaround and, in particular, how management had redesigned the business model. She announced cash-flow goals and included a frank outlook on the realignment of business sections, addressing the painful subjects of continued expense discipline and head-count reductions. She persisted in reminding employees of goals, assessed progress, and identified where they had fallen short.

Mulcahy carried out her quarterly conference calls with analysts and investors in the same spirit. She made the recovery plan transparent, and she gave a frank assessment of progress with each call.

Four years later, Xerox's debt was half of what it had been when Mulcahy took over. Accumulated expense reductions had reached $3 billion, and the company had registered 12 consecutive quarters of earnings growth. Its stock price had doubled.

Mulcahy had addressed the crisis with the only strategy that had a chance of turning the company around. First, she acknowledged there was a problem, and she had the same story for both internal and external audiences. Not only did she admit the full contours of the problem's seriousness, she taught it to employees and to the market. Then she set a clear strategy, making sure employees understood what was wrong and what they had to do to fix it. She was relentless in keeping the message and assessments of progress in the company's consciousness.

David Frishkorn, Xerox's ethics and compliance director during most of Mulcahy's tenure, says that companies who haven't been through such brushes with the precipice often exist in a state of dangerous complacency, which they fail to recognize. A diffusion of responsibility among decision makers filters down through the organization as a general assumption that somewhere, somebody is taking care of things. Frishkorn explains this state of mind as one that asks: Why would you question your coworkers or your revered leaders? Why would you question a policy that has been thought through by auditors and lawyers? Frishkorn and others with similar views often express admiration for the author Jim Collins, who popularized the notion that good is the enemy of great.

In a brilliant stroke of communication values, Mulcahy presented her view of how Xerox would look when the restructuring was complete. For internal consumption, she created a fictitious *Wall Street Journal* article dated several years in the future. "We outlined the things we hoped to accomplish as though we had already achieved them," she said later. "We included performance metrics—even quotes from Wall Street analysts. It was really our vision of what we wanted the company to become."

A good part of Mulcahy's success in accomplishing Xerox's turnaround was not only that she could see the entire arc of the transformation, but that she could communicate a vision to her staff and employees.

* * * *

A crisis, if the company grasps and executes the measures needed to survive it, can have long-term positive effects. All the companies discussed here who accepted responsibility for their own survival and acted on it became stronger. Anne Mulcahy captured this principle when she said, "My experience at Xerox has taught me that crisis is a very powerful motivator. It forces you to make choices that you probably wouldn't have made otherwise. It intensifies your focus, your competitiveness, your relentless desire to attain best-in-class status. I want to do everything I can to make sure that we don't lose that now that we're back on track."

In May 2009, Xerox announced Mulcahy's retirement as CEO. Her replacement, Ursula M. Burns, became the first African-American woman to head a Fortune 500 company.

CHAPTER 12

Strategy 7:
The Governance Imperative

Oversight, Informing the Board, Compliance

How to Judge Your Reputation Performance

Corporate directors read newspapers, and much of the concern in boardrooms today centers on efforts to reconcile disparities between what's heard outside and inside the company. Directors feel vulnerable on issues that range from accounting fraud to corporate social responsibility.

The growing sophistication of the workforce means that management is less likely to inspire its employee base toward a coherent set of principles by using words alone. The transformation of culture requires a specific set of values that management teaches, and against which it measures performance.

Most corporate value systems resemble one another. They nearly always represent some version of a list that includes integrity, emphasis on quality, accountability, personal responsibility, diversity, honoring commitments, focus on the customer, corporate citizenship, and enhancing shareholder value. An employee moving from one company to another will find at his destination more or less the same set of values he left behind.

Although the values are more or less universal, performance against those values varies widely. Why does one company excel while another falters? A management's seriousness about values, its care and expertise in communicating them, and the company's commitment to training all have a bearing on whether a set of values is alive in a company or a waste of words. And if it's the latter, does its emptiness indicate the general state of communication and candor within the company?

Boards are becoming ever more involved in running companies. The slow but growing trend toward a division of the chief executive and chairman roles gives boards a position from which they can observe the company more candidly than if the CEO doubled as chairman. The additional trend of naming lead directors who can speak for boards further increases the leverage they can exercise in forming strategy. This constitutes a significant and positive change from the rubberstamping of CEOs' programs that often prevailed in the past, when CEOs generally ran their boards. It's no longer unusual for boards to go into executive session, excusing the CEO in order to discuss his or her programs or personal performance. A board's responsibility for hiring and firing CEOs is embedded in the legal structure of the corporation, and the relationships between boards and CEOs are coming slowly to reflect that reality. Yet the new levels of responsibility and control that boards are exercising still depends on their access to information.

To carry out its duties to protect the company's reputation, any board must have the means for measuring progress and problems. Share price, one of the ultimate targets of a reputation program, is subject to so many diverse forces that it can provide a performance measure only in the medium and long term. So how do the CEO and the board assess the value of their reputation program while waiting for the market to respond? And how do they assess their vulnerability to reputation failure?

Values are meaningless unless the company achieves a clear understanding of its success in meeting its own standards. Leaders' approach to reputation assessment should be as systematic and as disciplined as their actions in building markets and selling products. Each company must develop its own methodology for clarifying its progress in building reputation.

Companies have available three tools which, when used together, can provide a comprehensive overview of their performance in supporting reputation. The first is the periodic trend report of the ethics and compliance officer. The second is a measure of the company's success in achieving conduct consistent with each of its values. We call such measures points of confirmation. The third tool is the reputation audit, an external inquiry similar to the perception study we addressed earlier.

The Ethics and Compliance Report

The ethics and compliance officer analyzes and manages the resolution of ethical problems that arrive from employees' reports, accountants, auditors, security departments, anonymous ethics hotlines, whistleblowers, and other sources. Depending on the depth of the ethics and compliance function, these can range over dozens of ethical factors, from stealing equipment and filing false expense reports to undue pressuring of customers, bypassing business reporting requirements, failure to maintain document security, use of computer systems for improper purposes, and harassment of other employees. The ethics and compliance officer tracks a specific list of ethical factors, reporting current data and extended trend lines to the board. He or she also brings to the board's attention issues of such concern as to merit prompt consideration at any time.

Points of Confirmation

The pursuit of an internal values-based program to support reputation requires that the company assess its own performance. The board, with the advice of management and outside experts if necessary, establishes specific reputational factors to be monitored. By showing the level of results the company has been able to achieve in each area, these points of confirmation reveal whether or not it is acting in accordance with its own standards.

The board derives its first point of confirmation from an examination of its own performance of investing in staff training. Do workers have sufficient grounding in the company's corporate values? Managers and the board must ask themselves, and answer, whether they offer adequate support in helping employees toward values adherence.

A second useful point of confirmation is available through the employee survey. The company can structure surveys to aggregate data on virtually any value and render a compelling indication of adherence across the company. Internal surveys can prove particularly valuable because their breadth can cancel out pockets of unrepresentative dissatisfaction. A survey covering several thousand employees that indicates a problem in one area will, on its own, confirm that the area requires attention.

Some companies use aggregated personnel performance appraisals to measure companywide values adherence. While quantifiable data is always attractive in making broad judgments, companies should also balance it with a consideration of subjective factors. Qualitative commentary is essential to individual employees' performance reviews.

Peter Drucker, the dean of all business writers, wrote: "No one has ever failed to find the facts he is looking for." In the case of the executive tasked with organizing information for the board, his or her approach must be characterized by a strong curiosity and an equally strong personal neutrality with regard to expected outcomes.

As the board gives its mandate, it must carefully consider the manner in which this person will perform his or her job. The judgments made in reporting on reputational points of confirmation will determine in large part the substance of the board's deliberations and will very likely influence the actions it takes. So this person must not only follow the board's instructions, but must share its purpose of achieving a balanced and unbiased view.

Qualitative points of confirmation on reputation might include:

- The company's success in recruiting. Is it able to attract talent among graduates or from industry peers? At positions requiring high expertise, is the net flow of talent to or from the company? Does it attract highly educated generalists who can broaden its vision of the world in ways that might lie beyond the reach of narrowly specialized individuals?
- Has the company achieved recognition as a "good actor" by NGOs? Or is it a target of negative attention? Has it become a target of complaints based on ISO Standards?
- Have executives responsible for specific areas such as corporate governance and social responsibility become recognized by outside organizations as contributors to professional thinking on their subjects? Have they published? Have they received invitations to speak at conferences?

- Aside from articles placed in the media by the company's PR resources, are the company's executives sought out by serious journalists as independent authorities on the industry, business, and financial trends, or on matters of technology or social responsibility?
- Has the company managed to remain free of shareholder resolutions criticizing it on the environment, human rights, diversity, or other issues? If shareholders have made it a target, what is its assessment of the validity of their complaints?

Press Coverage as a Point of Confirmation

Many companies attempt to monitor their coverage in the media as a means of assessing reputation performance. This is not entirely a passive domain, as they can hire media placement specialists who receive compensation based on the amount of coverage the company receives in the press.

New technologies can quantify the media coverage a company receives as well as the proportions of coverage that are positive, neutral, and negative. The creators of these technologies represent their programs as capable of identifying the features of a company that receive the most attention, and how its consideration by the media compares against competitors. Voice recognition software has come into use for the monitoring of radio and television reporting. Text recognition software does the same for print and digital sources, generally with emphasis on business and financial news outlets and blogs.

It is, of course, important that a company know when and where negative press appears so that it may respond. But media attention is a doubtful gauge of a company's reputation. No number of mentions of its diversity policy, for example, will balance the reputational damage of a chemical spill. And no company's leaders should confuse good press managed by an expert PR department with a laboriously earned reputation.

The Reputation Audit

We said earlier that one of the greatest impediments to making the business case for investment in reputation is the near impossibility of measuring its financial effect. You'll never know how much the disaster that didn't occur would have cost you. But calibration of financial effects aside, any company that considers its reputation important can measure its progress by asking stakeholders the right questions.

The reputation audit, in which an expert third party interviews diverse constituencies, delivers an external assessment of the company's reputation. The intelligence derived from such a study can inform decision-making in all spheres of the firm's activity. So when it comes time to announce decisions, financial results, or events, the reputation audit makes communication more effective by capturing nuances and complexities in the ways constituents experience the company.

Reputation audits are most valuable when their structure follows the company's core values. A company that takes this approach can use the reputation audit to establish points of confirmation for any value. If transparency is one of its values, for example, the reputation audit helps the company determine how stakeholders recognize good transparency, and what specific disclosure factors are missing when they consider transparency to be faulty. By taking its cues from what its audience says, the company can enhance its own ability to assess whether its transparency matches its goal. When the points of confirmation technique and the reputation audit work together in showing the company's performance as a rising line, the board can demonstrate with confidence that it's providing maximum protection for its franchise.

Off the Rails: When to Consider an Internal Investigation

There are times when no amount of staff training is enough to protect a company from ethical misconduct within its ranks. In large and medium-sized firms it's virtually inevitable that, over time, someone among a population of thousands will put the company's reputation at risk. Wrongdoing is made to be hidden, and although a board and management may become aware that a violation has occurred, its extent and the identities of all individuals involved often remain concealed.

Did members of a sales staff collude with competitors to align prices? Did a business division recognize revenue from contracts that hadn't been legally concluded? Did one of the businesses pay bribes to compete with foreign companies who functioned under different sets of laws? Regardless of who in its ranks has committed the unwanted acts, the company is responsible. And leadership's first challenge is to find out what exactly happened.

One of the first people to whom a company will turn for advice is its corporate counsel. With his or her guidance, leaders may ask an internal security group to carry out an investigation. External lawyers, forensic accountants, and auditors may also become involved.

While determining what happened is the first task, much depends on the choices management makes in handling the investigation. Legal counsel will be critical in deciding whether it's a matter for referral to government regulators or legal enforcement. If it is, at what point should the company make such disclosure? Should it complete its own meticulous investigation and turn a finished set of results over to the government? After all, you have to know what the crime is before you can confess it. In any case, an internal investigation and the disclosure of its results must be honest, complete, and swift. Anything else will seriously compound the problem.

The ability to present authorities with evidence of a rigorous inquiry may well affect penalties the company faces, both in terms of civil fines and criminal prosecutions. We saw earlier how the use of Federal Sentencing Guidelines in training helps companies understand how strong controls that pre-exist violations, and cooperation with the government if those controls should fail, can mitigate punishment. Both the board and management must bear such principles in mind at all times, but particularly in the moment misconduct comes to light. They should know that everything rides on their candid response to ethical violations, no matter who in the organization has committed them. And the implementation of remedial measures to reduce the chance of their recurring will heighten their opportunities to have reasonable conversations with the government at times when their careers may be on the line.

ORIGINAL TERMS IN THIS BOOK

communications of convergence Engaging an adversary without preconditions so that a mutual language develops around common issues. Enables a company to influence terms of the public dialogue about itself.

competence tribe / power tribe A distinction between two opposing approaches to work that often remains hidden until a crisis occurs. The outcome of the conflict between the two tribes determines not only how the crisis is resolved, but often the group's survival.

demand-driven communications Communication with stakeholders informed by an understanding of their concerns, as opposed to communication based on a story management may have grown accustomed to telling.

gapped communication Communication that fails to consider the listener's frame of reference, so the message is never heard as intended. Can also be called "lazy" communications. Sometimes results from weak commitment to transparency.

narrative-based research Inquiry into attitudes of investors and other stakeholders that explores the entire range of their opinions, regardless of the questioner's expectations. Requires unrestricted conversation that goes beyond a prepared questionnaire.

open perception study Expands the traditional, questionnaire-limited perception study by applying narrative-based techniques. Gives advance notice of themes that will appear in the public dialogue about a company in the future.

points of confirmation Objective performance hurdles that confirm the success or failure of a strategy. They allow a company to judge results of even the most subjective programs associated with reputation development.

structural corruption A condition, generally within an industry, in which standard operating procedure is unethical, illegal, or both. Often imposes irresolvable choices between the pursuit of acceptable conduct and competitiveness.

value paradox The distinction between management's ideas of how to create value in a company and those held by outside investors whose decisions determine the stock price—and therefore a large part of management's destiny.

vertical communications / democratic communications Terms that describe an attitude toward communication that gives attention to ideas and observations regardless of the level in the company hierarchy where they originate. A company with such an attitude solicits intellectual contribution from all its parts.

NOTES

2 "While no one knew the exact figure . . . perhaps by a factor of ten": John Lanchester, "Melting into Air," in *The New Yorker*, November 10, 2008. http://www.newyorker.com/arts/critics/atlarge/2008/11/10/081110crat_atlarge_lanchester. See also: Gillian Tett and Aline van Duyn, "Let the battle commence," in *The Financial Times*, May 20, 2009, page 7. http://www.ft.com/cms/s/0/d4a7adfc-44a5-11de-82d6-00144feabdc0.html

3 "many banks raised interest rates on cardholders who were still paying their bills": Alexis Leonidas, "Punctual Payers Face Higher Rates from Card Companies," at Bloomberg.com, February 13, 2009. http://www.bloomberg.com/apps/news?pid=20601213&sid=aqprj.W.xtY0&refer=home

3 "President Obama's new CIA director testified": Nelson D. Schwartz, "Job Losses Pose a Threat to Stability Worldwide," in *The New York Times*, February 14, 2009. http://www.nytimes.com/2009/02/15/business/15global.html?ref=business

4 "Contemporary life had moved us light years from the skills that would enable us to survive in tough circumstances": Stetson Kennedy, Remarks made at Memorial Program for Studs Terkel, Cooper Union, New York City. December 7, 2008. Available at http://www.c-spanarchives.org/library/includes/templates/library/flash_popup.php?pID=282901-1&clipStart=&clipStop=. Approximately 01:21:45.

8 "the concept of the meme": Richard Dawkins, *The Selfish Gene* (Oxford University Press, 1976 paperback edition), p. 192.

25 Monsanto. The following sources were useful in writing the Monsanto section: David Barboza, "Questions Seen on Seed Prices set in the 90's," in *The New York Times*, January 6, 2004. Carina Hum and Mope Ogunsulire, "Monsanto's Genetically Modified Organisms: The Battle for Hearts and Shopping Aisles," Case Study, *International Institute for Management Development*, Lausanne, Switzerland. 2001. Greenpeace Press Release: "Developing World Rejects Monsanto's Claims to Solve Hunger," August, 1 1998. Greenpeace Press Release: "Leaked Document form Monsanto Reveals 'Collapse of Public Support for Genetically Engineered Foods,'" November 18 1998. Innovest Strategic Value Advisors: *Monsanto Investor*

Risk Report, April, 2003. John Mason, "GM Crops Groups Accused of 'Trying to Lie,'" in *The Financial Times,* October 14, 2003. Henry I. Miller, "Global Food Fight," Hoover Digest 2000 No. 1. *The Hoover Institution,* Stanford University. 2000. Raphael Minder, "EU Poised to Allow Sale of GM Maize," in *The Financial Times,* April 26, 2004. Raphael Minder, "Brussels Set to Endorse Modified Seed," in *The Financial Times,* September 8, 2004. Michael Specter, "The Pharmageddon Riddle," in *The New Yorker Magazine;* April 10, 2000.

35 "immense pay packages": Michael Brush, "The 5 Richest Payoffs for Fired CEOs," on MSN Money, November 28, 2007. http://articles.moneycentral. msn.com/Investing/CompanyFocus/The5RichestPayoffsForFiredCEOs.aspx

35 "sick with stress . . . brought on himself": David Streitfeld and Gretchen Morgenson, "Building Flawed American Dreams," in *The New York Times,* October 18, 2008. http://www.nytimes.com/2008/10/19/ business/19cisneros.html.

35–36 "Stan O'Neil . . . largest quarterly loss ever" "The 101 Dumbest Moments in Business," in *Fortune Magazine* / CNN Money.com, January 16, 2008. http://money.cnn.com/galleries/2007/fortune/0712/gallery.101_dumbest.fortune/5.html

36 "Ivanov said years later": *Times* (London) obituary: John Profumo on TimesOnline, March 10, 2006. http://www.timesonline.co.uk/tol/news/ uk/article739657.ece

37 "His son wrote": David Profumo, *Bringing the House Down* (John Murray, 2006). Excerpted at Telegraph.co.uk, June 9, 2006. http://www.telegraph. co.uk/arts/main.jhtml?xml=/arts/2006/09/06/ftprofumo06.xml&page=1

41 "a survey conducted among more than 100 companies": Allison Maitland, "Reputation: You Only Know Its Worth When It Lies in Tatters," *Financial Times,* March 31, 2003. http://search.ft.com/search/article.html?id=0 30331000991&query=Reputation&vsc_appId=totalSearch&state=Form

47 "Not only was this practice prevalent . . . and Marsh convinced them to do so": Matthew Goldstein, "Spitzer Charges Marsh & McLennan in Insurance Racket," The Street.com, October 15, 2004. http://www.thestreet. com/story/10187969/1/spitzer-charges-marsh-mclennan-in-insurance-racket.html

48 "Under an agreement . . . 'unlawful' and 'shameful' conduct": Terence Neilan, "Marsh to Pay $850 Million to Settle Charges by Spitzer," in *The New York Times,* January 31, 2005. http://www.nytimes.com/2005/01/31/business/ 31cnd-insu.html?scp=1&sq=Marsh%20to%20Pay%20%24850%20 Million%20to%20Settle%20Charges%20by%20Spitzer&st=cse

48 "$108.5 million in restitution to disadvantaged investors" "forfeited over

$3 billion": John Hechinger, "Putnam May Owe $100 Million," in *The Wall Street Journal*, February 2, 2005. Page C1.

48 "$110 million in fines": Ellen Kelleher, "Putnam Adds $83.5 Million to Reimburse Clients," in *Financial Times*, March 4, 2005. http://www.ft.com/cms/s/ec23d1a6-8c51-11d9-a895-00000e2511c8.html

48 "Then, in March 2005 . . . total $204 billion under management": John Hechinger, ibid.

50 "Marsh's corporate counsel": Corporate counsel was William L. Rosoff. *Wall Street Journal* article of October 18, 2004, quoted in Joseph Belth, The Insurance Forum, Vol. 32, No. 1, January 2005, p. 142.

50 "In 2005, average CEO pay was up 298 percent over the prior ten years, the average worker's only 4.3 percent": Ben Popken, "CEO Pay up 298%, Average Worker's? 4.3% (1995–2005)," on The Consumerist, April 9, 2007. http://consumerist.com/consumer/executive-pay/ceo-pay-up-298-average-workers-43-1995+2005-250838.php

51 "Average CEO pay was 821 times the minimum wage": Lawrence Mishel, "CEO–Minimum Wage Raio Soars," The Economic Policy Institute, June 27, 2006. http://www.epi.org/economic_snapshots/entry/webfeatures_snapshots_20060627/

51 "a report to a congressional committee": "Executive Pay: Conflicts of Interest among Compensation Consultants," U.S. House of Representatives, Committee on Oversight and Government Reform, prepared for Chairman Henry A. Waxman, December 2007, page i. http://oversight.house.gov/documents/20071205100928.pdf

56 "'At present . . . not favorable'": Alex Berenson, Gardiner Harris, Barry Meier, and Andrew Pollack, "Dangerous Data—Retracing a Medical Trail; Despite Warnings, Drug Giant Took Long Path to Vioxx Recall," in *The New York Times*, November 14, 2004. http://query.nytimes.com/gst/fullpage.html?res=9B00E0DE143FF937A25752C1A9629C8B63

68–69 "Rather interestingly . . . didn't match up": Nelson D: Schwartz, "European Banks Tally Losses Linked to Fraud," *The New York Times*, December 17, 2008. http://www.nytimes.com/2008/12/17/business/worldbusiness/17exposure.html?scp=1&sq=European%20Banks%20Tally%20Losses%20Linked%20to%20Fraud&st=cse

69 "'The call came . . . smarter than the others'": Robert Chew, "How I Got Screwed by Bernie Madoff," on Time.com, December 15, 2008. http://www.time.com/time/business/article/0,8599,1866398,00.html

69 "In 2004 . . . to settle SEC complaints": Stephen Taub, "SEC Settles with Five Specialist Firms," on CFO.com, March 31, 2004. http://www.cfo.com/article.cfm/3012969/c_3042540?f=TodayInFinance_Inside

69 "Union Bancaire Privée": Henny Sender, "Madoff Had 'Perceived Edge' in the Markets," in *Financial Times*, December 22, 2008. http://www.ft.com/cms/s/0/4851399e-cfcb-11dd-abf9-000077b07658.html

73 "today it publishes the names and addresses of all its suppliers worldwide": Nike's lists of active factories is accessible at http://www.nikebiz.com/responsibility/workers_and_factories.html#active_factories

75 "'All control systems and the entire organization were geared to make such behavior possible'": Daniel Schaefer, "Ex-Siemens Executive Guilty of Breach of Trust," in *Financial Times*, July 28, 2008. http://www.ft.com/cms/s/0/0d4eb04c-5c8f-11dd-8d38-000077b07658.html

75 " 'There was a cultural acceptance that this was the way to do business around the world, and we have to change that'": Mike Esterl, "Siemens Amnesty Plan Assists Bribery Probe," in *The Wall Street Journal*, March 5, 2008. http://online.wsj.com/article/SB120465805725710921.html

75 "'soldiers for Siemens'": Richard Milne, "Fresh Twist in Siemens Bribery Case," in *Financial Times*, April 21, 2008. http://www.ft.com/cms/s/0/83899e0c-0ef1-11dd-9646-0000779fd2ac.html

75–76 "'I am deeply worried . . . nobody dares to decide anything'": Daniel Schäfer, "Siemens Enters Crunch Week in Bribery Scandal," in *Financial Times*, July 27, 2008. http://www.ft.com/cms/s/0/212c8876-5bf1-11dd-9e99-000077b07658.html

76 "at one meeting in Mexico an employee stood up and simply asked who this American guy was": Carter Dougherty, "The Sheriff at Siemens, at Work Under the Justice Dept.'s Watchful Eye," in *The New York Times*, October 7, 2008. http://www.nytimes.com/2008/10/07/business/07siemens.html?ref=business

76 "'schmiergeld" or 'grease money'": Nelson D. Schwartz and Lowell Bergman, "Payload: Taking Aim at Corporate Bribery," in *The New York Times*, November 25, 2007. http://www.nytimes.com/2007/11/25/business/25bae.html?ref=business&pagewanted=all

77 "$44 million fine in 2007": Schwartz and Bergman, ibid.

77 "The House of Lords took the same action against attempts to re-open the probe in mid-2008": Sylvia Pfeifer, "BAE Chief Warns of Fraud Probe Fall-out," in *Financial Times*, August 1, 2008. http://www.ft.com/cms/s/0/edf464a6-5ffb-11dd-805e-000077b07658.html

77–78 "The relationship between BAE and the Saudis, which had seen the sale of $80 billion in planes and weapons": Schwartz and Bergman, ibid.

78 "one of the biggest challenges confronting his successor . . . if the company's legal difficulties in the U.S. became too great": Pfeiffer, ibid.

80 "privatization of compliance": My thanks to Jeff Gracer for this term.

84 "Management has a self-interest in a healthy society, even though the cause of society's sickness is none of management's making'": Peter F. Drucker, *Management, Tasks, Responsibilities, Practices* (1974); excerpted in *The Essential Drucker* (New York: CollinsBusiness, 2005), p. 52.

84 "a terror campaign against the local population": Amnesty International: http://www.amnestyusa.org/justearth/indonesia.pdf

100 "describes the process": For an excellent description of Shell's scenario planning in the 1970s, see Peter Schwartz, *The Art of the Long View* (New York: Doubleday, 1991).

116 "'Presenting multiple versions of the same concept can be an extremely powerful way to change someone's mind'": Howard Gardner, *Changing Minds* (Boston: Harvard Business School Press, 2004), p. 10.

121 "a rock-throwing protest outside": Fernando Henrique Cardoso, *The Accidental President of Brazil* (New York: Public Affairs, 2006), p. 233.

122 "the number of cell phones": Ibid.

128 "the cause of the price rise": It appeared later that some of the volatility had also been due to financial speculation in energy futures.

134 "'people from the inside . . . retained the objectivity of an outsider'": Joseph Bower quoted by Stefan Stern, "Look Inside for the Best Outside Candidate," in *Financial Times*, November 15, 2007. http://www.ft.com/cms/s/0/16b175b0-931e-11dc-ad39-0000779fd2ac.html

137 "For employees, it confirmed beyond any doubt that their environment was changing": Perspective on Prince's campaign to restore Citi's reputation and its effect on attitudes within the organization from author interview with Michael Schlein.

139 "selection can also occur at the level of the group . . . sacrificing yourself for the group and be an individual survival trait": Nicholas Wade, "Taking a Cue From Ants on Evolution of Humans," in *The New York Times*, July 15, 2008. http://www.nytimes.com/2008/07/15/science/15wils.html?em&ex=1216267200&en=0c430acc141c196e&ei=5087%0A

145 "a list of core values": http://www.chiquita.com/CorporateCommitment/CoreValues.aspx

147 "'Healthy compliance . . . what the right thing to do is'": Siemens General Counsel Peter Y. Solmssen quoted by Carter Dougherty, ibid. http://www.nytimes.com/2008/10/07/business/07siemens.html?ref=business

150 "'[SocGen] has claimed . . . no economic significance'": Scherazade Daneschkhu and Ben Hall, "Kerviel Case Raises Difference Between Virtual and Fake Trades" in *Financial Times*, June 11, 2008. http://www.ft.com/cms/s/0/9e5415e6-3750-11dd-bc1c-0000779fd2ac.html

178 "taxpayers would almost inevitably be forced to cover the deficit to keep

the institution from sinking": Charles Duhigg, "At Freddie Mac, Chief Discarded Warning Signs," in *The New York Times*, August 5, 2008. http://www.nytimes.com/2008/08/05/business/05freddie.html?em

178–179 "'If I had better foresight . . . I would never have taken this job in the first place'": Duhigg, ibid.

179 "it had found nearly $2.3 million to spend on lobbying": Associated Press, "Freddie Mac spent nearly $2.3M lobbying in 2Q," on Forbes. com, August 12, 2008. http://www.forbes.com/feeds/ap/2008/08/12/ap5314988.html

179 "'I've had four other jobs . . . to save my reputation'": Duhigg, ibid.

188 "The Holder Memorandum": U.S. Department of Justice Memorandum, "Bringing Criminal Charges Against Corporations," June 16, 1999. http://www.usdoj.gov/criminal/fraud/docs/reports/1999/chargingcorps.html

188 "Thompson Memorandum": U.S. Department of Justice Memorandum, "Principles of Federal Prosecution of Business Organizations,' January 20, 2003. http://www.usdoj.gov/dag/cftf/corporate_guidelines.htm

198 "'shocked disbelief,' 'the self-interest of lending institutions to protect shareholder's equity'": Alan Greenspan, prepared text of statement to House Committee on Government Oversight and Reform, October 23, 2008. http://oversight.house.gov/documents/20081023100438.pdf.

204 Coca-Cola leader's op-ed piece: Neville Isdell, "We Help Darfur but Do Not Harm the Olympics," in *Financial Times*, April 18, 2008. http://www.ft.com/cms/s/0/18e084dc-0ce2-11dd-86df-0000779fd2ac.html

205 "'It's the 3 to 4 percent who try to influence the 96 percent by utilizing a symbol'": Jonathan Birchall, "Final Encore for a Man of the People," in *Financial Times*, June 8, 2008. http://www.ft.com/cms/s/0/1abcb2e8-33e9-11dd-869b-0000779fd2ac.html

206 "Florida Power & Light had deceived its customers under a false promise of helping a cause in which they believed": Investor Relations Newsletter, September 2008, citing, John Dorschner, "State Shutters 'Green' Program," in *Miami Herald*, July 30, 2008.

208 "Representative Brad Sherman asked the three to indicate by a show of hands . . . None responded": Daniel Dombey, "Prospect of Car Industry Aid 'Remote' After Corporate Jets Blunder," in *Financial Times*, November 20, 2008. http://www.ft.com/cms/s/0/ebe0cc82-b6a3-11dd-89dd-0000779fd18c.html.

208 "'There's a delicious irony . . . downgraded to first class or jet-pooled to get here?'": Ibid.

209 "'I don't trust the car companies' leadership . . . lose their jobs'": Daniel Dombey and Bernard Simon, "Ford Does Not Expect Liquidity Crisis," in

Financial Times, December 5, 2008. http://www.ft.com/cms/s/0/cf21bb34-c26e-11dd-a350-000077b07658.html

213 "a strong case for the noncharismatic CEO as a long-term performer": Jim Collins, *Good to Great* (New York: HarperCollins, 2001), p. 72.

217 "'provide independent oversight of the chief executive and management team'": Peter O'Neill and Neva Rockefeller Goodwin, "ExxonMobil Needs an Independent Chair," in *Financial Times*, May 21, 2008. http://www.ft.com/cms/s/0/3d82dbb2-2733-11dd-b7cb-000077b07658.html

217 "'To abandon that would not be wise'": Sheila McNulty, "Exxon Is Urged to Find New Paths," in *Financial Times*, May 1, 2008. http://www.ft.com/cms/s/45f3b3f6-1717-11dd-bbfc-0000779fd2ac.html

218 "'We don't talk a lot . . . That's our culture'": Sheila McNulty, "Shareholders Reject Split-role Calls at Exxon," in *Financial Times*, May 28, 2008. http://www.ft.com/cms/s/0/653cf2bc-2cee-11dd-88c6-000077b07658.html

218 "offered further evidence that companies respond to well-supported resolutions even when they fail": Ceres Press Release, "Investors Achieve Major Company Commitments on Climate Change," August 20, 2008. http://www.ceres.org/NETCOMMUNITY/Page.aspx?pid=928&srcid=705

219 "two major homebuilders agreed to greater transparency on energy-efficient construction": Jonathan Birchall, "Groups face climate pressure," *Financial Times*, August 21, 2008, page 13. http://www.ft.com/cms/s/0/8ddcc100-6f17-11dd-a80a-0000779fd18c.html?nclick_check=1

220 "an essay called 'The Moral Instinct'": Steven Pinker, "The Moral Instinct," in *The New York Times Magazine*, Jan. 13, 2008. http://www.nytimes.com/2008/01/13/magazine/13Psychology-t.html?em&ex=1200373200&en=180615d155579d74&ei=5087%0A

244 "an essential phase in assessing drugs for human use.": "A Controversial Laboratory," on BBC News online, January 18, 2001. http://news.bbc.co.uk/2/hi/uk_news/1123837.stm

244 "issued a rights offering that was twice oversubscribed": Christopher Cliffe, "Memoirs of an Overnight Pariah—Part 1," in *Financial Times*, December 27, 2001.

248 "he couldn't recall making the comment.: Lesley Stahl referred to a statement in which Perkins reportedly said he couldn't stand to breathe the same air as Dunn": CBS News, *60 Minutes*, "Tom Perkins: The Captain of Capitalism." Interview aired June 1, 2007. http://www.cbsnews.com/stories/2007/11/01/60minutes/main3442193.shtml

248–249 "A *Wall Street Journal* reporter later learned . . . gathered information on her husband": Pui-wing Tam, "A Reporter's Story: How H-P

Kept Tabs on Me for a Year," in *The Wall Street Journal*, October 19, 2006. http://online.wsj.com/public/article/SB116122600055097332-SMe_yumWlNpm_GtWJafxk__NJ5Y_20071019.html

249 "HP and its agents . . . in the news organizations": Damon Darlin and Kurt Eichenwald, "HP Said to Have Studied Infiltrating Newsrooms," in *The New York Times*, September 20, 2006. http://www.nytimes.com/2006/09/20/technology/20hewlett.html?hp&ex=1158811200&en=9ad88b9b669142c2&ei=5094&partner=homepage

249 "'I shouldn't have asked'": Darlin and Eichenwald, ibid.

249 "the very private wars . . . became front-page news": Michael Kanellos, "Lawyer for Former HP Chairman Vows Revenge on Perkins," on CNET News, February 28, 2007. http://news.cnet.com/Lawyer-for-former-HP-chairman-vows-revenge-on-Perkins/2100-1014_3-6163179.html?tag=mncol

252 "When the executive committee ended this moratorium . . . that addressed the basic functions of an energy company": Gregory S. Miller, Vincent Dessain, and Anders Sjoman, Harvard Business School Case Study: "Investor Relations at Total," August 18, 2006.

252 Xerox: David Frischkorn, chief ethics and compliance officer at Xerox, provided indispensable help in preparing the section on Xerox.

252 "'You have to talk to frontline employees.'" "The Cow in the Ditch: How Anne Mulcahy Rescued Xerox, Knowledge@Wharton Business Series, November 16, 2005. http://knowledge.wharton.upenn.edu/article.cfm?articleid=1318.

255 "'I had to bring in ten people to make a business decision'": Ibid.

255 "'I took out a lot of layers and think it was instrumental in improving performance'": Ibid.

256 "'I gave people a choice to . . . go to work, or leave Xerox'": Lisa Vollmer, "Mulcahy Took a No-Nonsense Approach to Turn Xerox Around," in Stanford GBS News, December 2004. http://www.gsb.stanford.edu/news/headlines/vftt_mulcahy.shtml.

257–258 "'We outlined the things we hoped to accomplish . . . what we wanted the company to become'": Ibid.

258 "'My experience at Xerox . . . now that we're back on track'": Ibid.

263 "'No one has ever failed to find the facts he is looking for'": Peter Drucker, *The Effective Executive* (1966), anthologized in *The Essential Drucker* (New York: CollinsBusiness, 2005), p. 252.

263 "ISO Standards": International Organization for Standardization can be found at http://www.iso.org/iso/home.htm.

ACKNOWLEDGMENTS

This book is the result of the generosity of many people who had nothing to gain but what they derived from saying the things they believed. As a group, they present a strong argument for the presence in public life and the business world of people who care deeply about the nature and impact of what they do. There is no crisis of character among the following, whom I wish to thank:

Sue Becht, Joseph M. Belth, David Berdish, David Bickerton, Joan Bigham, Elliott Bloom, Andrea Bonime-Blanc, Barnaby Briggs, Michael Brune, Charles Carter, Gilen Chan, Bill Coates, Kenneth Cohen, Steve Cone, John Crutcher, Sonya Delgado, Jim Fettig, Rose Firestein, Peggy Foran, Ken Frankel, David Frishkorn, Barbara Gasper, Fadel Gheit, Jean Gould, Jeff Gracer, David Greenberg, Jim Gunderson, Robert Hammond, David Healy, Deborah Hennelly, Joseph Hill, Greg Huger, Lauren Iannarone, Chris Jochnick, Tom Jurkowsky, Paul Kinscherff, Mary Jane Klocke, Terry LaMore, Christian Lange, Barry Leon, Sam Levenson, Jim Lindheim, Bob Micsak, Mike Mitchell, Patrick Moore, Michel de Montaigne, Thomas Nadrowski, MaryAnn Niebojeski, Amy Muska O'Brien, Steve Parrish, Sal Rasa, Clayton Reasor, Drummond Rennie, M.D., Tammy Romo, Jim Ryan, Michael Schlein, Toni Simonetti, Neil Smith, Tim Smith, Darial Sneed, Kevin Tarrant, Malcolm Theobald, Peter Thonis, Rich Wacker, Connie Weaver, John Wilcox, Robert Wright, and Luc Zandvliet.

There were others whose trust and belief in this project led them to contribute their thoughts but asked that their names not be included. You and I know who you are. Thank you.

I express my deep thanks to the people at the Union Square Press and Sterling Publishing who gave me the exceptional gift of

ACKNOWLEDGMENTS

being able to write the book I wanted to write. They dedicated their efforts to helping me get there. First among them is my editor, Iris Blasi, whose gentle, flawless professionalism made the process seem far easier than it really was. I am also lucky enough to have a team led by Marcus Leaver, Jason Prince, Michael Fragnito, Leigh Ann Ambrosi, and Karen Patterson. I am indebted to managing editor Rebecca Maines, my superb copy editor Rebecca Springer, designer Adam Bohannon, and to Elizabeth Mihaltse, who oversaw the jacket design.

I also want to thank Philip Turner for his commitment to this project.

And I am grateful to Maggie Cadman, whose careful, perceptive editing proved instrumental in helping me shape my original manuscript.

By far the most important force in this book's realization is my friend and incomparable agent Robert Shepard. His generosity of spirit made me see the book as a possibility, then his talent and dedication made it a reality. He never stopped. We should all have a Robert Shepard in our lives.

Finally, I offer my inexpressible gratitude to my wife, Sheree Stomberg, for her understanding and love, and to the three unique individuals who are our daughters. If the latter trio ever wonder what the fuss was all about back in the day, this book—in many ways *their* book—is here to help.

.

INDEX

ABOUT THE AUTHOR

Peter Firestein counsels senior corporate managements on reputation challenges in both capital markets and society at large. He is a former managing director of Thomson Financial and built the largest financial communications consulting business in Latin America at a time when governments were listing shares of giant privatized companies on the New York Stock Exchange. Peter is the originator of the Open Perception Study™, a technique for forecasting investor opinion about a company. He has headed Global Strategic Communications, Inc., since 2003.

Peter is a graduate of Stanford University and holds a graduate degree in English. His writing on corporate reputation has appeared in *Investor Relations* magazine, the academic journal *Strategy and Leadership*, and elsewhere. Peter has been a frequent speaker at financial industry conferences. He lives in New York with his wife, Sheree Stomberg, and their three daughters.